Connecting with China

Disclaimer

In writing a book of this kind, for a largely Western audience, which seeks to communicate the essence of the Chinese people within the business context, and how widely held preferences, values and beliefs inform their profile, my goal has been the breaking down of stereotypes. Nonetheless, to propose any meaningful profile of the Chinese people with which to engage, a degree of generalisation is unavoidable. I offer the insights into the Chinese character contained within this book with great respect for, and acknowledgement of, the huge potential for deviation from this profile of a regional, generational or individual nature in China.

My intention is to assist engagement without minimising the richness and diversity of the Chinese character which you will apprehend within your commercial endeavours. Since my intention is to build empathy and promote mutual benefit, I trust that both my Western and Chinese readers will forgive the necessary 'evil' of profiling and see this as vastly distinct from stereotyping in both its motivation and intended application. What I offer here, with great respect, is a point of departure for their China journey for those who read this book and their Chinese interlocutors actual or potential, and not judgements under any guise.

Connecting with China

Business Success through Mutual Benefit and Respect

JOAN TURLEY

A John Wiley & Sons, Ltd., Publication

For my daughter Grace and my partner, Dr Chen, for being the cherished inspiration and reward behind everything I do and everything I am.

For the families of all who made this book possible, particularly the families of the City of Shenyang and the Province of Liaoning who shared their love of China with me.

May you and your beloved country continue to thrive.

CONTENTS

Contents

ACKNOWLEDGEMENTS

Many people enabled and inspired the creation of this work and my heartfelt thanks goes out to them. Firstly those who contributed directly to the building of the content: Chloe Lee, IP Partner, Stephenson Harwood & Lo for her depth of insight, profound knowledge and culturally sympathetic approach to law and to Sino-Western commercial relations. Eifion Morris, partner Stephenson Harwood London for encouraging the project and fielding the Stephenson Harwood contribution so brilliantly. My thanks are also due to Phillip Moore at Andor for his powerful, insightful and assiduous contributions and for finding the time in a hectic international schedule to give the project his finest ideas and make it a priority.

I am also indebted to David Paice and James Hancock of Cathay Pacific for inviting me to the Cathay Pacific China business awards at the Dorchester, where I had the privilege of meeting and approaching Andor for this book and to Doctor Aislinn Rice of Andor for her sustained interest in and placement of this project. I would further like to thank Robert Bentley of Market Sector Research International Ltd for his professional, thorough and comprehensive contribution to the due diligence and governance chapter and for his sustained interest in the project since inception, which I greatly appreciate.

My sincere thanks are also due to the 15 Chinese CEOs who so kindly, generously and with such deference proffered opinions in the hope of promoting increased engagement, friendship and success with Western business men and women. We are grateful for your opinions and we will listen.

The process would not have been possible without the wonderful interpreting, interpersonal and intercultural skills of Professor Deng.

Acknowledgements

She is an example of the incredible talent China possesses within its younger professional classes. I am also indebted to the Government officials whom I met in Liaoning for their helpfulness, dedication to China and commitment to Business friendship with the West.

In making the work possible, I would like to thank Jana Hanušová for her kindness, support, belief and assistance in this project and her parents Jan Hanuš and Marie Hanušová who encouraged Jana to support me. Her help was invaluable and appreciated deeply. I would also like to thank Darina Vsianska for her vision, kindness, and gracious encouragement.

I would like to thank my late parents Sarah and William Molloy, and especially my mother for committing so generously to my education and talent, I thank them with all of my heart.

I would like to thank my sister Dympna Smethurst for generously supporting and inspiring me at important moments in my life.

A very special thanks to my brother, Patrick Molloy, for his active contribution to my work in China, his inspiring love of education and good management and his generous support of my career.

I wish to offer my deepest thanks to my sister Ursula Wilson for being a beacon of wisdom, understanding, empathy and unwavering belief in me and the work I do. Her love has always encouraged me to excel.

My most heartfelt thanks to Danny Smethurst for his exceptionally gifted, wise and informed understanding of China and international management. His mentoring and support have made this work possible, not least because he lives the message that I write about. I offer my deepest and most heartfelt thanks, respect and admiration.

I would also like include a very special thank you to Adrian Walthoe who has brought his incredible experience, fine Etonian training and superb brain to bear on this project. He is a consummate linguist and wordsmith who has supported me intellectually and emotionally at the critical stages of the project with unstinting generosity.

My deepest acknowledgement goes to my late husband, David William Turley, who gave me some of the greatest gifts in my life: my beautiful daughter Grace, a belief in my talents and the desire to write. He lives on through this book and in everything else I do.

I would like to acknowledge the kind support of Vicky O'Brien, Judy Aiken, Mary Creed and David Delaney who have greatly supported and sustained me throughout. My sincere thanks to a very special friend, Maitland Kalton, for showing me a new paradigm of relationships with reciprocity in a way which deeply inspired me and contributed to this book.

To Claire Plimmer, my commissioning editor and her team at John Wiley & Sons, I reserve my most heartfelt thanks. It was Claire's vision, sensitivity and cultural awareness which brought this book forward and nurtured and cradled my talent. Her rigour, commitment and dedication to her writers are exemplary. Julia Bezzant was always interested, available and supportive, while Michaela Fay and Samantha Hartley made the details of this book truly great. Wiley is quite simply an example of what I write about: people engaging across cultures and subjects with passion and empathy.

Finally, I would like to thank the people of China for trusting me and allowing me to befriend them. It is truly an honour.

INTRODUCTION

I went to China prepared to connect and it made all the difference. My experiences of the Chinese outside of China had shown me the value of relationships and the importance of people in making business and everything else work.

My experiences had also been positive, except when business agendas and timelines encouraged me to be hasty or to underestimate the importance of people and the health of the relationships in my China work. This had happened to me only once and had made me see that without the familiar blanket of meaningful relationships – well made and well nurtured – the Chinese run for cover.

But what struck me from the first moment on the very first business plane was the sense of togetherness and harmony among the Chinese. I remember being in awe of the feeling of contact, communication and, to some extent, collective warmth of the Chinese. This was something truly fundamental. This quality, which I later realised underpins everything positive that one achieves in China, is connection.

As interesting as the observation of this quality was, my reaction to it was equally revealing, as this collective quality, and the responses it demanded, provoked both attraction and resistance in me.

On arriving in China, I realised that relationships and connecting well were everything. We were welcomed as vitally important in each meeting we attended, with lunches and banquets organised for us as cherished guests.

The collective from the beginning. Chinese colleagues, interpreters and support staff were committed to accompanying me through long days without counting the cost in terms of convenience, personal space or tiredness. The meetings themselves were often twenty strong, growing in attentiveness and hospitality as the business dialogue deepened. They also included increasing numbers of people and were often filmed or photographed.

The sense of a journey was communicated through a profound 'getting to know process'.

Indeed, it quickly became clear to me that relationships were the most reliable indicator of both business prospects and progress. You knew where you were from the way key elements of the relationship were building. Central to all progress was a willingness to reveal self and connect with others. So, too, was a readiness to be open about factors such as character, social context, family place, position in society and age.

In essence, it was crucial to reveal and communicate one's identity – but significantly in China – as it related to others.

The early stages of my business trips felt demanding and arduous. With hindsight, however, I realised that they did not need to be. They were made so by my very Western concerns: What did I achieve today? When can I get some personal space? Which of these people in the meeting room is the ultimate decision maker? How do I communicate my talents for this project, idea, venture or cooperation? Within the answers to these questions lay the seeds of my own success as a business person in China. And I remember when the answers came to me.

As my business trips followed a helpful movement up through a hierarchy of government departments and referred private sector companies, I began to see how the questions I asked myself did not serve me well in China. Constant concerns of achievements, quick profits at all costs for stakeholders, excessive concern with personal space and privacy and the desire to prove professional credentials, as one would do in a Western professional setting, were deeply undermining and inhibiting my progress.

As I felt increasingly inspired and motivated by the cooperation and personal attention of my hosts and the endlessly devoted and capable services of our agent and interpreter, I began to ask what would work instead of these unhelpful questions which I could see were rooted in a comfort zone of professional behaviour and outcomes, informed exclusively by my Western culture.

I kept reiterating the question to myself at the end of each working day. What could replace these questions as a way of facilitating my work in China? The answer came back clearly and unequivocally: Connection. I can remember watching colleagues from a Chinese team praising and toasting each other and feeling the very real way in which collective, participative relationships drive this culture. More importantly, I felt the warmth, bonding and success that emanated quite naturally from this collective way of working and being.

It was the same feeling I experienced in watching the pure joy our interpreters and assistants felt when they had helped us reach our business goals, or the unstinting cooperation that Chinese Government officials, business and city mayors extended to make those goals work.

At such moments, I realised the pure magic of connection in China and the power of having better, different questions in my head to motivate me and measure progress. Questions such as: How can I be part of it? How are my relationships today? What can I contribute here? How well am I playing my part in building the reputation of my Chinese colleagues? – and the most magical of all: How can I handle this situation for mutual benefit?

The power of these simple shifts in attitude was phenomenal. I was able to achieve reputation, outcomes and strong business results in record time and without any of the strain and arduousness of prior business trips.

It was at that moment of realisation that this book was born.

Beyond the obvious business criterion of having something that China wishes to buy or partner you on, it is relationship and connection that will ultimately determine your success in this business culture. It is in the area of relationships that energy and skills, well invested, will produce phenomenal results.

This was my journey. This has been my China experience. The techniques and insights distilled in this book reflect that experience. Writing this experience of relationships in driving success has been my destiny moment in respect of China. I hope that in the application of these techniques, you will begin to create your destiny moment.

You have within you the seeds of success with China, right here, right now.

With the help of this book, your business journey can be full of successful relationships, prosperity and shared reputation. You need only dare to connect.

CONTEXT

In today's world, there are few of us who do not seek to better understand the mysterious and apparently inscrutable force that is contemporary China. The powerful appetite that we hold for China is not really for the facts and figures or for the details of the economic ascendancy of this nation, inspiring though this is. Increasingly, it is a desire to know China from a place which will permit real contacts, exchange, relationship and understanding which we crave.

This is a wonderful shift and it parallels the change China has made. With President Hu Jintao's[1] recent ideal of a 'Harmonious Society', China too has committed to walking the journey towards real empathy, understanding and meaningful relationships with the West.

You are about to make that journey successfully where many others have failed. Why? Because you will make it from a relationship base which makes it possible to understand, bond with and know this race.

The premise of this book is that so much of what is considered vital in the Chinese order of things runs on relationships and emotion.

---

[1]Chinese President and General Secretary of the Central Committee of the Communist Party of China (CPC) Hu Jintao proposed this important goal at the opening ceremony of a 7-day training course in Beijing, on 19 February 2005. The course was offered by the Party School of the CPC Central Committee and attended by major provincial- and ministerial-level leaders. (*China Daily*, 20 February 2005). http://www.chinadaily.com.cn/english/doc/2005-02/20/content_417718.htm (accessed 18 January 2010).

Traditionally received wisdom from Confucius and the Bing Fa texts has been used by Westerners as a useful point of entry into understanding the psyche and relationships of China and, indeed, for shedding light on the Chinese emotional profile – the real route to building and maintaining relationships.

Understanding the forces that shape Chinese strategic thinking, however, will only partially assist us in progressing up the very formal hierarchy which the Chinese use to codify relationships and signal degrees of trust and the will to cooperate. Since the Chinese create success on the basis of partnership and measure it by the strength of a relationship status, it is in this area that we must build real strengths and create new resources.

Viewed from a purely cultural intelligence standpoint, the journey could be a long one. Our cultural habits, values, mores and protocols, particularly around trade, money, and partnership, are vastly different. However, viewed from the perspective of emotions, we share a common landscape; our emotional impulses and intuitions have, indeed, much in common.

When we are looking at the similarities and not the differences in our cultural and emotional profiles, we discover an entirely new terrain on which to build enduring friendships with the people of China. This common emotional framework may be wrapped in different cultural codes and use different means of communication or behavioural signals; nonetheless, it represents a common ground.

We have the opportunity at this crossroads to relate to China. Not just to manage, contain, or respond to, but rather we have a seminal opportunity in our lives to understand at core and relate to the Chinese character and emotions. While the tools for this lie in the intellect, the resources needed lie in the area of relationships.

'China from the Head' approaches have become the predominant response to this task. These do not inspire, they terrify. The simple fact is that China cannot be understood exclusively in this way. Despite appearances, emotion and character in China are paramount – good news, theoretically, for the West which has spent decades developing emotional awareness through self help, therapy and leadership courses.

But this amazing advantage is largely neglected because often we do not know how to apply this knowledge in China.

So, relating for success needs a whole new set of tools in a game where the stakes are being perceived globally as increasingly high. However, there remains currently a widespread feeling of bewilderment in respect of China which has spawned endless think tanks, consultancies, and experts in the West. These, however, ignore what those of us who have succeeded in China know at a very committed level: the way to reach the Chinese is through emotion, trust, sincerity, and relationships – ones which are built from the inside out.

You are about to make the critical journey towards a deep basis for relating to this nation with tools which are powered by the intention to connect. Moreover, you will make it from a comprehensive base of relationship skills. As stated, this journey is not possible to make satisfactorily from the intellect alone, especially with a race such as the Chinese whose strategic thinking powers have been honed since birth and who guard both privacy of mind and mental processes at all times, ensuring that total access through an intellectual route is barred.

To capture the spirit of this people and bond at a meaningful level involves looking closely at our respective emotional make ups, embracing, where needed, new common definitions of concepts like trust, character, respect, relationship and communication. It is a journey, not just to the heart of China but to the deeper recesses of our own emotional profile, our preconceptions, our ways of interacting and responding. In making this journey, we have the chance to know ourselves better. This, in turn, will make our relationships with China infinitely more solid, for we will approach them with the confidence of the self-aware in a nation which cherishes self-mastery.

In this book, you will not be given statistics, geographical or economic facts – important though these may be. Instead you will hear a distillation of wisdom from someone who has devoted almost seven years of her life to living with, working with and sincerely appreciating the Chinese.

This is a soft lens analysis of the Chinese, accentuating the areas of common ground; an antidote, I trust, to the recent plethora of 'China Scare' texts which serve neither us nor China. Here, we are seeking to cast a sympathetic but accurate eye on the feelings which power this amazing people. This book advocates a new subject basis for interaction, another approach to engagement and bonding, which recommends that we bring more authentic feelings and higher intentions than we have hitherto had the opportunity to demonstrate.

This book will provide tools, insights and examples to help us journey to this goal. It is a journey for business readers who want to gain fluency and confidence in relating to China, by offering richer definitions of what it is to be in a relationship with a culture for whom this word is as important as breath and for whom emotion and sentiment are life energy. There will be an opportunity for you to lose certain things in the reading of this book: fear of China, anachronistic views of this culture, notions of inscrutability, and even the occasional resentment.

There is an old Chinese expression,[2] 'Give a man a fish and you feed him for a day. Teach him how to fish and you feed him for a lifetime.'[3]

---

[2]Sources consulted for the identification of pertinent quotations include Confucius I, the Analects translated by Arthur Waley; *Confucius II – The Wisdom of Confucius* translated by Lin Yutang, London 1958; *The Sayings of Lao Tzu* translated by Lionel Giles, E.P. Dutton & Co, New York, 1905; *The Sayings of Confucius* translated by Lionel Giles; and *The Art of War* translated by Lionel Giles.

As we refer frequently to the wisdom of these three great Chinese thinkers, and do so extensively in Chapter 7, we have chosen to apply more contemporary forms of these sayings whilst ensuring their authenticity and fidelity to original thought.

[3]Lao Tzu, c. 6th century BC.

Observing the complex business protocol necessary for success in China is not easy. Some Western books on business manners will list up to two hundred dos and don'ts in the areas of negotiating, naming conventions, meeting etiquette, accessing decision makers, participating in business banquets, handling financial and legal matters and appointing staff. The purpose of this advice is to prepare you for the key contingencies you may meet in order to avoid the situation where culturally non-adapted behaviour or protocol lapses lose you business – or, given the importance of relationships, in China, lose you your business.

While helpful in intent, however, the array of behaviours to be learned is daunting. And what happens if you are clear on what to do in situations A, B and C, but situation D arises?

It is this kind of terrifying scenario, akin to walking on eggshells, which leaves you, as the Chinese proverb states, at best with 'a fish for one day'. But successful business cooperation with China requires 'a fish for life' skills and ones that reveal mutual benefit for both parties.

So what is the solution? Simple. The Chinese are incredibly forgiving of any protocol breaches *if* the correct attitude to relationship is in place and *if* we demonstrate commitment to relationship from the off, with wholehearted sincerity and an obvious desire for the creation of mutual benefit.

Understanding how to provide this reassurance through your business and personal behaviour as well as your attitudes and actions in China is the real skills set you need – the one that will drive success for you and create longevity of relationship and harmony; the kind that does not mind how you hold your chopsticks or what colour your business card is.

This is what this book provides. This is what will allow you and your Chinese partners to feel safe and help you find your 'fish for life' with China.

Relating well to China and influencing her for good is an investment in our businesses, careers, children and the environment, as well as in the wealth of future opportunities that exist with China across myriad fields of human endeavour. It also represents the most seminal moment in global relationships in recent history. With the right tools, the task is to be embraced and enjoyed. But while the tools for analysis lie in our intellects, the resources to fulfil this task lie in our hearts.

Let's see how the way of 'a higher plane', as it was described by Wen Jiabao,[4] illuminates our path to a bright future of rich relations, mutual kindness and win–win success: a world the Chinese president has dubbed a 'Harmonious Society'.

To get the best from this book:

- Enjoy the cultural explanations and observations
- Absorb the feeling observations of Chinese character and business culture
- *Search your heart for how you would respond*
- *Look for the similarities, not the differences*
- Search your heart again; think how you could respond better.

This book will ask more of you than more conventional business books, but it will generously reward your efforts. It is best read in its entirety first, then used as a reference or manual at intervals in your work with China.

Firstly, I would ask you to release preconceptions and judgements and to enjoy and absorb the first section of this book as we explore the Chinese emotional landscape and values – the beliefs, ideas and feelings which animate and define them. While 'lighter' to read than the later sections, you will find yourself coming back frequently to

---

[4]Wen Jiabao is the current Premier of the State Council of the People's Republic of China. During Premier Wen's last state visit to the UK, he affirmed the following in respect of Sino-British commercial relations: '… both sides now stand at a higher plane and look to the future with a broader vision'. *The Times*, 3 February 2009. http://www.timesonline.co.uk/tol/news/politics/article5645533.ece (accessed 18 January 2010).

this section of the book for the deeper wisdom and insights it contains about your Chinese partners. In a society which values character and relationships, the 'map of the heart' becomes the most pragmatic of guides.

In the second section, you will feel very at home; these are the chapters that reward your investment in reading this book by demonstrating that relationships are bottom-line assets in China, that they constitute very real business collateral and that they truly are the hidden drivers of success with this market. There are also very practical illustrations of our theme from business experts, legal experts and companies who have built and sustained considerable success in China. This is real 'inside track' guidance, offered respectfully, to allow the significant business success you are already demonstrating in running companies to migrate well and fluently to the Chinese market.

Uniquely, this section is completed by the views of 15 Chinese CEOs and business commentators on how we work with them to build success and mutual benefit.

At every stage, I have highlighted and culturally explained what it means for your business and why the business and relationship approaches the chapters contain are so sound for China and constitute a template for success. In doing so, I have emphasised, and at times re-emphasised, the cultural reasons behind the relationship approaches we are asking you to adopt. This is not unconscious repetition, rather a deliberate strategy of reinforcement. Knowledge turns into acquired skills only when the information provided is absorbed in sufficient depth and with sufficient frequency that it becomes a reflex – something you 'do' automatically. And this is what I wish to achieve with and for you: the emergence of reflexes in relationships and business behaviour with China which will not let you down – whatever the situation – so that you become your own cultural mediator in China; in other words, your own best friend.

And because I ask much of you as Western businessmen and women in understanding and embracing the Chinese business relationship model, my summary contains a balanced view of how and why China and the West can shift on key areas of contrasting business approach to overcome difficulties and build great levels of connection and enduring relationships.

I have advocated the goal of mutual benefit and reaching this goal with respect as both medium and facilitator. The practical results of such attitudes are exemplified in the success stories of companies who have used this approach – and the fact that they continue to operate profitably in China today.

Finally, because you are busy and because there are always moments in China where you need 'instant wisdom', not lengthy explanations, I have included a Quick Reference Guide section to help you with the challenges you will meet and make you confident even on the longest day or amidst the most baffling protocol. This is a short guide to remind you of what you already know: that China wants what you have to offer and that you are entirely equal to the task of relating for success to this country and business culture.

PART I

PART I

Chapter One

EMOTIONAL FOUNDATIONS OF THE CHINESE CHARACTER

By nature, men are nearly alike; by practice, they get to be wide apart[1] – Confucius

As we begin our journey of looking at relationships, we are about to lose some misleading stereotypes about the 'Chinese' character. From the imperious Mandarin to the inscrutable, calm exterior of Chinese business, to the diffident, non-personality driven face of the Chinese Government, we are about to see beyond these intimidating exteriors into the unfathomable depth of the Chinese heart.

Would it surprise you to know, for example, that the Chinese are one of the most emotionally intense and deep people in our world? It did me. Like many others, the more stereotyped views of the Chinese – their pragmatism, their ambition for skills and knowledge, the importance of money and status in their society and their apparently controlled, occasionally imperious exterior – kept the emotional base of this culture rather veiled from me.

Perhaps the greatest bar to seeing the deeply personal and emotional facets of the Chinese identity lies behind another facade: that of

---

[1]The quotations which head up this and subsequent chapters are taken from the seminal writings of three great Chinese Thinkers: Confucius (the Analects), Lao Tzu (Tao Te Ching) and Sun Tzu (Bing Fa/Art of War). Fuller biographical and analytical detail on the above is contained in Chapter 7.

the driven, busy, ever-achieving, ever-acquiring way in which the Chinese appear to operate in life.

This deceptive acquisitiveness is perhaps the strongest masker of the depth of feeling and sincerity of friendship the Chinese embody.

This 'busyness' confuses the intentions, hides emotions and muddies motives in the eyes of the undiscerning Westerner.

It is helpful to dispense with it immediately by putting it in a context that explains the constant achievement goals and pursuant that the Chinese exhibit.

In a society where there is a cherished responsibility on the younger generation to provide for lifelong parental care and financial security, the urge to achieve has, in fact, a deep emotional basis, whereas the West has often viewed this as being a symptom of an over-developed acquisitiveness or competitive nature.

To achieve within this definition of responsibility is to display your ability to care for those you love and to give proof of living life fully and deploying life force to good consequences for one's loved ones.

To the Western perception, however, the acquisitive stereotype makes us wary of believing that a deeper emotional profile powers the Chinese character. Yet it does so indisputably. Far from being proof, as some Western perspectives would have us believe, that the Chinese deprioritise emotion in favour of achievement, wealth or status, the act of achieving is much more about contributing to family pride and wellbeing than seeking personal recognition. In such a context, prosperity is worked towards in the spirit of creating stability, life force and harmonious conditions for loved ones.

Moreover, the absence of strongly communicated individual personality and overt ego also deflects us from observing the deeper aspects of the Chinese character. Within the Chinese profile, emotion is often tempered with highly developed and evolved powers of logic and strategic thinking as well as training in achieving balance and stability from life mentors such as Confucius.[2]

Yet behind all of this emphasis on logic and discipline are the emotions which fuel Chinese life and power everything from business to family relationships. Emotions, and sensitive approaches to emotions, are the key to making China accessible and moving towards a shared emotional framework.

So, moving past these deceptive facades, we are now able to look more closely at the real emotional world of the Chinese and to a better, more respectful, understanding for the purpose of building real connection.

In this exercise, it is helpful to consider the classically defined, key emotions which are identified within the Chinese holistic view of the person and used to underpin ancient Chinese approaches to the wellbeing of the individual.

Within the classical analysis of primary emotional states, five emotions are given prominence: happiness, fear, sadness, anger, and grief. Let's begin by looking at happiness, because it provides a unique key to the hopes and dreams of the Chinese and a strong basis for the goals which they establish in relationships.

The emphasis on happiness is one of the central keys to the Chinese character, often undervalued in the process of bonding.

For the Chinese, who see providing for previous generations as well as the next generation as a lifelong process, and who seek consistently in life to work hard, prosper and acquire skills, it is crucial to

---

[2]c. 6th Century BC sage and teacher, credited with founding China's first school based on merit and renowned for his vision for achieving social order and harmony which has influenced generations of Chinese thinking up to, and including, the present. A fuller description of the biographical details and highly influential teachings of this seminal Chinese thinker and mentor is contained in Chapter 6.

enjoy the journey. A life slavishly spent controlled by time and driven by deadlines is not a life for this people.

Every day is a unit of time. This time is to be deployed in the pursuit of goals that enhance one's family and reputation but, equally significantly, this must be combined with a quality of life. The Chinese like to have clear aims or subjects for their life, but insist on pursuing these in a rich, leisurely way while celebrating life and enjoying the view as much as the destination.

In China, the state of happiness is a daily organic goal. The search for happiness through simple pleasures – balancing duty and relaxation, appreciating the diversity of relationships, the art of engagement, the deep enjoyment of food and the aesthetic appreciation of sights and sensations – are what constitutes the movement towards this goal.

Whilst the West professes a similar dedication to the goal of happiness, the state of happiness as a daily objective is often eroded by ever-increasing work hours, fast food and poor work/life balance. So how can we bond around this core emotion and use this prized state of being as real common ground?

The lesson is to savour the process of living as the Chinese do, to see everything as opportunities to connect with people, the rituals of eating as an opportunity to bond rather than refuel, and to see engagement in business or work with the Chinese as the exploration of common goals rather than the achievement of outcomes, time-driven goals or deadlines.

A key factor is to understand and share the appetites that constitute happiness for the Chinese: relationships well developed and richly sustained (it is interesting to note that in China wealth is described as being rich in relationships and connections, not money); the daily rituals of life made beautiful and the time taken to enjoy them; intellect well deployed with successful outcomes; intelligent living, growing in knowledge and skills; the replenishing of energy through sharing rich experiences, and the rituals of hospitality; cultivating a sense of creating an infinity of time to give relationships the nurturing they require at any stage in any day – no matter how busy.

Since the Chinese believe that stress is counteracted by happiness, this becomes an emotional state much sought after in Chinese daily life. While few Westerners would dismiss the state of happiness as an aspiration, within Western culture, it is more often viewed as a by-product of other positive factors such as a successful professional life, a win, a promotion, the acquisition of things translated into gains and rewards.

However, if we can invest in the emotional experience of happiness as a basis for exchange and success, and release our time-driven approach to goals and limiting definitions of relationships, we will have found a central key for engagement.

At the other end of the primary emotions identified by the Chinese is anger, not an emotion we comfortably tolerate in the West outside of the strictly personal arena. The Chinese see anger as a natural emotion which, when spontaneously expressed, quickly dissipates.

It is a response to the frustration about anything that publicly plays to a loss of face and dignity: unintelligent living, failure to seize the opportunity to assist others (especially *in extremis*), the feeling of being excluded or not needed, being deprived of the joy of rendering service and being deeply reproached for the same.

Above all, it is a response to disappointment in all its forms. If, as it does in China, the business of connecting and engaging well governs all of life, then the following are to be scrupulously avoided: jobs poorly done; promises not kept; relationship ethics breeched; inflexibility and putting outcomes before relationships or handling important connections indelicately or without kindness.

If we can participate in the appetite for happiness and provide opportunities to achieve it in the way we request help, accept support, provide opportunities for service and honour the rituals of life and the simple pleasures they enshrine, we will build a hugely rich emotional terrain and make meaningful progress.

Amidst the cherished goal of happiness in the Chinese character is the profound ability to experience sorrow and grief. The Yin/Yang face of such an intense desire for happiness is the capacity for profound sorrow, experienced not just in moments of loss, but also in instances of missing or when failure occurs.

The Chinese see adversity as a chance to grow relationships and boost their strengths. When ultimate failure occurs, if it has affected relationships, much deep sorrow is experienced even when the context is professional. This is something we Westerners would tend to experience with a much more dispassionate set of emotions – regret, concern or displeasure.

Sorrow is also experienced when relationships are not supported by communication. In such circumstances, it feels as if skills which to the Chinese are as natural as breathing are not reciprocated or are neglected through carelessness.

Communication is life force to the Chinese. It is the platform for discernment of and creation of relationships through empathy. It needs to be consistent, frequent and authentic. As a nation steeped in the duty to provide for multiple generations, the Chinese easily discern what is cursory and poorly intentioned or, conversely, what is supported by heartfelt emotions.

Sorrow and sadness are frequently felt when the Chinese are not permitted to render service to those they value or are in any way blocked from doing so.

The impulse to protect, assist, support, guide and mentor those whom the Chinese embrace into close relationships is of primal intensity. Those who are adopted as friends by the Chinese are considered to be the natural beneficiaries of the entire impressive gamut of Chinese skills, resources, energy and care; a rare and often lifelong privilege akin more to our definition of devotion than of mere relationship.

This cherished place, dealt with shortly in our analysis of relationships, makes the winning of a common ground and the task of relating an unexpectedly nurturing destination where we meet with truly able co-creators in the business of happiness and success.

Continuing to look at the primary relationship emotional states, we approach fear. Fear has a hidden, but heavily neglected, place in the Chinese character. It is always contested by another hugely powerful Chinese quality – courage – and manifests more as a low-grade anxiety.

In a society with high perfectionist tendencies, goals and strong levels of competitiveness, the will to excel and succeed has spawned a residual low-grade anxiety that runs as an emotion through Chinese character and aspirations. Intensive, multisensory, stimuli-based living does much to quiet the anxiety or provide a distraction from it. However, in a culture where an individual carries three generational reputations and is the public face of a range of his most cherished relationships, anxiety is not to be dismissed.

The anxiety manifests as perfectionist tendencies and the need to live and work intelligently at all times and for this to be in evidence in all situations. It also gathers around critical concepts like keeping one's word, presenting pleasing externals to one's life and having the wherewithal to meet one's life goals.

Few of us in the West would deny the performance anxiety that characterises our working practices and the expectations that result in increasing life stress. However, our anxieties tend to focus on the material implications of survival, success or failure, and the ability to expend talents and manage relationships.

Our public face is not subject to the daily task of maintaining the dignity and reputation of a whole range of people, based on our behaviour and speech in every circumstance. This is an existential anxiety and presents a wonderful opportunity for those who seek to make a positive contribution to China.

By demonstrating understanding, by increasing the sense of wellbeing experienced in and around relationships, by being reliable partners in the business of creating and maintaining meaningful reputation, we will render a deep service to the very heart and spirit of Chinese responsibility.

However, going further, we have the opportunity to show sensitivity to this anxiety by carefully conducting our part of the relationship with the Chinese in a way that alleviates these inner existential burdens. When we do this in a committed, open-hearted manner, the Chinese are profoundly grateful and often apply their superior knowledge of implementing decisions and creating outcomes to help us realise our most cherished business dreams.

The core, classical emotional states we have reviewed set the scene for an emotional framework that we can build on with the Chinese. It paints a brief picture of true impulses that act as primary catalysts for the Chinese character.

When we have further explored relationships, we will return to the key area of emotions and look at how to use a common emotional framework based on emotional signals around central Chinese values: trust, integrity, sincerity of intention, authenticity and empathy to build deep, meaningful, successful and enduring relationships. For many Western business people, this begins as an intellectual goal in respect of China. In the course of its execution, it often becomes a powerful channel for their business success as well as a heartfelt desire and intention.

Chapter Two

CHINA: RELATIONSHIPS AS BUSINESS MODEL

Look at the means which a man employs, observe his pleasures. A man simply cannot conceal himself – Confucius

As you may have already begun to discern, in order to understand the Chinese and to trust them wholeheartedly, it is important to look behind formal and inscrutable masks and see the primary place emotion, relationships and character hold in their world. This is also the beginning of our capacity to build relationships for success and mutual benefit.

This is a culture passionate about family and steeped in relationships as a way of life. The collective 'we' implies an emotional commitment to shared experiences and a deeply cherished and permanent undertaking to provide financially for parents, which powers everything the Chinese seek to achieve.

Where individualism is valued in our culture, the ability to think, feel and succeed collectively is valued in China. The most cherished word in the Chinese lexicon is 'we', the most cherished word in our Western lexicon is 'I'. This is both the challenge and the opportunity.

Relationships are powerhouses of action in China. They are at once a state of being and a permanent, active disposition towards service and assistance, in favour of trusted family, friends, colleagues and business partners. They are the lifeblood of all aspects of achievement and success. They get things done, wrap commitments and agreements around all forms of business, life and cooperation and promise longevity, where relationships are made with care and underpinned by shared experiences.

Relationships are ties in this world, they are bonds and bonds act as the momentum, the glue, the facilitator and, ultimately, the arbiter of the success of business dealings.

This is what awaits us in China, and behind the dignity and formal, quiet exterior, this is the silent call to arms if we are to find our way through to mutual business ground, successful deals and relationships.

The Chinese apprenticeship in 'we'-based thinking and relationships begins with the close involvement with family – a Chinese person is first and foremost a member of a family, then an individual, just as an individual is, above all, viewed for their place in the greater social context as a 'unit of humanity' before being an autonomous centre of achievement, productivity or ambition.

With happiness and commitment, the Chinese grow up aware of a responsibility to their senior generations which is inclusive, financial and comprehensive. The collectivist style of relationship and mindset makes this a cherished relationship with no on/off or pause button, no conflict with a sense of individual liberty or aspiration – and it sets the scene for both the place which they hold as well as the way in which relationships are executed.

The energy and enthusiasm which the Chinese bring to the business of achieving and succeeding has often been misunderstood as acquisitiveness and a desire to stamp territoriality on ideas, products, services and initiatives. This view fails to grasp the kindness and passion that underlie the Chinese in their effort to nurture their primary relationships and responsibilities through the provision for all generations of family. When viewed in this manner, the Chinese begin to emerge in a different light, driven not by ambition but by a passion for relationships and a desire to provide for those they hold dear.

And this is not merely in terms of finances, it is also about the provision of reputation, assistance and protection, and the greatest of these is reputation.

When you give the gift of face in China to an individual, you give something even more precious than the gift of self – you give the gift of 'we'. By building a joint face and a shared reputation, you agree to underpin this by a joint commitment to maintain and cherish the 'face' which has been built.

When we begin to look at how agreements are reached and, more importantly, at their safety, it is in the arena of sincerely built and expressed 'common face' that we must first seek the real protectors and powerful guarantors of contracts and hard-won deals.

In essence, China takes our Western formula 'we have a deal because the business has gone well; and metamorphoses it into 'we have a relationship first, so that the business will go well'. Interacting well with the Chinese model of relationships is to understand that life, wisdom and behaviour guide relationships – and how these are rooted in living the collective 'we'.

Firstly, the Chinese are magnificent adapters to people, and to the demands of tasks, routines, rhythms, other cultures and, above all, to events and their direction.

The Chinese tend to take events as they come and adapt themselves to them. Partly this is a matter of disposition and training for a race that values mastery of self, partly it is an indicator of the priorities in the Chinese order of things, particularly in the area of relationships. Within the Chinese model of life and business, the order is always as follows: relationships first, then tasks, events and outcomes second. Indeed the Chinese maxim 'hard times make good friends'[1] is an indicator of the crucial equation underlying all Chinese thinking, that nothing can harm or undermine the relationship which is well made.

So they seek common ground and consensus, both in their behaviour and language. Because work symbolises life energy and Western divisions of work and life are not made by the Chinese,

---

[1]Ming Jer Chen, *Inside Chinese Business*, (Boston MA: Harvard Business School Press, 2001), 59.

a harmonious working context is part of a harmonious life. Work, colleagues, partners and associates are not dispensable at a fundamental level – after a certain time in the day or week, project or work cycle. They are integrated into one's life, bonded with, and offered mutual interdependence, assistance and protection indefinitely.

The collectivist approach confers an early and sustained skill on the Chinese: that of listening – real listening. Relieved of the burdens cherished by individualistic cultures and their performance codes of 'shining individually' and achieving distinction through differentiation, the Chinese are free to listen without simultaneously preparing their response which results only in a partial or superficial and inattentive listening ear, and ultimately poorly-managed engagement, connection and negotiation.

Good listening Chinese-style is further assisted by the acceptability of silence in dialogue, particularly serious commercial or professional dialogue. The Chinese feel silence is needed for natural reflection on what has been listened to wholeheartedly, and to prepare a respectful and considered response.

It is the sign of a thinker, not a hesitator; of an experienced business person, not a slow or passive interlocutor.

So, listening as an active process of respect is a communication tool for building the deeper foundations of a relationship upon which talking, exchanging ideas and goals will build.

In approaching a relationship with the understandings detailed above, we already have a strong template that will be highly proactive in helping us reach our goals. But in developing and sustaining the relationship, it is helpful to understand another, often misinterpreted aspect of the Chinese model – its intensity.

In order to achieve success in China, there is a very real extent to which you must trust deeply and be willing (within the realm of what is ethical, professional and respectable), to go to any lengths to achieve it, for the Chinese 'relationship' is sacrosanct – wholehearted, intense and comprehensive.

Constraints of time, personal space, energy, convenience or personal preference are easily and frequently cast aside to make room for the enormous respect relationships are held in and the energy invested in them – as well as the sustained outcomes in personal and professional wellbeing and success constantly produced in China.

If relationship is your goal, method and means for all the successful business and other definitions you seek in your life, then you will invest heavily and consistently. This is the case in China. Moreover, if our passion is to go the distance for our relationships then, as in the Chinese model, we are expected to not count the cost or look permanently for balances of gains made and time expended, for resources given or exchanged and for an exact parallel in forms of giving with the Chinese, which we can monitor and deem equitable.

If reputation is also individual reputation – with far-reaching public and private consequences for any loss of face – then you will seek to establish that prospective business suppliers, dealers or partners have the same approach. As ever, in China, what we see is that apparently 'emotional' ideals and standards are, in essence, very practical business rules.

This acts as a kind of commercial prenuptial flushing-out process, which discourages the poorly-intentioned or those for whom relationships are simply a means to an end, as it does those of inferior or unsuitable character or shady agenda. Instead, it allows the latter to be identified before unhappy partnerships can occur with loss of face and multiple compromising effects on reputation and personal/professional networks. So, while the received wisdom is that China requires 'deep pockets', experience suggests that what China requires is an openness. 'Deep pockets' may be little more than a facilitator of the more meaningful cultural goal of 'deep relationship resources' – the true skills necessary for success in China with the added perk of making the need for 'deep pockets' less acute. When trust is earned, money loses its primacy of sway as the currency of exchange and facilitation.

And since relationships are more about actions than theorising, the Chinese then like to proceed to achieve together for two reasons. The Chinese are superb strategists and implementers. When they do not feel controlled, pressured or over-monitored, they bring creative and very old wisdom to the accomplishment of business and partnership goals. They also bring networks of cherished relationships that offer them further assistance.

Secondly, shared action and experience is the glue and the forward propeller of relationships, whilst shared actions taken to achieve a common goal give the joint relationship a destination and cement it through shared experience. Outward demonstrations of a common relationship journey which has borne fruit and created joint face and reputation are what matter. Reputation is paramount as both social and business collateral.

Relationships – not controlling events, not targets, outcomes, processes or structures – are the enduring drivers of success in China. They ensure that, in the pursuit of success, the joy and richness of Chinese society and engagement are not lost, and that time in one's life has not been exchanged for a purely sterile outcome but for glorious achievements that have enriched and consolidated relationships. This primary and most cherished asset in the Chinese approach to the collective has the effect of disarming any self-centred fear and the compulsion to win at all costs that highly individualistic cultures can display at their most pressurised moments.

If, as in China, the basis of your achievements, goals and aspirations lies in supporting materially and making long-term provision for a network of cherished family, preserving face and providing active assistance to business colleagues and friends, then the goals tend to be freer of self-interested fear and the route towards them more relaxed and comprehensively win–win in outcome. Conversely, within our definition of investing in business and professional relationships in the West, our goals are assessed by standards of professionalism, deployment of financial and skills resources, accountability, shared outcomes and positive results – and the absence of litigation.

For the Chinese, however, it is about investing in mutual exchanges of a different nature: insights into one's character, intentions, goals and gifts chosen with care. Through this we can nurture and mark the developmental stages of the relationship and solid commitments to shared face which withstand adversity, business contingencies and challenging events.

So a win–win spirit of endeavour and relationship resources will achieve much in China where winning is about shared relationship models and goals, and not about winning at each other's expense.

We have the opportunity to be ambassadors for the mutual benefit model of which we seek to be a part and we must take the lead. China has already expressed its desire and commitment to such relationships as the future model for true success and business achievement in contemporary Sino-Western relationships and because China wants its trusted business friends to prosper and succeed, you will – if you dare to stand for win–win relationships, tap into the well established seeds of these within the Chinese model for making and sustaining business and other relationships. You will not only prosper individually but take your place in one of the most dynamic success stories of our time – one which, like the business friendship you build, will endure.

Chapter Three

REFLECTIONS ON CHINESE VALUES AND PRIORITIES

If I am walking with two other men, each of them will serve as my teacher. I will pick out the good points of one and imitate them and the bad points of the other and correct them in myself
– Confucius

Authenticity

One of the most important and most misunderstood qualities of character and behaviour in the Chinese psyche is the search for the authentic in behaviour and in emotions.

Yet it is not a term many Westerners associate with being of fundamental importance to the Chinese. Surely cultural priorities for the Chinese, in terms of emotional approaches and behaviours, lie in strength, efficiency, responsibility to family, adherence to the collective and to social order. So why have we chosen to focus on authenticity as a common emotional ground for engaging and relating well to the Chinese? We return obligatorily to the primary importance of relationships.

You will remember the high value the Chinese place on relationships to support and order their lives, the primary role in terms of personal identity that is fulfilled by being a responsible member of the collective and displaying relationship finesse at all times. This is the very basis of emotionally intelligent living for the Chinese, and at the heart of this relationship skill and finesse is the ability to choose those with whom one will bond, invest life energy, share face, and journey in relationship ties that carry huge privileges and obligation.

So the search to assess authenticity is really about the flexing of important judgement skills that must be in evidence at all times in a reputation-valuing society like China. If a relationship is built with the poorly intentioned, dishonourable or inauthentic, it is not the relationship that will be called into question, but the judgement skills and prowess of the Chinese partner.

The deeper reason for the primary place authenticity holds in the 'litmus tests' for friendship and partnership worthiness is the desire the Chinese have to protect their emotions and avoid disappointments. In a world where perfection is considered the norm, not an unattainable goal, the fear of disappointment and the deep sadness it engenders are not to be underestimated.

But what constitutes authenticity of emotion, behaviour and character for the Chinese? The authentic, like that which has integrity, is very much about one's place in the order of things and relationships with others.

An authentic person cares for the presentation of relationship and reputation. They never do anything that would 'cut' the relationship, so behaviour, including emotional responses, needs to be steady, discernible and even predictable. This consistency is considered the bedrock of an authentic, developed character. However, it is never meant to be a cold, uniformly emotional profile. Consistency with warmth, nurturing and true dedication to relationship, wellbeing and mutual support is the ideal in a Chinese view of the authentic.

Most of all, however, authenticity must be the articulation of what is dignified, and it must be present over time and in all circumstances.

The best of times and shared adversity alike permit the Chinese to discern authentic motives and authentic emotion. It is the ultimate proof that they will not be 'let down' or compromised in their emotions through disappointment and that it is safe to engage their deepest emotions in the act of trust which, once given, is not easily or lightly withdrawn.

Authenticity calls forth, in the Chinese view, emotions and behaviours that are always sensitive to 'the other' and to the collective reputation of one's social fabric.

So at the heart of authentic behaviour is that which is rational and reassuringly steady. It is here that there is often a departure in what we Westerners would consider authentic.

We tend to look for authenticity in an individual commitment to self, in an honouring of inner promptings and impulses even if it means a departure from, and a rejection of, collective thinking. Authenticity is less about being responsible, mindful of collective reputation or emotionally steady than it is about being true to self: emotionally courageous and willing to modify ideas, life decisions and situations to reflect our true emotions and desires.

Western definitions of authentic living would rarely take as their epicentre or field of application the wellbeing of the social order or constitution or the collective stability of a social fabric. In the West, an authentic life is one that, whilst encouraging good citizenship and integrity towards others, is defined primarily with reference to self. In China, it is defined in terms of the collective: you and me, our collective face, our responsibility both shared and individual not to disappoint.

This imperative often comes accompanied by the mandate to protect reputation in a way we are tempted to view as insensitive and expedient. A topical example was furnished by the 2008 Beijing Olympics whereby the little girl chosen to present the most authentically pleasing image of China, fronted a singing voice which was not hers. This created a whiplash of politically correct judgements from the West, with words like 'inauthentic' being bandied about in weary tones, as if this was almost to be expected of China.

However, the Chinese commitment was to invite the world and its people, and to present the best face of contemporary China. It kept its word by presenting the best child's voice and the most pleasing physical aspect of the Chinese young. For both girls and their families, it was a great honour. To be the voice and face of China respectively at such a tender age is an honour both self and parents will never forget. As for the judgements we in the West have made, they contain a certain degree of inconsistency. Do we not also seek to field athletes/ambassadors who represent or embody excellence and deselect those who do not match this standard as individuals or nations? In any event, what is excellence but presenting our most superior athletic face?

Yet, here we have revealed a core area in creating a bridged East–West definition of authenticity. We so often mean public acknowledgement, credits, transparency, highly ethical individual actions and even departure from the collective if it serves deeper personal definitions of authentic being.

The Chinese see the private meeting of public obligations, the maintenance of harmony, proofs of good faith, steadiness of character and the ability to relate well under all conditions as the dignified, responsible basis for authentic emotion and behaviour. This, for them, is true life and authentic being and all activities carried out in the service of these objectives are considered worthy and notable.

Emotional harmony

Emotional harmony is one of China's most cherished values in recognition of its transformative effect on cooperation, stability and perspectives within relationships. Emotional harmony enables us to see the difference in races as enriching, positive, abundant and stimulating.

Emotional disharmony makes us view the differences in perspectives as threatening, problematical, inconvenient and troublesome – something which encourages us to be defensive and territorial towards those we view as different.

At the core of emotional harmony within the Chinese model is the capacity for sharing trust and sustaining it. One of the great potential barriers to relating well around the issue of trust is the quality of control, a quality that is necessary in huge areas of life and business affairs, but which can seriously temper the glow of trust and the climate it takes to build it.

Control is a response to the challenge of providing resources in the face of needs and uncertainties, the need for survival, to reach material and career goals and to provide for self and others. It is also a response to dialogue which is unfamiliar and uncertain. As such, it can act as a helpful ally, a way to martial resources and focus the mind to handle one's life better. In this area, given the importance of managing one's life well, the Chinese value control and exercise it strongly over matters practical, financial and in the pursuit of life goals.

Yet it is in the area of emotional discipline that the Chinese are often perceived as having a tendency to exercise the greatest control – and by Westerners this has often been viewed as one of the greatest barriers to emotional connection and trust.

In China, however, exercising control over emotions is a sign of trustworthiness. Within China, demonstrating it is a proof that one will contribute positively to the business of reputation and will not break the area of relationship trust by undermining the public face of others.

Self-discipline is one of the characteristics that denotes trustworthiness, just as understanding the primacy of relationships denotes an understanding of one's part in the collective.

For us therefore, it is a matter of moving past 'inscrutable' exteriors and seeing the emotional discipline of the Chinese as a sincere marker of trustworthiness, not as coldness, lack of will to engage, or a barrier to trust.

The Chinese put their faith in the relationship. Unlike the West, they are not overly comforted by the processes in which relationships can be wrapped, nor do they consider resorting to law when relationships go wrong as a straightforward or easy option, as we do.

So trust is built by emphasising the relationship. Similarly, it is nurtured by identification. The Chinese have not had as much international experience to predispose them to look for similarities. The process of opening up to the outside world is historically recent for China, and whilst ability to empathise is strong, they have had less time to apply this to a range of relationships outside their nation than we have in Western society.

Here, there is huge potential for meaningful contribution. By providing the means for identification, we can highlight the similarities as common denominators which act as a basis for trust building and business connection.

A key area is family. Revealing our own attachment to family, being willing to talk about our feelings, and show our care and emotional vulnerabilities around the area of family brings us so much closer to the spirit of China and to winning trust in business and professional contexts.

Drawing out other similarities, shared interests and paying attention to the detail of other's needs, aspirations and biographies creates enormous trust. As does emphasising your sincere interest in the wellbeing of the Chinese family and being ready to invest self in any form of help that can be given to support the family or extended family, especially if this displays your willingness to go well beyond the constraints of space, time and convenience.

This is building trust, China style, around themes that are dear to the Chinese heart, showing the sincerity of your character, the authentic nature of your intentions and the depth of your commitment. It is a prioritising of relationship over process and structure, it is a play for the primacy and longevity of relationships built together painstakingly, as a demonstration of 'thinking with the heart' (the Ancient Chinese approach to the concept of trust[1]) and a prelude to business actions and mutually beneficial, exciting levels of success.

Sincerity of intention

Among the most important questions you will ask yourself on your journey are *What do I want from China?* and *What are my intentions towards China?* If all your energy and richness of focus centre around the first of these questions, it is best not to seek engagement.

---

[1] For a fuller definition, please refer to page 33.

Let's defend this bold statement. China is now being courted for every possible objective, by every major nation, group and entity, and this will intensify as China's unsolicited mandate to influence and shape many areas of Western life becomes apparent.

A common thread dating back to the nineteenth century, however, from a Western perspective, has been to approach China from the standpoint of what can be gained, what riches can be extracted and what professional gains could be realised.

So China has, at times, braced itself when approached by the West against self-seeking business objectives of some form. Added to this the difference in relationship skills, with the task-based, objective-driven way business relationships are approached and nurtured in the West compared to the deep primal importance of creating strong bonded relationships in China, and you begin to see how directly goal-led and peremptory the Chinese sometimes perceive the opening phases of relationship building with Western people to be. Perhaps you have already begun to see the potential for our goal-led behaviour to support the view within China that the opening phases of our relationships are indeed motivated by self-interest alone.

A good beginning with China requires a very different set of skills. Does this mean, however, that we cannot have pragmatic goals and aims in relating to China or that they do not, in turn, have aspirations and goals for the associations they form internationally? Of course not.

But what comes first? If empathy for the Chinese, a sincere desire for relationship, understanding and a common terrain of advantage, truly underpin the approach to our practical dialogue with the Chinese, then we will see outstanding results, if we persevere.

This approach to China is really more about winning hearts than converting cultural thinking, redolent still with examples of outcome-driven behaviours from the West, where the bonding of people and the emotional dialogue that cements practical dialogue in a world of empathy was significantly absent. Begin well and intend the connection with people to be authentic and sustained, and you will be amazed at the relief and the ensuing desire to bond the Chinese will exhibit.

Intention reveals deep and powerful factors for the Chinese. A sincere attitude, the great determinant and a by-product of sound character, is what the Chinese seek, above all, to discern and give their trust to in the early phases of connecting to those who seek relationships with them.

The Chinese want to see what manner of sustained attitude we bring into the all-important, life-determining area of relationships. To invite lightweight, exploitative or inconsistent character into the inner sanctum of our relationship base is to reveal faulty judgement and undermine our relationship face by associating with those who possess no skills in this area. To show lack of finesse in appreciating relationships, lack of commitment to the empathy and interest in others' wellbeing – inherent in the core friendships of the Chinese – rules someone out in matters of trust, joint goals or sustained relationships in China, whatever their objective.

It is within this context that we can look at how good character, attitude, sincerity and positive intention can be signalled. What do we need to reflect on within ourselves, and what signals can we give to the Chinese that impart our deeper heart and higher intentions in the task of relating to them?

What the Chinese insist on knowing today is the depth and commitment which our intentions reveal.

If we have come with aspirations, things to offer that mutually enrich, and even ideas for joint advancement, the Chinese will take a considered look, providing we are basing all this on their model of meaningful relationships. This includes the desire to bond, earn and win trust, and provide the kind of deep insights into character through which sincerity can be fully proven.

Character and its analysis is often a lengthy and diligent process in China as a prelude to partnership, friendship or cooperation. What the Chinese mean by sincerity is critical to understand:

firstly, sincerity in Chinese terms, defined by the collective and by relationships, means a profound and sustained interest in others, in people and their interactions, in needs, mutual favour obligations and biographies. It is a permanent disposition of openness to a world view that sees self and others bound in a voluntary, profound and inextricably linked dance of being and identity.

It is surrender at all times to the notion of the collective and a developed sensitivity to the signals and emotions of other people in the joint responsibility all Chinese feel to build and maintain face.

Within the Chinese definition of sincerity, this commitment to others, this attitude of awareness of others, is tested for its depth, and rejected if found to be superficial or short-termist.

The Chinese, for example, show their sincerity in seeking to build relationships or celebrate their continuity through the rituals of food and drink, the ceremonies of formal dining, tea taking and banqueting. Yet, notably, the Chinese, who lavish these rituals as a work of true friendship, abhor what they term 'meat and wine friends'[2].

Superficiality, partisan or insincere intentions and motives in the construction of friendship or partnership are a source of deep mistrust and potential rejection by the Chinese. They, who welcome any adversity for the strengthening effect it has on relationships, value sincerity of attitude and a willingness to build their relationships with passion and perseverance. Measured against this yardstick, they find some aspects of the Western approach to relationships superficial and poorly intentioned.

The early stage of relationships, in the cradle of any form of enduring partnership, requires an ability to show sincerity of attitude and dignified intention.

The Chinese would much rather be invited to one's home at the appropriate juncture than to the most lavish of restaurants because

---

[2]Ming Jer Chen, *Inside Chinese Business*, (Boston MA: Harvard Business School Press, 2001), 53.

of what this means in terms of respect, appreciation and the sincere proof of a desire to bond.

Similarly, the often criticised system of gift giving is much misunderstood in terms of what it represents and its relationship to good intention and sincerity of attitude. The Chinese see gift giving as a celebration of the stage of developing relationships and relationships themselves; their health, diversity and strength, as markers of one's true success in life.

In such a climate, the Chinese are not looking for extravagance or ostentation in gift giving, but for thoughtful, sincere choices. Indeed lavish gifts are a source of anxiety and embarrassment to the Chinese who find them hard to reciprocate.

It is the thoughtfulness of buying something of everyday usefulness to a particular individual's life that really touches the heart and makes the gift memorable and desirable: in other words, it is the investment of self, as well as the motivation and sincerity of intention that the gift reveals about the giver, which is of true interest to the Chinese.

The other element so fundamental to the Chinese in the assessing of sincerity and intention, is time. Everyone can present a good face for a day, a week, a month. The Chinese process of getting to know you is prolonged and acts like an extended due diligence on character and on intention. This is why adversity is welcome, and challenge relished.

If relationships are your stock in trade, as they are in China, and you believe that core relationship fundamentals such as sincerity, good intention and positive attitudes will be improved by testing times, then adversity holds no fear.

It is as if the Chinese take the 'clay' of character and sincere intention and put it through the heat of the furnace to watch if it will become fine porcelain: if it undergoes this metamorphosis successfully, it is to be cherished and nurtured.

Many commentators on China remark that to deal with China you need 'deep pockets', referring to the prolonged timelines often required to make business work and associations successful. My experience, as mentioned earlier, is that we need deep emotional resources to relate well and meaningfully to China.

First, we need to review our own intentions and sincerity of agenda. In this, we need to remember that China respects those with goals and aspirations. People who do not have a 'subject', as the Chinese call it, for their life, work or talents are considered aimless or marginal in this country.

So goals, ambitions and the desire to prosper are all respectable 'subjects' for one's talents and life force. This was, as mentioned earlier, the race that invented money. However, relationships driven primarily, exclusively or too obviously by these material concerns are simply crass and unacceptable to the Chinese.

Firstly, they reveal a distressing lack of finesse in relationships skills – as fundamental in a relationship-centric society as breath or air.

Secondly, they show an approach to life which is too limiting and departs from the appreciation of life and expanded living the Chinese insist upon, even when they are striving hard to meet goals, acquire skills, and grow in knowledge.

Since the latter is a lifelong journey, appreciation of surroundings and quality of relationship constitute the very fabric of a journey well made.

Someone who pursues goals and subjects to the exclusion of all else and to the detriment of all else is not considered assiduous or a mild workaholic as in the West, but an insincere, small person who has not understood the tools for living or mastered the art of being in a relationship.

So we must rely on our intentions, our sincerity of approach, and the particular balance of our own agenda on China. If we risk putting sincerity firmly alongside any 'subject' we may have as the goal of relating, the Chinese will discern proof of good intentions.

They may wish to see perseverance added and so continue to view our intentions over a rather protracted time – but they will not revise their good opinion providing no superficiality, inconsistency or shallowness in the face of adversity is detected.

Since for the Chinese, 'bad times make good friends', sincerity and intention must not be fair-weather and must certainly not be inconstant, but in such a climate, once relationship is achieved, it need never fear hard times, litigation, absence, distance, competition or longevity.

It will reside on solid ground: the truth of the sincere and well-intentioned relationship, made with depth and sustained in the face of challenge.

Integrity

Integrity is an extremely important quality in China, yet one which many Westerners, at times, believe is insufficiently demonstrated by the Chinese themselves. Interestingly, the Chinese also believe that Westerners have failed, historically, to exhibit sustained and meaningful levels of integrity with respect to China. Which makes it all the more important, when creating real bonds with China, to revisit this quality which both cultures are failing to signal satisfactorily to each other, as a prelude to essential trust building.

The word 'integrity' is derived from the Latin *integritas* – meaning 'strong/strength'. It has a fundamental importance in our culture and, indeed, in China, as the glue which makes relationships possible and the mechanism by which trust is engendered in personal alliances, business affairs and ventures.

Yet the definition that is adhered to, and the kind of predominant reassuring tone that emanates from this definition of integrity, is overlaid with vastly different signals and codes in Western and Chinese cultures.

In China, integrity corresponds broadly to three areas of primary importance: reputation, strength and responsibility.

Within this framework, reputation has precedence because it constitutes the hallowed goal of Chinese life. It is a fundamental premise of Chinese life that public reputation, or 'Mianzi',[3] is what every Chinese person needs to have, seeks to preserve and is conscious of, at every moment of their life. This is a precious and universally accepted goal in China, so much so that the Chinese naturally support and partner each other at all times. In matters of face, within a fundamentally collectivist society like China, your face is also mine and mine is yours.

There is no exception to this burden of reputation and no leave periods, so behaving in a way that gives and preserves face becomes an act of consideration, integrity, trustworthiness, even social responsibility.

So how is integrity, as reliable participation in the building and maintaining of face, communicated in China? In myriad ways, from a dress code that is correct, to the appropriate attitude to punctuality, to concern for how people and situations are represented, to maintaining dignity and never making oneself look small, weak or needy, even in adversity. As such, it involves judgement about 'never putting our weak leg forward' and being conscious and alert at all times, and in all situations, of the face one carries for other people.

It is about being an individual but also being guided by the collective; an individual as a 'unit of humanity' for whom acting appropriately, on behalf of all those one stands for, is as natural as breathing, dressing or grooming.

It is at once instinct and daily ritual, something that is assumed by all Chinese without the need to verbalise or articulate. It is a fundamental part of what constitutes personal dignity and wisdom in China. Lack of integrity, on the other hand, is defined as actions, attitudes and behaviour that fail to support the collective and those for whom one carries face. It is almost the inverse of our value code in the West. We often define integrity as choosing to stand out from the crowd and admire individuals who differentiate themselves from

---

[3] **Mianzi**, or **face**, idiomatically meaning 'dignity; prestige' is a fundamental concept in the fields of sociology, sociolinguistics, semantics, politeness theory, psychology, political science and Face Negotiation Theory.

prevailing societal choices or dispositions where these have been questioned and found wanting.

The cherishing of collective wisdom and order, as well as the privilege of upholding collective face, is what delineates acts of integrity in China. So, it follows that certain attitudes and behaviour are considered unseemly and lacking in the goodwill that characterises the state of integrity within the Chinese emotional landscape: displays of public challenge, disrespect for accepted hierarchies and for the dignity and supremacy of age, lack of attention to received wisdom, over-insistence on individual opinion and the excessive reliance on all forms of non-precedent-based analysis.

Challenge and confrontation offend another important aspect of the Chinese sensibility associated with the display of integrity: harmony and being a contributor to harmony.

The Chinese thrive in harmonious conditions and emotional climates. Their principal language (Mandarin) is built for consensus and this is reflected in their dislike of the unequivocal or the absolute, which tend to engender strong positions and debate. The fundamental 'Yin/Yang' holistic way in which they view choices, alternatives, opinions and analysis also reflects this overarching instinct for harmony of being and collective identity.

The Chinese desire to contribute to harmony, to public reputation and to the harmonious and aesthetic aspects of creating and maintaining face is intense. This is also reflected in the efficient presentation of intelligent, disciplined living which is cultivated as an ideal within the Chinese code for living.

With the state of integrity comes a further mandate within the Chinese definition: that of responsibility. Responsibility is first and foremost to those for whom one cares, the most serious face being reserved for 'Jiaren'[4] or family/adopted family. However, it extends

---

[4]**Jiaren** denotes the closest possible relationships in the Chinese context – relationships with extended family members. While blood relations certainly constitute the strongest bonds of obligation, the Chinese will

in expanding circles to include all our contacts and schoolmates as well as fellow city, province and homeland cohabitants.

Responsibility in China is twofold and requires the third property of integrity (in China, strength, both inner and outer), as manifested in 'good character', keeping one's word and perseverance.

For the average young person in China, responsibility means a life-long dedication to supporting the emotional, financial and familial needs of their parents and grandparents. Since their achievements contribute to family, city and regional face, pressure on them to succeed and excel is enormous and yet it is considered a cherished pressure, a 'touchstone' for excellence in the name of all those they love.

The strength comes from the endurance in terms of character, effort and physical stamina needed to 'carry' those one loves throughout the space of a life and to adhere to myriad conscious and uncon-scious definitions of face, reputation, responsibility and integrity, as one navigates the journey through business and life.

Trust

Trust has a unique definition in China. The verb *to trust*, as men-tioned earlier, translates as 'thinking with the heart', and tells us so much of the deep importance of this emotional state. 'Xin' (heart) in the Ancient Chinese philosophical paradigm was thought to do the thinking. 'As for the organ of the heart, it thinks' – Mencius. The Tao Te Ching states: 'In *Xin* (thinking and feeling), it is the profun-dity that matters (Gao, 255). In the Book of Poetry, the earliest col-lection of Chinese folk and royal songs, heart is at the centre of emotions and sentiments (...) elsewhere, it is made clear that the

---

consider highly trusted non-blood relatives as family members. If any person, Chinese or non-Chinese, is accepted as part of an extended family, he or she is considered *Jiaren* and accorded the status of a true insider. Ming Jer Chen, *Inside China's Business*, Harvard Business School Press, 2001.

heart is the source of intellect and understanding. So trust within this paradigm becomes the synthesis of properties and impulses of the heart and mind[5].

For the Chinese, analytical processes and strategic thinking are of the highest order, and capabilities in these areas have been developed over five thousand years of mentoring from famous analysts and strategists, from the Art of War through Confucius, to leading alumni and the elite public administrators created by prestigious universities like Tsinghua in today's world.

The importance of thinking and focusing clearly, taking the long view and constantly analysing life and opportunities powerfully, is a cherished aspect of Chinese life and identity. It constitutes wisdom, proficiency and maturity in life. King Solomon's biblical imperative 'Get ye wisdom' could be the inner dictum that motivates all Chinese.

So to move such a critical and respected function to the heart and marry it with emotion to emerge as trust, provides a poignant and tender insight into the depth of connection that trust constitutes for the Chinese mind and heart. Indeed trust, and degrees of trust, represent so much for the Chinese that it is codified within the Chinese system. Beginning with low levels of risk of emotion and resources reserved for strangers and foreigners, 'Shengren' to 'Shuren', where familiarity bonds and trust exist with attendant expectations, it rises to 'Jiaren', the cherished 'family' category, where committed trust is unbreakable and all resources and goals are commonly cherished.

Foreigners can enter into the higher category of 'Shuren' on the basis of prolonged acts of good faith, sincerity of intention, shared experience and reliability of well-nurtured reputations. It also resides in a permanent willingness to show the kind of commitment to the meaning and implication of relationship and collective reputation that the Chinese themselves exhibit effortlessly at all times.

---

[5]Gao, Ming. 1996. *Commentaries on the Silk Scroll Book of Laozi, Boshu Laozi Xiaozhu*, Beijing: Zhonghua Shuju. Schwartz, Benjamin I. 1985. The World of Thought in Ancient China. Cambridge, MA: Harvard University Press. SZ. *Commentaries on the Thirteen Classics, Shisanjing Zhushu* 1979. Beijing: Zhonghua Shuju.

To codify degrees of trust in such detail shows the unique importance of when, where and how trust is bestowed and is evidence that the commitment to trust, once given, is not withdrawn.

To facilitate this journey, let us present our own 'thinking with the heart', an emotionally intelligent approach to relating to this great nation. Let us be aware of our own cultural preconceptions, respond with mastery and secure emotions, display authenticity, and be clear in our intentions. To move from a boundary-conscious, space-valuing society to gaining the trust of the Chinese requires a series of shifts, but these are simply the kind of shifts those of us who desire even greater mastery of self and connection with others would be willing to make. Let us illustrate.

Gaining trust in China, as we have seen in the sections on relationships, intention and sincerity, is about a willingness and discipline in handling our emotions combined with a consciousness of our deep connection to others at the level of identity. So trust is the ability to apply logic (mastery) and emotion (heart) to the task of relating, rooted in a concept of our common identity.

The practical demonstrations are about working towards common goals, publicly supporting reputation, keeping one's word, observing strong availability of time, protection, favour, support and assistance in one's relationship and showing commitment to the relationship as a journey.

Above all, trust means observing the complex codes that avoid loss of reputation and acceptance by social groups and here, to achieve understanding, we have to enter deeply into the cultural context. In China, social acceptance is life; if you and I are one and I facilitate your loss of reputation, negative outside perceptions or demise, I am harming myself, rejecting my hopes, denigrating my own reputation and compromising my prospects, present and future.

So the attention to detail is great. A common commitment to support each other's faith extends even when one is tired, beyond financial constraints, beyond barriers of space, time, distance or convenience.

The trust resides in the earnestness of one's commitment to the extended unwritten code of reputation and harmony. There is much here that we can build on. It requires that we extract the best of the Chinese model: attention to others; awareness of others' needs, goals and feelings; self-discipline and restraint; openness to less polarised views of self and others; relationships of a deeper level, i.e. not bound by constraints of time and convenience; a respect for the communality of relationship face and for the very human need to be perceived well.

Yet there is a new opportunity to go further. The last decades have brought many opportunities in the West for self analysis and, with them, more sophisticated tools for a more aware style of living authentically in tune with self and others.

The single biggest attribute of this growth has been an increase in emotional awareness and, to some extent, emotional tolerance.

We have a chance here to bring, through our enriched self-awareness, a model of relating which is wide and deep and can provide additional power to the Chinese whose trust now, once again, has to extend beyond its comfort zones to embrace foreigners of all types.

Made successfully, Chinese-style relationships take us to new levels of experiencing how nurturing, intense and fulfilling the sharing of emotions and goals can be against a backdrop of a committed view of ourselves in a common humanity with others.

In conclusion, we need to be mindful. We have to ensure that the commitment to relating with trust must be deep and wide; it must not fear time, adversity or distance; its perseverance must be intense; it must wear the badge of lifelong association and protection along almost family lines; and it must be willing to participate wholeheartedly in the business of reputation, harmony and 'beautiful perception'.

It is this partnership that is the trust opportunity for East and West; a heart able to read itself and another is the key to all relationships, but in China, where intelligence of the heart can be enriched by the extended matrix of relationships on offer from the West, it is a seminal moment for us. It is the chance to redefine what being in a relationship means, and expand the limits of our comfort zone and of our capacity for trust to new levels of enthusiasm and awareness of interdependence with others.

Empathy

Empathy is a critical emotion in our strategy to build a common terrain for relating and, as such, belongs alongside our analysis of core Chinese values and priorities. It is also a difficult faculty to develop and sustain across different national and cultural boundaries.

Cultural intelligence can offer us much in this critical task of explaining what constitutes empathy, how it is built and when it is solicited or displayed. Firstly, it is helpful to consider what empathy constitutes for the Chinese and how it is meaningfully demonstrated.

Empathy in a collectivist or relationship-centred society is all built in. Without it, you cannot live in a society where personal identity and reputation are defined in terms of 'the other'. It is an essential component of the daily building of rapport, interacting well and creating trust-based relationships. It also helps us 'feel' intrinsically where the boundaries of others' lie and when their, or our, boundaries are infringed.

To live fundamentally in a community is to have built-in resources which are deep and sustained in order to cope with the kind of cheek-by-jowl living for long periods of the day that would have most of us Westerners running for the cherished cover of personal space.

And yet the Chinese, too, when living communally and empathetically, need to withdraw to physically replenish their store of empathy. How is this space achieved? By withdrawing into self for periods of inner calm and regeneration, by taking excellent care of self physically (Tai-Chi) and mentally (the meditational aspects of Tai-Chi), so that one is not giving from deficit and empathy is available as the natural lubricant of highly communal living.

To empathise, we must first be 'filled up' in terms of our own inner resources. We must have filled ourselves up emotionally to step outside our own needs and have a subject of positive emotions: reassurance, identification, attention to similarities not differences, comfort, strength to offer a person or situation which we are touched by or where our empathy is solicited.

In a highly communal society like China, people instinctively nurture self through care of body, exercise and massage and release emotions through song and game, to be sufficiently resourced to live in a permanent state of allowance of the other.

To live in strong self-nurturing, whilst being focused on others, seems contradictory to many in the West because our strong emphasis on the individual is wary of collective demands on our emotional resources and being drawn in to what we deem to be co-dependent alliances. In a society where there is no separation of self and other, such definitions become obsolete and empathy becomes an important component of simply being able to function successfully within the daily, myriad demands of nurturing strong relationships and collective harmony.

How is empathy shown in China, and what is the means by which it is solicited and expressed?

It is very common to phone someone Chinese and, even in a difficult moment emotionally, to be asked first of all 'have you eaten?'. This is a strange and potentially irksome question for a Westerner at a moment or need of difficulty. However, within the Chinese rationale, empathy is, above all, a quality that engenders the desire to take care of, and the primary focus therefore is the physical body. It is this attention to the maintenance of physical strength and wellbeing in others which signals the first level of Chinese empathy – but the focus on 'caring for' rather than providing 'tea and sympathy' will be discernible as we discuss the other levels of Chinese expressions of empathy. This is because empathy is seen as providing something valuable such as supporting self-care in the all-important area of physical wellbeing.

Moreover, since the Yin/Yang philosophy of life prevails, the Chinese accept that life can be difficult if it can be easy, sad if it can be joyful, and financially challenging if it can be prosperous.

Complaining is to rail needlessly against the order of things rather than to deploy valuable Chi in building stronger relationships to support adverse conditions and to work with trusted friends to strengthen oneself in hard times and to find solutions.

There is no victim or complaining culture in China, and as such the kind of empathy that is given emotional expression is reserved for the kind of natural disasters, family losses, or deep collective sadness of national tragedy.

On a smaller scale, empathy is, above all, a call to arms to solve problems and alleviate distress. Since a given situation, problem or difficult emotional dilemma is not first 'yours' but 'mine' in a collectivist 'You and I' society, concrete help will be speedily forthcoming and acts as an expression of empathy. Such help, typically, will be intensely practical.

Within my own personal experience, in a former period of professional challenge the Chinese colleague who was the least verbal in his expression of sympathy was still there many months after sympathetic Western colleagues had moved on, offering solid support, practical care and strategic solutions for regrouping unscathed.

This is empathy for the Chinese. It is 'care in action' and it is a permanent state of being, based on a deeply shared existence and fundamentally common humanity.

The negatives, as perceived by our Western consciousness, are that the Chinese seem unsympathetic to the emotional flow and vagaries to which we pay attention and to our words and states. The inner dilemmas caused by our perceptions of the world and the way in which others treat us, do not typically engender much overall sympathy.

This kind of inner dilemma the Chinese call 'fighting yourself'. If something is wrong or uncomfortable, take steps to change it or transmute the pain of the situation through accepting or moving on, so as not to waste valuable Chi on what is painful or destructive.

So when in a time of challenge for our friends in the West the first and most empathetic question might typically be, 'How are you feeling about this?', in China it would be, 'What can we do?', and this would usually follow the questions that check on wellbeing such as 'Have you eaten?' or 'Did you sleep?'

Sympathy and care may be facets of the emotional state that is empathy, but they are born of fundamentally different attitudes to collectivist living, personal space, emotional resources and the handling of adversity.

So how can we create a common terrain for empathy to flourish? How can we provide a bridged definition going forward?

A simple but important shift of emphasis and expression would achieve much in mediating our understanding of this emotional state.

For us in the West, we have the opportunity of thinking more collectively, embracing the concept of more communal ways of living and formulating empathy more overtly in terms of evidence of support, willingness to solve problems and the provision of concrete help.

In China, the challenge is to embrace the task of expressing pure sympathy, and understanding that attention to the emotions of others can be expressed in ways other than the provision of concrete assistance, such as in respecting the rich flow of personal emotions which can deepen relationships and increase self-understanding and mutual awareness.

Above all, a commitment to empathy is a commitment to draw closer, embracing a greater understanding of each other, our thoughts, feelings and what makes us feel valued.

Most of all, it is a willingness to embrace another's truth as valid, even if it's not our truth, and know that from the higher plane of the emotions, at the level of our deepest impulses and yearnings, we have a common humanity. We are one.

Chapter Four

COMMUNICATING FOR MUTUAL BENEFIT WITH CHINA

Kindness in words creates confidence – Lao Tzu

The task of communicating with another culture is always deliciously daunting because of the sheer richness of contrasting emotional intelligence and cultural intelligence at play in the interaction. With cultures close in thought and communication styles, such as near neighbours within Europe, there is a comfort level of shared assumptions.

With China, however, we are looking at a highly contrasting set of cultural assumptions, and a radically different cultural filter. Our filter on spoken language comes from a whole series of definitions of what is normal, defined by our culture, way of life and values. This, in turn, is then put through the cultural filter of the Chinese listener who 'hears' our words and conjures up an image of what a breakfast, friendship or contract might be, as defined by how he or she views these individual states, objects or feelings.

Meaning is determined by culture. So there are many clues, which we will now offer, about what helps us to be understood by the Chinese. These are mainly practical and will be invaluable cultural aids to building relationships well and adapting through a China-friendly, communicative style. Beyond this, however, it is important in the context of our theme to remember that language is the transfer of information, while communication is the transfer of emotion.[1]

---

[1] I am indebted to Nick Marston of the *Parallel Mind* for this distinction and his enlightened views on Emotional Intelligence.

Firstly, it is important to understand that since in China self and other are one, the language is built for consensus and agreement. There is no single word for 'no' in China, and 'no' is rarely used – as is the case with other direct and judgemental statements.

Politeness and indirectness mark the communication style as well as a dedication to respecting and handling others' feelings well. This is also true of talking quietly (unless celebrating with friends and family) and not emphasising or underlining points through increased loudness or strident tones.

Seniority extends to pride of place in communicating respect and is particularly due to the opinions of those who are older, higher in status or publicly prominent. Received wisdom is considered sacrosanct and precedent honoured, particularly where it is delivered by those seasoned in business and senior in years.

It is also important to allow those who are powerful or prominent to lead, and for business friendships to move gently from formal language to more relaxed tones and the use, for example, of first names or friendly epithets.

In China, respecting the prominence of family, the surname is used first and accompanied by the first name. To hear only one name (the first name), strikes the Chinese as strange, dismissive of their family and oddly incomplete. While they will offer English first names, it is so much more conducive to learn to pronounce their 'real names' even if we then need to put these with a title of some manner or description.

In discussing things or agreeing outcomes, it is important to put harmony at the centre of communication and not to use language to gain personal recognition, score points or win arguments. Do leave spaces for silence – the sign of a mature thinker in China that in no way signals passivity or inarticulate delivery, as it sometimes does in the West.

Persuade through a genuinely holistic approach to win/win and remember the dignity of the individual face. So never confront people with unprepared questions or force individual opinions.

Giving views is an enormous duty in a society where public reputation is precious, so engage in discussion rather than debate.

The Chinese follow the topic/comment structure when ordering their speech, with very little context. This is a sign of respect for the listener. That which is not necessary wastes life force. The act of listening in China is intense for reasons of respect and face. To facilitate this, it is advisable to strip out idioms or figurative phrases such as 'belt and braces' or 'ball park'. These kind of expressions are informed by experiences within our culture and values, do not always cross national borders and are embarrassing in the extreme to the reputation-conscious Chinese if poorly understood.

Understanding the differences in body language is also important. Avoid pointing, particularly to individuals, in this team culture. Equally to be avoided are extreme gestures, excessive movements, gesticulating or ways of speaking and moving which draw particular attention to the body. The Chinese consider these distracting as they put too much emphasis on the speaker, not the message.

Similarly, aggressive delivery or sensational ways of getting or sustaining audience attention is inadvisable. Communication is a slow dance of progressive wooing and, as such, is carried out harmoniously, with respect for all participating and always approached gracefully.

Among friends or with family, especially around meals, communication is often loud and joyous, and even contains cross-talk and banter, interruptions which are profoundly unwelcome in more formal communication.

Beyond these helpful signallers, we will have unexpectedly positive results if we can minimise our own levels of cultural filter and communicate in a way which permits the Chinese more ease of access not just to our thoughts, but to our feelings.

The Chinese understand language as the transfer of emotions. It is often through communication that we can create the appropriate emotional climate for building engagement and trust.

Chinese songs and words are redolent of an intense level of emotion, hidden behind a calm, disciplined exterior. Communication can act as the pathway to the deeper recesses of the Chinese emotions and be an able guide to a privileged world of access to Chinese relationships. While cultural knowledge will take us there, it is the deeper intention to communicate our emotions honestly and courageously that will ensure success and win over those we have dialogue with.

Communications and relationship best practice

As you can see from this communication overview, the greatest challenge, and therefore the greatest opportunity, when dealing with China is in reconciling different styles of communication between Chinese and Western cultures. Typically, experts have chosen to date to deal with this by finding linguistic bridges across the seeming divide, or issuing ever more complicated guides to Western businesses in the selection and use of interpreters in China.

Whilst acknowledging the merits of this advice, my starting point will be different. Based on the communication I observed take place, one key point of contrast, if dealt with effectively, liberates us to be in genuine and successful dialogue with the Chinese. In my view, the difference between effective and ineffective communication with China relies on one key factor: intention.

If we examine the primary purpose behind the task of business communications from a Western perspective, we will quickly be led to acknowledge that our motivation is that of drawing closer to, and fulfilling, our business goals. If we apply the same analysis to the Chinese way of communicating, the primary purpose is to maintain relationships, harmony and face. This disparity of starting point contains huge implications for the way communication differs between China and the West and shows how it can become a source of unrealised business goals and unfulfilled business partnerships.

If, as is the case in the West, the primary motivation is to achieve a goal, then clarity, directness, efficiency, proof of professional credentials and the explanation of gains will be to the fore.

If, however, as is the case in China, your primary goal is to build and maintain deeply textured relationships and shared face, your concerns in communicating will be of a different order. They will be those of communicating respect, situating yourself in terms of status within your company and the broader professional context as a proof of good character, and establishing your trustworthiness in the business of face.

Your goal of preserving harmony will push you to embrace a less direct, more sensitive and responsive approach to communication, where attention to body language, mood and expressions assists you to engage in a business dialogue tailored to the needs of the developing relationship – in the knowledge that relationships drive business outcomes and success in China.

So, by embracing from the start that communication will now be the servant of the relationship and seeking, at all times, to develop this relationship, we place ourselves immediately on the same wavelength as the Chinese – and it will show.

We can further signal China-friendly communication by embracing relationships in all forms and putting the 'collective' at the centre of our speech. In other words – communicate 'we' to show that we are thinking 'we'. Put in its most basic form, communication tends to reveal the essence of a culture's approach. In China, it is 'we', in the West, it is 'I'.

So, by situating yourself collectively, by presenting your place in a company hierarchy and team, by sharing your contacts, you are creating deep levels of engagement and trust from the outset. What you are in fact doing is saying how much you value relationship and what a priority you will make it in your dealings with China.

You are also making it clear that the opinions you offer are those of your team, your company and your shareholders. Since harmony is the ultimate goal and arbiter of success in China, you are staking your claim to 'real partnership' by communicating your commitment to relationships as the *modus operandi* and facilitator of the business dialogue you have opened with the Chinese.

So, having set a great foundation, how do you consolidate it? By remembering the key characteristics of a collectivist society, i.e. knowing one's place in the business and social order and maintaining harmony, preserving social values that help the group's wellbeing, and at all times being careful to represent collective opinion in a positive format. Above all, it is in allowing these values to seep into and permeate the way you exchange ideas, discuss views, establish plans and negotiate deals.

In summary then, think collectively and generously, speak in a way that promotes harmony and consensus, explore rather than dictate views, plans and goals, share opinions rather than argue them, and communicate your desire for the success of the relationship rather than only success in its own right.

Presenting your views, always 'on behalf of' the team, the company or the board, and making evident your sincere allegiance to the collective talent, makes you a trustworthy and attractive proposition to the Chinese.

Put simply, they admire and respect people – as we have emphasised elsewhere in this book – who are willing to be 'part of' and are not set on rugged individualism, in business or in life. Nor do they value, understand or like those who seek to self-aggrandise or promote their individual talents or profile.

The Chinese do not engage in self-promotion; rather, they attribute success to their place in the collective talent and to the fulfilment of group objectives. So, 'attraction', rather than 'promotion', is the key to success in China. If we are inclusive, collectivist, generous and modest in our communication and behaviour, the Chinese will recognise us as business partners who act and communicate in a way which they find trustworthy and which will preserve their public face and reputation.

At this critical point and with the necessary reassurance in place, they will begin to invest seriously in the relationship and in the creation of shared outcomes and success. This magical moment, which no longer needs to elude Western businesses as it has in the past, could be likened to the *De Qi* moment when a Chinese doctor truly makes contact at a deep level with the specific energy point needed to rebalance the *Qi (Chi)* or healthy life force flow, which the Chinese believe is central to all health and vitality.

Like an individual body's 'Chi', relationships in the context of a collectivist culture constitute the 'Chi' of the group, organisation, business partnership or deal. Maintaining them is paramount and causal in the creation of business success and prosperity.

To sustain relationships with China, communication must be gentle. A moderate approach and dialogue are valued in this culture as signs of business acumen and wisdom – not, as is the case in the West, the skills of business debate or argument. Nor does China rate, in the way which we do, the charismatic individual business approach and methods epitomised by our iconic company leaders.

Indeed, showing respect by varying our manner of communication dependent on the age, status or hierarchy of those we are dealing with in China is a natural skill. Also, it should be accompanied by a talent for choosing non-conflictual ways of expressing opinion and communicating your place without ostentation within the team and its contribution to business dialogue.

These are skills which, when deployed by the Westerner, place us on such a positive and common communication terrain with our Chinese partners.

But we can go further. Remembering the importance of face, we can take care that we are giving and preserving face for our Chinese business counterparts, not undermining or taking it away. We need to do two simple things to reach this goal. If we do, then we already mark ourselves out as talented Chinese-style communicators and candidates for success.

First, we need to learn to listen. This capability is a mark of all things good in the Chinese mind: humility, collective thinking, respect, willingness to learn and be informed, as well as maturity and the propensity to reflection.

All Chinese exhibit this capability in business – great Chinese business leaders are great listeners. We have highlighted listening in building trust, creating reputation and handling negotiation. Here, we are defining it further in terms of contrasting cultural significance.

Listening well in China means that you are listening intently. The silences, so valued in Chinese interaction, then allow you to prepare a mature response. Listening within the more time-driven Western model, which places such strong emphasis on meeting participation as performance and indicator of professional talent, is often partial. It is less about focused listening, more about absorbing key facts while preparing a response which supports a position or stance in the dialogue to advance the business objective in hand.

This often leaves detail undigested. In a society where listening well is a sign of respect in business and the ability to reflect a detailed understanding of business dialogue is a matter of current and future 'face', the Western-style 'key points' with lots of further cut-and-thrust debate and personal opinion-giving, strike a jarring and potentially relationship-breaking note.

If we are to communicate for partnership success with China, we must give proof of our ability to listen. By listening well, we meet the demand of the second, most sacrosanct dictum in communicating with China: that we preserve the decision-maker's face. To underpin this, it is wise for any and all conversations, particularly in front of third parties, subordinates or non-team members, to preserve the individual and collective 'face' of your Chinese counterparts.

So the key second skill after listening is that of moderation and restraint in speech. If opinions are given sparingly, points made with caution and respect, and areas of disagreement and dissent expressed tentatively or, better still, privately, the progress of your business negotiations will amaze you.

To motivate you further, it is important to remember in all your business communication with China that 'shared face' is the ultimate protector of business success – not merely legal contracts, crucial though these are, or sums invested.

Communication in times of great progress and adversity also needs to move closer to some core values, for these too are allied to the importance of 'face'.

You will recall that the Chinese believe that 'hard times make good friends'. In the West, however, we believe that good corporate governance and the demands of due diligence compel us to spot problems, slowdowns or inferior results and subject them to analysis and public criticism if the all-important business goals are to be reached.

This is a goal- or process-driven rationale, very typical of cultures with a functional approach to business and results-only definitions of success.

If, as does China, you define business success primarily in terms of a business relationship well built and maintained – from which mutual benefit and profits derive – then you will be careful how you deliver critical or bad news or communicate business setbacks. Equally, you will endeavour to give lots of leeway and to admonish gently and privately when mistakes or inferior results occur.

Indeed, the key to communicating with China is to be restrained in what you say and do now, in favour of the long-term health of the relationship and the joint success it will promote.

To maintain a successful balance in relationships also means the careful handling of communication in good phases as well as bad. In the West, our emphasis on charting our individual career paths, justifying the faith of our superiors, and gaining performance-related salary and bonus structures, means that achieving and receiving praise is seen as the Mecca of professional progress.

Yet this is not so in China. Singling individuals out makes artificial distinctions that place employees above their leaders and directors in the professional hierarchy. Whereas acknowledging collective ability and privately marking someone's achievement with a discreetly, but thoughtfully, chosen word or gift maintains the harmony of the whole and demonstrates your fluent understanding as a Western businessman of the way the Chinese behave in business relationships.

Such understandings – carefully demonstrated – are powerful gateways to your business goals and, even more importantly, to enduring engagement and connection with China.

The final, critical stages of business dealings, when we are most focused on the 'conversion' into deals or partnership of all the dialogue we have had with the Chinese, is the moment when we most need to deploy our communication skills and emphasise our commitment to success through relationship.

Many pressures will crowd in at this point to deflect you from being your own best friend as a cultural mediator in China: stakeholder pressure, Western timelines, your own professional pride, beliefs that 'business is business' and 'profits are profits', etc.

Resist them! Now more than ever, stay focused on the relationship and the precious channel that you have created through the trust-building communication skills you have learned, to transform those relationships into success.

The Chinese work to preserve the relationship. At critical times, therefore, they will say yes when what they mean is no, not yet, or not in this way.

Learn to read the deeper signals on outcomes they give you – especially privately – and know that when the Chinese cannot realise the goals of cherished business friends and 'face partners' in one way, they will find another.

To ensure their continuing motivation to do so, embrace patient progress, release attachment to the specific forms outcomes must take or means by which they must be reached. Be delicate, patient, ask questions at moments when you are feeling relaxed, not pressurised – and show faith in the creative ways the Chinese circumvent obstacles on behalf of valued business friends and partners.

In summary, while the individual techniques and communication tactics can be elaborated on, like all good communication, it is the underlying attitude and intent that ensure success and a dialogue which is respectful to Chinese business counterparts. For China, this can be summed up in two phrases, 'Build relationship harmony' and 'Build and protect shared face'.

Dare 'to be part of' a collective thought and talent bank when you communicate while according generous body space, avoiding gesticulations and extroverted signs of emotions.

This is the internal journey we as Westerners must make away from the 'I'-based model of communication to the 'we'-based model which is the gateway to great communication with and success in China. It reassures and it builds trust. Ultimately, as well as being helpful in our business dealings with China, it sets the scene for a much deeper long-term participation in the business ascendancy of cultures like China that value careers, ventures and lives which seek to celebrate the collective and create mutual benefit in all they do.

Chapter Five

WHAT MATTERS TO CHINA

If you think in terms of a year, plant a seed; if in terms of ten years, plant trees; if in terms of 100 years, teach the people – Confucius

Understanding what a culture values is one of the surest and speediest ways of making connections and forming vibrant, sturdy relationships that will sustain and propel robust business progress and the navigation of contingencies.

If you truly understand what matters to a culture, it is infinitely easier to communicate, engender trust and foster mutual success. Moreover, it offers us a security and a surefootedness that no amount of mere cultural protocol and rules-of-engagement-type advice can offer. It gives us access to deeper pathways for connecting. Signalling an understanding of these values as Western business people is tantamount to offering respect and – perhaps unexpectedly from our point of view – demonstrating acumen. Since China does business on character, values and relationships, individuals who have taken the time to acquaint themselves with these aspects, and to deploy respect through playing conscientiously to these values, pronounce themselves as astute and business-minded, as well as 'well-intentioned', in their business strategy and partnership plan.

Relationship skills, as this book has demonstrated, are everything for the Chinese who expect commitment, finesse and even elegance in the way we seize the finer points of what matters within their culture to an individual, a company, a board or an organisation, and to act upon them. And the Chinese excel in this area; watch them achieve their business goal through the elegant and mutually beneficial interaction with those who can collectively help them achieve this and it appears as elegant and effortless as water flowing.

Moreover, it shows not only great commitment to relationships and an astute, intuitive ability to deploy them simultaneously as goal, means and end – especially means – but it also reveals another aspect of China: the Chinese are consummate and highly respectful adapters, without losing any of their innate Chinese identity, dignity or characteristics in the process of adapting to other cultures.

In many ways this is what they hope for from us: an ability to stay grounded in who we are as individuals, companies and citizens of our nation, while having the relationship finesse and elegance to see what matters to them, fundamentally, within their culture and business culture, and to 'relate' with empathy and consideration towards those cherished priorities, preferences and values.

The way for us to feel motivated to do this, and to open ourselves up to empathy for a nation which appears at quite a cultural distance from us, is to overcome our natural feelings of apprehension. To assist us, it is important to look behind the stereotypes about the Chinese and to see the similarities between their deeper priorities and impulses and our own. By dispensing with the stereotypes, we can identify and relate to those values closest to the Chinese heart and psyche that colour their life and business at every stage. In previous chapters, we have already cast a helpful eye over how the Chinese relate to core states and emotions and how this informs their behaviour in business and life.

Now to help us develop the active, natural and surefooted skills we need in order to relate to the Chinese, it is important to understand the hierarchy of what matters deeply to them and what drives them, and to develop the willingness to reflect our understanding of these values in our business behaviour and interactions with the Chinese.

But first, the troublesome stereotypes.

First let's look at avariciousness. This is the one used to engender the most fear and anxiety in those trading or aspiring to trade with China. This uncomfortable stereotype for those of us who know and respect China's industriousness is particularly misguided. Let's deconstruct it. What is perceived as a 'grabby', 'we want it all' or 'what is yours is ours, and what is ours is our own' mentality is a misinterpretation of one of the core Chinese motivators and values: achievement, and doing what one does to the best of one's ability.

This is a cherished concept in China, demonstrated in a range of situations. The Mark Twain adage, 'if you are a street sweeper, be the best street sweeper that has ever lived', is perhaps most appropriate to this culture. To do something well, to the very best of one's ability and with talent, industry and inventiveness means so much in China. It is proof of living one's life fully and passionately (remembering the minimal boundaries and fluid relationship between work and private life – and that work is life in China). It is also a responsibility, a cherished one at that, to present the best possible version of oneself and one's talents on behalf of self, family, organisation, city, region and nation. This is fundamental. Striving is noble in China: maximum effort is expected, opportunity is cherished and rarely wasted, and achievement is seen as a constant contributor to the expansion of one's own life and the wellbeing of those one cherishes. It is the ultimate maker of reputation, a reputation you carry for cherished others in your life – and it is a sign that you have deployed your talents and your *Qi*, or life force, to positive results. In other words, it indicates two values which the Chinese hold very dear: intelligent living and growth.

Chinese people seek to achieve so that their life continues to grow and expand. It is the same for their desire to acquire. For the Chinese, it is less about the objects or effects, more about the exchange of one year of one's life, talents and, above all, energy against tangible outcomes for oneself and one's family. But it is truly the demonstration of growth and expansion of a dynamic movement in the lives of individual professionals, companies or the culture as a whole, that is deeply important to the Chinese and it is this which represents the true Holy Grail.

It is for this reason that the Chinese appear hungry for success and seek to be renewed through ongoing challenges rather than to remain content with the last achievement. In this sense, the Chinese are always pushing back the barriers. They live their lives and conduct their businesses aspirationally; seen in this light, their striving is inspirational and considerably easier to relate to for Westerners, whose careers, company performance and national identity are not linked so critically to public and collective reputation, as is the case for every Chinese person.

Moreover, the kind of striving we have described would not, of itself, produce success if it were not for other cherished Chinese values such as intelligent use of energy, brilliance in strategic thinking and the kind of teamwork which is the envy of other cultures, because it is not orchestrated, but born of a genuine, minute-by-minute awareness of collective living and working which the Chinese learn as infants at their parents' side.

It is this collective mindset and attitude that is the greatest value we need to relate to. In essence, we, as members of individualistic Western cultures, think collectively when it is important, ethical or helpful to do so – but our primary responsibility, field of reference and concern is self – and, then, our place in the collective order. As explained elsewhere in this book, a Chinese person is first of all defined by their role in the social order and the collective and then as an individual person, identity, profession, etc. In our review of values, what we need to understand is that concern for collective face, achievement, reputation and advancement is so strong a mindset and a behaviour pattern that it represents a value – perhaps the greatest value we must seek to understand and relate to.

Yet this has often confused the issue for Westerners. A Chinese professional will seek to push him or herself extremely hard in the pursuit of achievement only to field and then 'deflect' (in Western terms) the credit or praise towards a team, a company superior or board or a cherished government trade facilitator. Moreover, all public acknowledgement of this achievement takes account of family, heritage and regional/national citizenship, and the role they have played in shaping the success in question.

As Western professionals, we first seek to achieve through our individual talents, ideas and knowledge bank. When we do so, we expect to be rewarded first as an individual (something we have come to expect in a meritocracy), and then for our company, board, family, etc to bask in the reflected glory. We are, however, essentially expected to take responsibility for our own talent, for charting our career path, for succeeding in our own development, in adding value to our professional structure and professional goals.

These are more than just contrasting starting points, they are contrasting means of operating, ways of thinking and behavioural fields of reference. Elsewhere in this book, you will find real dynamic strategies for bridging this gap on this massively important value. But to give you an overarchingly effective strategy for meeting this aspect of China, consistently well, ask yourself one question:

Would I think differently towards this (person, situation, company or task) if the collective harmony were all important to me, and if reputation were more important than results?

Use this over and over as a way of reprogramming the more individualistic mindset of our Western business cultures, and as a surefooted way of respecting this core Chinese value at critical or problematical junctures in your business journey. It will serve you well.

An extension of the aspirational and collective aspect of Chinese values is the sharing of information, ideas and expertise. People with teams in China see themselves as part of a think tank and talent pool, and operate with huge levels of loyalty, cooperation and concerted effort. There is no question of hiding information or saving and protecting useful assets for one's individual profile and glory. If I am the team, then to fail the team is to fail myself; to compete with the team is to compete with myself.

This core principle, that of sharing fundamentally, comprehensively and consistently to support the collective, is another of the big pillars of the Chinese value system and it has given rise to misinterpretation and unhelpful stereotyping by other cultures.

When sharing is what you do, whether information, skills, or ideas, it is expected to extend to those whom you trust as close business associates, partners and colleagues. In the West, this is not the case, automatically or comprehensively. Even in major business relation-ships or the closest of business ventures, we reserve the right to control, protect and select the information assets and ideas we possess, at times to the cost of what might otherwise be collective successes.

And why? Partly, because we believe that this is what gives us an edge. Protecting what we have rather than cascading or innovating to keep our competitive edge is always a more apparently secure option. Yet those Western companies who have generously engaged in knowledge share, such as Philips[1] with their IPR projects in Tsin-ghua and Beijing, have won more than cooperation from the Chinese, they have won respect and multiple platforms for continuing success.

There is a second, deeper reason why sharing of ideas and informa-tion proves difficult for us and desirable for the Chinese. Ideas define us in a process-driven business system, they are our core property and advantage – to let these go easily or cascade them naturally can feel to many Western professionals like a loss of essence, a kind of theft. To the Chinese, despite their enormous respect for intelligent thinking, whether this is practical strategy or analytical data, relation-ship skills and networks constitute the real tool for living and their true armoury. So the passing on and around of ideas, information and insights in the service of successful business relationships is a natural action.

Viewed in this way, the unhelpful stereotype of an 'ideas grabbing', intellectually 'acquisitive' China finds a healthier perspective.

And perhaps we need to consider one final contrast in values to dispense with this stereotype and begin constructively bridging cul-turally informed preferences in approaches to knowledge, talent and skills share.

At the basis of our protectionism in regard to ideas, skills and knowl-edge in the West, is an aversion to being 'copied'. It feels like someone is taking from us that which makes us unique, defines our talent and creates our sense of 'specialness'. In essence, it feels like

---

[1]The excellent initiatives promoted by Philips within and in close coopera-tion with China is described and referenced in Chapter 10.

our own history as a professional and individual is under threat. In the case of companies, it feels as though someone has usurped our version of entrepreneurial spirit and minimised the achievements of our business journey.

In China, the story could not be more different.

In China, to emulate, to 'copy' a business idea, skill or strategy is the greatest of compliments – it says that your ideas are great, your skills impressive and your business outcomes admirable. Above all, it says that your knowledge and skills have passed into the area of 'received wisdom' – something to revere and emulate, something to esteem. Moreover, if we are in a business relationship with the Chinese, they probably expect our relationship and commitment to collective success to extend to a voluntary desire to share and cascade some of this successful intelligence.

While Western sensitivities about intellectual property protection have encouraged China to journey rapidly and admirably towards an understanding of our point of view and preferences, we need nonetheless to concede this fundamental value in China and to find a way of becoming comfortable with it. Our approach can then be different to the examples of respect-based emulation and reproduction of that which the Chinese esteem to be intelligent and admirably efficient and successful in our business and professional profiles.

I would suggest that if we were to apply our energy to learning the hugely effective way in which the Chinese deploy relationships to achieve business tasks, targets and ambitious goals, and to incorporate these into our reactivated skills base on relationships, we would find the 'exchange' and the whole equation more equitable and we would more happily contribute what we have into each other's business 'creation box'. We might find, as the Chinese do, that as we lean more heavily and effectively on our relationship skills to achieve brilliant outcomes, our utter reliance on and anxiety towards the sphere of ideas and its watertight protection might rebalance. Now that would be a dynamic, equitable, mutual skills share for our dealings with China in the coming months and it would undoubtedly yield wonderful results.

As stereotypes go, the one that paints all Chinese as dominant and controlling, specifically in business and finance, is the least helpful to a positive business dialogue for success and mutual benefit. Once again, this is born of poorly-understood cultural values. The Chinese value stability and continuity, it makes them feel safe and capable. Despite huge modernisations and opening up to the outside world (evidenced by the rate of change since joining the WTO), the Chinese revere that which is tried and tested, such as the timeless wisdom of their great thinkings on life, conduct and business affairs (Confucius, Lao Tzu and Sun Tzu) and the comfort of established business relationships and partnerships. This makes them incredibly loyal to their core values, to learned wisdom and, equally importantly, to those partners with whom they have created sound business relationships; partners who have acted in predictably safe and ethical ways, thereby allowing the joint network of face to be constructed and preserved.

And this is the key point: what can look like extreme control or will to dominate to a Western audience, is really something completely different and here some understanding and vision is needed on our part.

Imagine if your business actions caused less than glowing results and were a source of potential loss of face, not just to you, your team, your company or your stakeholders but for the entire business, familial and community networks, and that these networks constituted your most significant reality and resource personally and professionally. Difficult to imagine for a Westerner, this level of pressure on the Chinese and the consequence for their reputation, for while our actions have consequences and ripple effects, the various aspects of our lives, both personal and professional, tend to be more compartmentalised and negative effects contained by process, structured corporate governance and law, and distinctions between the personal and professional.

Nonetheless, it is only a small leap of understanding for the many entrepreneurs and directors of small- to medium-size enterprises to understand the level of pressure and consequence to reputation and family, of businesses that are not run with predictable levels of organisation and the negative effect of partnerships which are not soundly chosen and maintained.

So what are we looking at really? Control or dominance, no, but extreme scrutiny of business intentions, behaviour and actions as a prelude to sound relationships and a sense of safety as guardians of collective face, yes.

The Chinese do not take the same comfort as we do in relying heavily on law and the possibility of potential recourse to litigation in times of difficulty. They do not like conflict or overly process-based approaches to business, nor do they like the, at times, compromising nature of the kind of discussions necessary for conflict resolution. Their goal is harmony, unhampered relationships and continuity of business networks.

So they do not seek, as we do in the West, to control business processes heavily, for these do not allow business to live in an organic way, nor, they feel, do they provide the room to modify and breathe new life into tired business dialogues. The Chinese choose to exercise strong interest, effort and monitoring in the area where they believe their power lies in the quality and health of their business relationships. It is here where attention is directed. They seek to nurture, document, communicate about and take the temperature of relationships frequently and with intensity and passion.

To us, in the West, the constant attention to and checking on relationship status in our business and professional lives feels like control and we, conditioned by a strong individualistic culture, shrink from any feeling of over-monitoring or over-exposure in relationships, both business and personal. Instead, we believe that our power is best exercised on the structures and business processes that make us feel safe – holding them ever tighter – and remembering the legal underpinning we hold in reserve.

You see the contrast. But in understanding the core value that stability and continuity constitutes for the Chinese and how they seek to achieve this through healthy, well-maintained business relationships, we can begin to see this stereotype as erroneous and the Chinese attentiveness within our business relationships with them as non-intrusive. If this understanding sits alongside the efforts the Chinese are making to respect the comfort that processes and structures (including healthy legal support) offer to the Western business psyche, we have an exciting movement towards common ground. In time, this will dovetail into a committed business relationship model, supported by healthy structures and processes that helpfully monitor the health of the relationship as well as the deal, without a hint of the overbearing or the intrusive. This is a fusion of the greatest strengths of our respective business models and it is achievable now.

Yet another unhelpful stereotype is that of the remote Chinese business person who is inaccessible, difficult to read and, therefore, a challenge in diverse business situations, from making a sound business beginning to negotiating with, fairly or robustly. This stereotype has intimidated many Western business people in both the seminal early stages of their China journey and the later defining moments of dealmaking. It is exaggerated and confusing. At first glance, the difficulty is that this stereotype is supported by the formality of the style of speech the Chinese deploy, by their receiving skills and by the manner of conducting banquets and business meetings.

And it is not merely a matter of communication styles, it is the approach to business which contrasts with our expectations.

The Chinese business culture values the formal structures that provide a safe context for real business friendships to be made and sustained. First name, instant intimacy type business styles which proliferate in some other Western business cultures ask too much of them and do not provide the visible framework for the respect they find essential for serious business dialogue.

So, yes, you will arrive in rooms containing very serious looking meeting participants and large circular groupings, sometimes with many more people than in Western meetings. Yes, there will be a great deal of formal speechmaking and turn taking. And yes, there will be a post-meeting formal banquet where you will be indulged as we would indulge a friend, and yet with the formality we in the West reserve for business gatherings of a high profile, prestigious nature.

This is because business is prestigious in China. When I presented myself as a then CEO of a company to a group of undergraduates at a major North-Eastern university, I was given a prolonged standing ovation before I even spoke, because I was a CEO, a business woman, a leader.

So formality – when understood as a mark of admiration, an initial context of respect which, when well established, leads us into solid but increasingly less formal business friendships – is easier to understand and relate to as a value.

And here is an additional motivator: we in the West may move more quickly to the use of informal, egalitarian structures such as first names, we may also treat everything increasingly informally, from meetings to business lunches, but our goal remains formal – to do good business for one, two, five, ten years. The Chinese are looking to form and cement business friendships, ones that will last even if the business structures alter around them, ones that make you mutually available as cherished 'guanxi' for assistance and concerted effort in the realisation of joint goals. In a word, for lasting relationships.

Viewed from this perspective, the formality of context in the Chinese business relationship yields in time, under the correct conditions, to strong business friendships, capable of huge levels of support, intensity and longevity. Our informal structures for business settings in the West rarely seek to produce such an outcome, remaining with the more formal, though admirable, goals of profits, professionalism and due diligence.

Viewed in this way, the impact of that first large, crowded, formal meeting space and ultra-formal banquet loses its power to intimidate. Remember the intention behind the formality, be yourself, show warmth (the Chinese adore this when appropriately and genuinely displayed), and remind yourself that what is really happening underneath all the discussion, behind all the formal speeches and toasting, is the appraisal of your character and your worthiness on behalf of your business, to become, in time, a trusted business friend.

Act in ways that signal your willingness and worthiness to enter into this category, using the knowledge gained from this book, and watch how gratefully responsive the Chinese prove to be towards you and your business.

Two final stereotypes need to be eradicated from the Western consciousness if we are to relate well to China. First, the notion of a competitive culture which needs careful monitoring by virtue of this characteristic. Second, the notion of business inconsistencies in Chinese behaviour: frequent changes in the nature of the business stance, deal directions which change often and in significant ways, making it difficult to 'connect' and 'feel' deals and implement them in clear, unchanging contexts; and wavering decision-making processes.

Both of these stereotypes, while milder, are potentially troublesome and without foundation.

The Chinese always do their best, using the most intelligent means and the best information, knowledge or business intelligence available to them. As we said earlier, doing one's best in China is not just a matter of business and professional pride, but of reputation and dignity.

So, my experience is that the Chinese do compete, *but primarily with themselves*, for increasingly better results in life and work, on behalf of those for whom they carry cherished face.

Conversely, a commitment to the collective and to harmony will always look to make the result of the work beneficial to all, and to draw out others to do their best. It is not the kind of internal competitiveness we have been led to believe. Remember the solidarity of the Chinese team, the protectiveness of Chinese leaders towards employees and the collective responsibility taken for results, whether poor or impressive.

The inconsistency issue is equally easy to put to rest when we remember the cultural value behind this 'apparent' inconsistency. As we have discussed, the commitment of the Chinese is first and foremost to the relationship, and their view of business is that it is an organic process which is subject at all times to the superior importance of the relationship and its healthy development.

So, it is not surprising that opinions are modified and that the living 'entity' that is an ongoing business dialogue changes in function of relationship developments and priorities. These are the cherished primary goals and minute-by-minute values-driven responsibility of every Chinese business person at all times, and in all situations.

It is interesting how a closer look at unhelpful stereotypes, and a willingness to see how a more informed understanding of China's core business values and characteristics can refute these stereotypes, leads us automatically and helpfully to deeper understanding and connection.

By understanding and appreciating Chinese values, and seeing within them a core of similarity with the best of our own business and relationship goals and ethics, we will approach China in a spirit of those who seek connection, and it will make all the difference.

China will respond to that which we expect of her and the reflected view we offer. No one strives to do their best when shown a distorted, unflattering mirror. For this reason, many of us who have worked with China are persuaded that positive perception and expectations alongside a sincere disposition on our part to connect, will bring superb results – and ones that last.

Chapter Six

BUSINESS CULTURE IN DETAIL

Can you imagine what I would do if I could do all I can – Sun Tzu

We have had the opportunity to look at some of the factors that contribute to Chinese styles of relationship and to understand what feelings are of primary importance. In building sincere, effective skills for relating to China, it is important to become a good observer; to be able to access and interpret behaviour and values, and to know what signals – both given and received – elicit trust and assist with bonding as business associates. Watch, listen and learn might be the specific watchwords of initial good practice with the Chinese.

Once we know the practical background to Chinese preferences and the behaviour they value, we need to recognise how these translate as work style, communication preferences, negotiating approaches, contract making and attitudes to such critical strategic qualities as analysis and planning, as well as the 'softer skills' of deploying character and emotion in relating person-to-person.

What follows is a generalised route map to the Chinese business culture and style of operating as it reflects their deeper values, thinking and preference.

The truism that people do business with people needs to become our maxim if we are to understand why we need to use the material found in the following pages.

Firstly, we will identify the preferred Chinese business style which helps us to situate it in regard to our own. Then we can link it to our business culture and preferences. Most important of all, we will see how simple, thoughtful behaviour and attitudes on our part can help us to find a mediated way which creates win–win business and positive feelings between the Chinese and ourselves.

It is this part of our China journey that turns knowledge and relationship insights into skills. In relationships, as we have seen, the Chinese epitomise a collectivist culture, one in which the first concern and allegiance of an individual is to the group. Within this business relationship model the leader is paternalistic, taking care of subordinates like family and expecting uncommon levels – in Western terms – of adherence to group face and loyalty to the seat of power. The Chinese believe that leaders should clearly hold power, but use it with accountability.

In business, leaders value their team's opinion but have very top-down ways of canvassing opinion and utilising talent. Accountability is strong – but so is protection of individual liability because of shared company and public face.

In this model, relationships come first and business status is not accorded merely on rank and position but on the basis of more socially defined values such as family, class, education and religion.

To relate to these elements of the Chinese business character, we need to make some adjustments to our more individualistic, achievement-based approach to business hierarchies and relationships to accommodate a model that favours consensus and less rigid hierarchy. Yet, reaching a middle ground requires only a few shifts on our part to which the Chinese will prove gratefully responsive.

Instead of presenting individual achievement, we must from the beginning situate ourselves in terms of the collective: our family, our team, our company. As described elsewhere, we must be willing to 'be part of' and not use business opportunities and meetings to increase personal collateral as we are encouraged to do in the West.

Showing concern for the collective is the biggest indicator of willingness to reach middle ground for the Chinese – and it needs to be comprehensive and sustained.

So, when you present, present as part of a team. When you negotiate, do so as an enthusiastic communicator of the team's ideas, aspirations and will.

Communicate slowly, thoughtfully and with respect for silences to allow individual and collective reflection. Respect the high social and professional collateral of relationships by being willing to do 'real business' outside of formal structures: in bars, cabaret suites and tea houses, valuing people above processes and structures. Let the Chinese know that a fundamentally common terrain exists for fulfilling business goals and reaching decisions when they are ready to be reached and not when process demands that they be met.

While respecting the group, it is important to acknowledge decision makers and to accord them respect. While we may prefer more 'equal' relationships in today's Western boardrooms, great levels of consulting happen internally within teams in China, and great affection is present in the way leaders guide and mentor the strengths of their subordinates.

If we remember this so as to relate well, i.e. non-judgementally, we will make the leaders and influencers more comfortable with our business messages and goals. They will then judiciously and more enthusiastically contribute to using their team in ways that enhance the progress of negotiations and deals.

It is important when showing respect for Chinese business associates to match the status of teams. Once again, paying attention to such detail shows our respect for Chinese relationship preferences and our willingness to accommodate them. In a world of collective face, the business of matching status is a serious one; age, length of service, wisdom and experience all become important criteria in ensuring that the 'fit' around a negotiating table or business banquet is the one most likely to produce a sense of safety, protected face and respect – signallers to the Chinese that we value order, experience and the careful deploying of human talent.

Avoiding ostentation in dress and manner further consolidates this safety. The Chinese respect character and accomplished, well-rounded or experienced people – but they see the need to over-differentiate ourselves by allowing such qualities to shout rather than whisper as revealing a need for excessive personal attention. This, in turn, is viewed as the sign of a weak, insecure or needy individual.

A single attitude shift can make us come across strongly here: 'be willing to be part of', see the wisdom of allowing our goals, targets and talents to surface in a collective framework, 'each shining more brilliantly in the other's company', *Xiang De Yi Zhang*,[1] as the Chinese express this mutuality and willingness to act as a positive foil for each other.

The key imperatives for good relationship practice in China, then, are: be willing to be part of, observe, listen and watch respectfully and avoid ostentation.

These are all excellent guides and insights in relating to China in a way that promotes positive perception and mutual benefit.

A willingness to give of oneself in the business process – specifically the respectful gift of time – is also crucial. Take the time to appreciate your Chinese counterparts, colleagues and clients. Mark the milestones of the relationship with thoughtful gifts that add dignity to the development of the relationship. Help the family and friends of Chinese counterparts where possible and ethical. Why? Because, if family and social networks are the most cherished asset of an individual, company or race and the latter are your preferred partner, then gestures in this area will be received with exceptional gratitude, and gratitude is the ultimate sealant of relationships in a favours-based, collective society like China.

For the Chinese, more used to Western individualism, it suggests a generosity that makes them feel safe about the relationship and optimistic for its success and longevity.

---

[1] John B. Stuttard, *The New Silk Road,* (John Wiley & Sons Inc., 2000), 88.

The handling of communication is another area where we can truly create mutual benefit through simple empathy and the application of thoughtful insights about Chinese preferences. In China, a talent for speaking and a talent for listening are equally prized; like Winston Churchill, the Chinese also believe that 'courage is what it takes to standup and speak. Courage is also what it takes to sit down and listen'.

This talent for speaking in China tends to take the form of small speeches, either representing the collective or offering a contribution to the key 'subject' of a business dialogue. It is not a lively cut-and-thrust interaction or debate and never includes sharp dialogue, contentious opinion or excessive profiling of personal views.

To relate with empathy, we need to understand the importance of each of these 'speeches' as the individual delivery of a collective opinion and face. So, listen with care, respond slowly without gushing and always respect silences.

Listening to learn, quieting our mind so we can listen with full attentiveness is one of the skills of a true winner in business dealings with China. It demonstrates two of the valued skills in the Chinese armoury: respect for others and maturity of reflection as a sign of commercial acumen.

In communicating with a culture where trust, character and relationships are paramount, it is also important to understand the relative weight of the spoken and written word.

The Chinese tend to listen rather than write or annotate a meeting. This is particularly true of leaders or senior negotiators. They enjoy the entire process of communication as a means of getting to know, expressing shared objectives and exploring negotiating scenarios.

The point at which this process converts to 'hard deals' and is supported by the inclusion of lawyers is much more fluid than in the more time-contained, linear, process-driven model that is Western business.

The relationship will dictate the timing and outcome. So it is better to invest in the quality of the dialogue and in achieving real connection than in seeking to define and record stages of progress and results that may later be overturned or modified.

The safest way to a happy outcome is to ensure a strong development for the business relationship and to adjust fluidly, flexibly and courteously to the negotiation and the relationship momentum. Never panic. Do not force issues. Adjust to fluid changes, contingencies or shifts of position and, at each moment, protect the quality of the relationship and the face of those you are dealing with.

Finally, at all times, highlight the continuing mutual benefit to be gained from the work you are doing together. When agreement is reached, introduce your lawyers sensitively, viewing contracts as a means of celebrating the stage relationships have reached and the progress of shared objectives. China has good historical reasons for being cautious about excessive reliance on law,[2] and is tempted to view our insistence on law at a premature stage of negotiation as an early and powerful statement of poor faith.

Be flexible in demands but sparing with promises, as these can be the true trust breakers in negotiations with cultures that value character, oral communication and trust-based partnerships.

Another key building block in our skills for successful connection with China lies in an understanding of their attitude to the vital business resource of time. Where our handling of time is viewed as

---

[2]Legalists. While other major movements, notably the Confucian and Daoist philosophies saw man as perfectible through instruction, the Legalists saw man as propelled by inherent imperfections and base motivations. The antidote was to provide rigorous laws, reward those who subscribed wholeheartedly to them and punish, with increasing severity, those who did not. Highly influential during the Qin Dynasty, Legalism also contributed heavily to its violent demise. Since this time, the Chinese dislike and often reject anything which reminds them of the excesses of the Legalist movement. This extends to an overdependence on laws and an overly codified way of recording human interactions and relationships.

a strong professional asset to be managed and controlled, in China time is viewed as circular, seasonal, something which you use and command and are never controlled by.

The treadmill of a time-dictated professional life is highly unattractive to a culture where one's work and private life boundaries are fluid, and where relationships require constant nurturing and the generous investment of one's resources – including, and especially time.

It is important in such cultures to give time ... *time.* Allow things to unfold and show respect for the expanded timescales – knowing that these are not wasted moments but markers of business relationships well made.

Do not hurry or harry the Chinese. Control rarely elicits the best in people; it is specifically difficult for cultures which carefully assess people, character and organisational harmony as a prelude to any joint business association.

Set an agenda, confidently and early on – but with a clear willingness to allow the discussions to move you around as well as through the agenda. Give time generously when planning. Stay flexible, and adjust rather than insist on a precise business trajectory or pre-ordained time for accomplishing objectives.

Ironically, you are more likely to reach business objectives successfully and, equally important for the Chinese, harmoniously, if you adopt temporarily a more 'easy does it' approach. Patient progress achieves results in China, as well as the confidence to command time rather than be controlled by it – especially if this is in the service of the most important of goals, the nurturing of relationship for success in business and in life.

Finally, on handling time for the building of success, it is important to know that, at this juncture in China's business development, it is very important to come prepared to demonstrate something other than a quick profit motive.

In many sectors where it is being courted as partner and consumer, China has the luxury of choice and it is crucial, therefore, that we give proof of serious business intention, continuity to the relationship including face, and a sincere desire for longevity in business dealings.

The Chinese prefer that which is known and familiar to that which is new, whether this is in the sphere of tradition, values, business practices or crucially, business relationships.

So we are looking not just at the largest and most profitable of contemporary business markets but, potentially, the most loyal. However, to be part of such values, we need to demonstrate that we respect them by acknowledging tradition, investing time generously in our business relationships and arriving in China armed with motives and a disposition which promotes long-term, mutual benefit.

Maintaining this trust also requires a few adjustments to our handling of business rules and accountability as it relates to the business we seek to do and the relationships we seek to build.

We have placed significant emphasis in the West on the adherence to fixed rules around our business in an effort to make business dealings more secure. We rely on rules, they make us feel safe. We have spent a great deal of time codifying them and judging the abilities of individuals and the seaworthiness of companies by them. To protect the rules, we rely extensively on the application of commercial law.

In cultures where both glory and accountability are more collective, and the primary duty is to the group wellbeing and 'face', the rigid application of rules and the early and extensive use of lawyers in business dealings may compromise our ability to give or maintain face and support to the group.

Rigidity of attitude and reliance on the letter of the law in such a culture makes for a feeling of lack of safety – for, if this is an individual's overriding concern, then the protection of shared reputation and face is not. Put simplistically, the choice appears to them to be: What do you trust more, your relationships or structures and process?

By reassuring the Chinese on the primary importance we are according in our business dealings with them, we will elicit cooperation on the 'process' relationship aspects of our business and in a manner and spirit much more likely to protect consensus and avoid litigation.

To do this, we may need to move more firmly to trusting, as the Chinese do, the intuitive approach to business already displayed by so many successful Western entrepreneurs and SMEs. It is also advisable to show respect for the beliefs, customs and traditions which inform 'lucky' or prosperous business practices.

Feng Shui, for example, is a serious concern in China in creating harmony between business and environment, as are the use of prosperity-inducing numerous numbers, symbols and icons.

Showing a flexible approach to the use of auspicious symbols and dates that are culturally informed elicits gratitude from the Chinese. Whilst never fearing to modernise, the massive opening up that China has undergone makes it appreciate Western business friends who allow it comfort in its traditional business values and iconography of prosperity amid the sea of change in which it has willingly and admirably participated.

Chapter Seven

PAST CHINA WISDOM – CURRENT BUSINESS PROFILE

Kindness in thinking creates profoundness – Lao Tzu

We have referred several times in this work to the Bing Fa texts. In this context, few Western business people who have read widely on the area of strategic thinking in recent years can have escaped the many references and frequent quotes from one of the most prominent Chinese writers, Sun Tzu and his renowned text, *The Art of War*.

There is good reason to take seriously the guidance of such revered thinkers, analysts and strategists as Sun Tzu, Lao Tzu and Confucius. They still mould and exert influence over the business people you will meet and deal with in China and, indeed, they represent a whole tranche of the latter's thinking. The Chinese consider their advice as relevant today and to as many spheres of activity as, in the case of *The Art of War*, it was to 6th century military tactics and stratagems. This is because, in a world of change and of internationalisation where China has once again opened both commercially and in terms of its relationship borders, the perennial wisdom of its great thinkers prove a source of inspiration as well as practical assistance and reassurance.

I have seen Chinese people draw on this wisdom when suddenly confronted with challenging business and relationship situations, and in some cases real adversity, where their responses were both unexpected and extraordinary, providing a profound insight into their character.

Firstly, in the presence of difficulty, instead of judgement and anger, there is often calm. Next, the words of great sages are often cited to uplift the situation and remind all concerned that somewhere, in prior times, this kind of adversity has been met and overcome. They then offer wisdom to guide one out of the problem and into the solution. This process is something to behold. It is not some kind of sleight of hand or blue skies thinking; it is pure, distilled wisdom, covering a comprehensive range of aspects on life, behaviour, character and relationships which help the Chinese feel in possession of an inner template for business and life.

And when you reflect on the wisdom and observe its often masterful application to success and strength in business by the Chinese, you realise what an immense resource it is. Moreover, you become aware of the extent to which you are observing it in action, in the most important business decisions and dialogues.

It is all the more disappointing, then, that Western experts and management consultants have chosen to focus on the 'know thine enemy' military-style stratagems of some of the writings of say, Sun Tzu, while missing vital clues and signals about character, attitudes to stress and mastery of self in order to relate well. Rather, they have emphasised the tips given by the Chinese strategists as being ways to discipline and marshal talent to enable the more competitive, astute, even manipulative elements of business dialogue to become even sharper.

What is often missed, then, in the analysis of individual writers – whether it is the military-style precision in planning, thinking and 'outwitting' enemies or competitors (Sun Tzu), or the kind of probity and self-restraint in figureheads and leaders advocated by Confucius – is the sheer breadth of advice on 'knowing oneself' before relating to others contained in these writings. They are, therefore, relevant not just to the strategic thinking prowess of the Chinese but at a much deeper level, to how they handle emotions, make judgements, manage impulses and experience relationships.

This is the true value of analysis of these texts for us – to facilitate an understanding of the Chinese character and emotional landscape and, in so doing, to become respectfully familiar with truths and wisdom of great import to them.

And the motivation to do so lies in the undeniable fact that when we are talking to a Chinese colleague, when we are strategising with a Chinese partner, and when we are relating well and deeply for engagement and success, it is these truths we are speaking to, strategising with, and relating to. It is these, the silent pathways and quiet mentors of everything from China's logic to its admirable strength in business adversity. So, it is through the lens of character, relationships, attitudes and values that we will approach the work of these three influential writers and analyse their effect on the business world and, more importantly, business people we wish to relate to in China.

In choosing to include Lao Tzu, much of whose wisdom might be described as 'aimed at the heart', I would like you to remember two things: first, that the Ancient Chinese approach to trust fuses properties of the intellect and the heart and that this, in turn, is the prerequisite for the kind of relationships which power success in China.

Second, in this model, remember that wisdom of the heart is business wisdom, wisdom on life and character and is, in essence, strategic and commercial advice. Viewed from the perspective of China's commercial rise, this wisdom has proved its effectiveness; viewed from the enabling effect it has had on the Chinese focus on relationships at the heart of this rise, it has proved both its essential quality and unifying effect.

And, overall, it suggests that absorbing this wisdom is a key factor of relating well to China from a basis of shared knowledge.

While it is tempting to provide a great deal of context for our analysis of the wisdom of these great thinkers, not least out of respect for their contribution to Chinese and, indeed, world thought, it is the wisdom and its application to business relationships rather than biography which we must concern ourselves with here. So the brief portrait we now offer of these great thinkers will act as a preface to our look at the instruction they provide, as well as the implications of these principles for both China and those of us who are in relationship with her. Our goal will be to focus on what distinguishes them and their instruction, followed by identification of key principles and, significantly, how these manifest today in the people and relationships we encounter in China.

Confucius (K'ung Fu-Tzu – 'Master Kung') perhaps the most widely-known Chinese thinker of all time in the West, has shaped Chinese thought, behaviour and organisational patterns to a degree for which there is no parallel or analogy in the Western history of thought and social discourse. Yet we know little of his life before his middle years. He is thought to have been born in 551BC into minor nobility and to have worked as a clerk, during which time he is believed to have largely educated himself. In this period a more formal education was reserved for the offspring of the wealthy and carried out by a private tutor, whilst more vocational training was provided by officials who groomed the next generation of administrators.

The latter is what Confucius aspired to become, a goal he did not achieve – fortuitous, perhaps, for China and for all of us, in the light of what he did accomplish. This essentially was to create what is generally believed to be China's first school and to establish a meritocracy that replaced the privilege-based criteria in use at the time in selecting students to benefit from this mentoring.

The idea of merit defining intellectual and social prospects and the importance of the growth knowledge brings as a prominent goal in one's life are fundamental aspects of and aspiration for the Chinese character and are a direct result of innovative Confucian concepts. However, it is his 'template for creating social order' by which he structured an otherwise potentially unruly and chaotic universe which made Confucius' influence so significant, perennial and respected in China.

Confucius' vision of harmony in society and affairs relies first of all on balance and ethics within the individual and then on this individual playing his part honourably in the hierarchy of the family, which in turn plays its part in respecting the community it finds itself in. Harmony here is a goal whereby the macrocosm (society and hierarchy) is an image of the microcosm (balance and inner order achieved by individuals) in the broader social framework. And contained within this model lies so much of China's desire for self-mastery while standing in a rich relationship with others and contributing to the social fabric which houses these relationships. Some of Confucius' deepest wisdom, however, is reserved for what he considers to be definitions of a 'superior man' and how such an individual's actions, behaviour and relationship would reflect in a better, and ultimately wiser, route to his goals, as well as a sounder management of his talents. It is a kind of character and relationships template for all seasons and all times, and the influence of its key truths is widely discernible in Chinese business and life.

Confucius's advice on character can be divided into two categories: virtue and ambition. Much of this is visible in everything from the Chinese approach to leadership to their attitude to decision-making, adversity and partnership – even to the unexpected specifics of business, such as the ethics of selling: 'the superior man understands what is right; the inferior man understands what will sell'.

Confucius has much to say about sound ethical character and the rewards this brings in business and relationships. His concept of the superior man or leader is what we describe as 'sound and effective' in today's business terminology and profiling. It is the profile of a character which is ethical and aspirational in equal measure – but first and foremost, ethical.

Many things define such a character and give proof of its ethical nature. Confucius explains that a 'superior man is modest in his speech, but exceeds in his actions', and does not 'impose on others what he does not himself desire'; values learning and thinking in equal measure, leads by flawless example, and instinctively knows what is right and ethical; possesses gravitas and relishes adversity for the opportunity to show moral courage and strength of character, 'the superior man makes the difficulty to be overcome his first interest; success only comes later'.

It is a template for the ethical man of affairs who thinks deeply, values silence and is not afraid to learn from those who are senior in rank or knowledge, 'never contract friendship with a man that is not better than thyself'.

Although this picture suggests an ideal – or perhaps to some, an idyll – it is nonetheless reflected in the aspirations, wisdom and gravitas of the Chinese character. You will engage infinitely better with these aspects in relationships once you understand the kind of guidance which has given birth to them. This virtuous, responsible character, however, is far from staid, wooden or lacking in proactivity and business aspirations. In fact, Confucius urges this side to come forth. But from the beginning he suggests that this should be about the use of one's deepest talents and the calling out of same in others, in order to achieve success. He exhorts: 'I want you to be everything that you are, deep at the centre of your being' and he encourages that such authentic contact with self be used to fuel powerful determination and winning attitudes, 'the will to win, the desire to succeed, the urge to reach your full potential … these are the keys that will unlock the door to personal excellence'.

So, with determination, the ethical, aspirational business man or woman sets goals and is resolute in moving towards them, including demonstrating flexibility of means in carrying through these goals: 'when it is obvious that the goals cannot be reached, don't adjust the goals, adjust the action steps'. This includes a sense of when to hold to or relinquish a stance, decision or opinion. It is a sign of fluidity and open-mindedness: 'when you know anything, hold that you know it, and when you do not know a thing, allow that you do not know it'.

And this aspirational element is encouraged to be bold and not to fear the imperfect (better a diamond with a flaw than a pebble without) or setbacks. Nor, according to Confucius, should our ambitions ever be half-hearted: 'wherever you go, go with all your heart'.

To strive is both Confucius' imperative and recommendation: to be and do the best, to call this forth in others and to know in depth the character of those you deal with: 'look at the means a man employs, consider his motives, observe his pleasures, a man simply cannot conceal himself'. Above all, he advocates that we are willing to learn from others and are constantly seeking to enrich ourselves and those we deal with at the level of character and success: 'if I am walking with two other men, each of them will serve as my teacher. I will pick out the good points of the one and imitate them, and the bad points of the other and correct them.'

Thus Confucius shows us the ethical and aspirational side of this proposed, well-rounded character and further suggests how strong ambitions can be grounded in the soil of preparation, honed talent and high levels of cooperation: 'the expectations of life depend upon diligence; the mechanic that would effect his work must first sharpen his tools'. And finally, we must have empathy for our tasks. Confucius was one of the earliest proponents of what has now become a human resource truism: that what we excel at, we love, or, as he advocates, 'find a job you love and you will never work a day in your life'. And in doing what we love, Confucius advocates perseverance, the true mettle of success and litmus test of strength of character: 'our greatest glory is not in never falling, but in rising every time we fall'.

It may well be that as I offer you connections with, and demonstrate the influence of, this wisdom about the Chinese business character and its cherished insistence on relationships, you have already identified some links for yourself. Such moments of insight are precious in your developing business relationship skills with China, and they will, I promise you, become more frequent. What is hopefully apparent is that these combined aphorisms and adages have become constants in Chinese thinking and have a part to play in our understanding of them.

So how do these understandings translate as business profiles and behaviour, how do they colour relationships and help with motivation and self-management?

Well, here are some of the notable characterisations which this wisdom has engendered and created.

First, the balanced presence of aspirational and ambitious qualities in business planning, linked with strong individual modesty, is the hallmark in China of an excellent team player. And this is an entire culture of team players. Equally, at leadership level, daring to direct brilliantly but without ostentation or overt presence of personal charisma is a decidedly Chinese phenomenon. Success on a large scale may be present, but the emphasis will rarely be on one central talent or 'ego' propelling this success forward. It is more likely to be about business, families, partnerships or cooperation. Yet the virtuous and discreet man of affairs of Confucius' vision is nonetheless capable of ambition, aspiration and the confidence to 'have a go', to shoot for the stars. I have often been in awe in prestigious gatherings in Western business settings of how those who dare to ask questions are young professional Chinese people, confidently and politely 'taking the floor' while others wait with a very Western reticence at such moments. I have also witnessed this in China; when there is an opportunity, the Chinese will step forward – despite whatever inner anxieties or doubts they may have. While some would assert that this is a product of high competition in terms of people numbers, I believe it to be more the result of the boldness – at least in terms of goals, determination and strength of character – which has been engendered in them by their great thinkers.

Similarly, Confucian wisdom has built the resilience and stamina of the Chinese in adversity, one of their most endearing strong suits. What their great thinkers advised – fluidity, flexibility of means while resolutely following the goal – is an entirely Chinese way of navigating setbacks and contingencies. This makes them incredible partners because following this wisdom makes them creative and resilient in reaching shared objectives without being deflected from important goals.

And Confucius' attitude to the nurturing of successful partnerships with others is always brought back to the nature of the individual's relationship with self. Inner concord is reflected in ease of relationship with others. This takes the form of 'inner and outer harmony' working toward the realisation of common goals between individuals of sound character with high degrees of trust, for 'it is more shameful to mistrust a friend than to be deceived by one'.

This capacity for introspection, for polishing of character and talent while simultaneously nurturing relationships with others, and seeing relationships as constant learning, is also a decidedly Chinese phenomenon and yet it is a brilliant model for our time. Only, however, if carried out in the presence of the undisputed Chinese prerequisite for business success and life: respect. As Confucius rightly posits, 'without feelings of respect, what is there to distinguish men from beasts' and, conversely, with respect, in the Confucian model, all things are possible.

Lao Tzu, generally translated as *old master* or *old teacher*, was a contemporary of Confucius but, unlike the latter, he believed that the goal of creating harmony in the social order of his time could only be obtained through inner fulfilment within individuals. He largely rejected that which seeks to codify, make hierarchies or create conventions as, for him, these represented distractions which deflected men from that which is in harmony with nature – both inside and around them. Lao Tzu is seen as the father of modern Daoism, which is the other most significant influence on Chinese society and thinking. His original philosophical thought was much modified when it later became the basis of an organised religion. Nonetheless, the wisdom provided by Lao Tzu's original principles was, and is, a counterbalancing of Confucian teaching with its emphasis on the pragmatics of social order, balance and hierarchy.

Unlike the more prominent Confucius with a visible and distinct attachment to the social order, Lao Tzu advocates different routes to success and different templates for relationships.

These begin with knowing the self. Lao Tzu affirms that 'at the centre of your being you have the answer; you know who you are and you know what you want'. This is a crucial beginning, for all Lao Tzu's definitions of success begin with finding an authentic relationship with self and expressing it. To do this, we may need to consider less routinely accepted versions of the self we have come to know and dig deeper, and this may well involve surrendering the old in favour of the new: 'when I let go of who I am, I become what I might be'. And in this surrender, this relinquishing of control in favour of more fluid being, lies the key to success and fulfilled relationships: 'he who controls others may be powerful, but he who has mastered himself is mightier still'.

This philosophy of non-control extends to the handling of talents, situations and people. Lao Tzu cautions that 'if you fill your bowl to the brim, it will spill. Keep sharpening your knife, and it will blunt.' It is a template for living which suggests that true relationship with self, an absence of over-structuring in life and affairs, striving for high ideals and being a powerful example, are the real catalysts to success with harmony.

To demonstrate the power of this approach, Lao Tzu uses a simple but powerful metaphor: 'in the world there is nothing more submissive and weak than water. Yet for attacking that which is hard and strong, nothing can surpass it.' Strength is not control in this model, but self-knowledge and preparedness. It also involves high degrees of trust in the natural unfolding of events and interactions with others: 'he who does not trust enough, will not be trusted'.

Within Lao Tzu's counsel, example, trust and inspiration replace the more control-based structures and resolute aspirations of the Confucian model. Direction emerges from non-interference and trusting the flow, doing what is in front of one well – 'anticipate the difficult by managing the easy' – and keeping all ambition simultaneously grounded and rooted in a higher nature – 'ambition has one heel nailed in well, though she stretch her fingers to touch the heavens'. And Lao Tzu repeatedly urges us to be courageous in order to allow the natural order and rhythm to prevail in our affairs. He also encourages us to be plain dealing, reflective and to have faith in outcomes based on this approach: 'by letting go it all gets done. The world is won by those who let it go. But when you try and try, the world is beyond the winning.'

Apply courage, intuitive understanding and gentle approaches since 'the softest things in the world overcome the hardest'. Perhaps most powerful of all within his boundless wisdom is the counsel he offers in cultivating a calm and serene mind, and the effectiveness such serenity brings to the achievement of our goals: 'to the mind that is still, the whole universe surrenders'.

There is much to recognise and acknowledge from Lao Tzu's influence in the attitudes and behaviour of Chinese business people today. His wisdom is prevalent in so much of the quiet self-mastery we sense in our Chinese interlocutors and in the pace and approach they use to move towards objectives or pursue goals. The fluid approach, the slower pace, the reflective, even contemplative response to moments of business pressure or crisis, are a product of this calmer mind and accepting stance towards unfolding events and factors which Lao Tzu advocated. When we have noted the Chinese reticence to act when undecided and about their resistance to action for action's sake, we are reflecting the basic principles expounded by Lao Tzu.

In preferring not to be over-directional or heavily monitoring of business tasks and progress, the Chinese reveal more of this approach, which might be described as a prudent 'allowing' of the process. In this way, great outcomes can occur as a result of thoughtful actions, inspiration, trusting events and the cooperation of individuals who are fully developed and authentic.

This has nothing to do with compromise. Lao Tzu's 'allowing' stays firmly grounded in personal and what we would now see as business virtues and assets. He counsels against letting these deteriorate into inauthentic versions of what we are trying to create in business and in life: 'when virtue is lost, benevolence appears, when benevolence is lost, right conduct appears, when right conduct is lost, expediency appears. Expediency is the mere shadow of right and truth; it is the beginning of disorder.'

In relationships, Lao Tzu counsels a similar fluidity and modest presence: 'respond intelligently even to unintelligent treatment'. He further advocates that we seek a calm state of mind for management and that we are neither emphatic nor belligerent in our opinions: 'one who is too insistent on his own views, finds few to agree with him'.

The Chinese reticence towards the strong expression of personal views, their dislike of chaotic or pressurised conditions and their mistrust of fast-paced proactivity without periods of reflection is redolent of Lao Tzu's words and profound advice. This is further reflected in the Chinese aversion to excessive control of events and over-accountability and the high value they place on trust, especially in the business arena.

For this reason, in the cherished areas of relationships, values and behaviour, the inspiration Lao Tzu offered in the 6th century is as valid today, as its truth is perennial.

The last of our three thinkers, Sun Tzu, was the probable author of *The Art of War* (Bing Fa), written whilst in the service of the state of Wu as a renowned General.

The goal of this work was to demonstrate how to achieve maximum yield for least effort. The route advocates the use of psychological tools: intelligence, subterfuge, deceit, surprise and concealment, identifying the enemy's weak points, and developing advanced strategic plans. Originally written with a military goal in mind, the application of the texts to fields such as business planning and market competitiveness has appealed greatly to Western analysts over the last years. Nonetheless, it is the concept of the 'bloodless battle', a series of 'benign coups' and strikes which is the goal of Sun Tzu's strategy. The latter, despite its manipulative elements, lacks the relentless aggression with which it is at times characterised in the West.

The key principle of Sun Tzu's approach was to conceal much of oneself, one's character and motivations as well as one's talents, while forcing the opposing side to reveal itself. This amounted to a kind of absence of centre, a disorienting omission of any exchange of character which resulted in a weakening effect on the talent of the opposing side: 'be extremely subtle, even to the point of formlessness. Be extremely mysterious, even to the point of soundlessness. Thereby, you can be the director of the opponent's fate.'

He counsels prudence, providing visible advance rewards for those who support you and amassing information on those you compete with, while flushing out their least flattering behaviour and greatest points of exposure: 'pretend inferiority and encourage his arrogance'. Yet this is not a rallying cry for aggression: 'supreme excellence consists in breaking the enemy's resistance without fighting'. Moreover, discernment is constantly at the fore of the ideal leader's character that Sun Tzu depicts, and this must take the form, above all, of discernment about human character and relationships: 'the skilful employer of men will employ the wise man, the brave man, the covetous man, and the stupid man'. His supreme message, alongside caution, intelligent preparation of resources, intensive knowledge of the enemy and consummate levels of advance intelligence gathering, is to guard closely that which makes your strategy successful.

Once again, you may recognise some of these traits in the business profile of Chinese partners and counterparts. For example, the Chinese do not like aggression in their relationships, and they prefer to achieve intelligently and in a way that protects harmony and face, a predilection foreshadowed by Sun Tzu's 'bloodless battle'. In keeping with this advice you will notice that even the most rigorous negotiations are never vociferous or aggressive, they are merely consummately skilful.

Much of the confident, determined manner and self-mastery we alluded to before within the Chinese character is contained in Sun Tzu's insistence on the power of mental preparation and on the confident visualisation of beneficial and successful outcomes in business and life: 'victorious warriors win first and then go to war while defeated warriors go to war first and then seek to win'. And to inspire, reward and carefully select those behind you is identified as the critical task of the true leader, especially when accompanied by timely decisions – 'the well-timed swoop of a falcon' – and the ultimate efficiency of an attitude which seeks to 'subdue the enemy without fighting'. Many of these skills are visible in the excellent leadership and bonded teams of the Chinese business world. Whilst these are now acquiring a decidedly international and even intercultural look and feel, Sun Tzu's influence is present in the gravitas of the leaders and the immense loyalty shown to them by their teams.

Finally, the man of affairs and leader must have vision to see and anticipate things before others, thus proving his proficiency at leadership and worthiness for the task: 'to see victory only when it is within the ken of the common herd is not the acme of excellence'. Western consensus on the degree of excellence in Chinese planning and strategic vision owes much to the influence of such great thinkers as Sun Tzu with their emphasis on forward thinking and longevity in framing goals and their brilliance in strategising the means to accomplish them.

Authorities on these great thinkers will forgive this cursory look at such a profound body of wisdom, but my purpose has been to see how these principles inform the behaviour, values and relationships that we all meet on our business journeys in China. Collectively, such wisdom undeniably illuminates much of the Chinese character and its considered, reflective approach to business and life. Alongside this perennial wisdom, China, and particularly its young, is exposed to an ever-increasing body of international information and China's business processes are also changing in response to greater degrees of partnership with the West. But there is a level at which this wisdom, which has so guided and informed the Chinese heart and mind, will always be discernible in important moments of our engagement with them. Of all the concentric circles I drew when mapping out the areas of common denominator between these great thinkers and their wisdom, it was on one specific value that they were united in voice: respect. It is this value, which they advocated towards self and others, that unites the wisdom underpinning the business cultures of both China and the West, and it is this same value, respect, which makes such wisdom truly intelligible and meaningful to each other.

Chapter Eight

GETTING THINGS DONE

Do the difficult things while they are easy and do the great things
while they are small – Lao Tzu

Nowhere is cultural contrast more evident in terms of starting points
between China and the West than in the area of implementation and
the balance of action and inaction, proactivity and patient waiting
which each culture perceives as necessary to achieving goals. We
have touched on this in other chapters. However, because it is an
area of challenge, it also represents an area of great opportunity in
achieving a bridged definition when implementing business strategy
for profitable outcomes and success. If you were to ask a focus
group of Western businessmen what words come to mind when
terms like 'implementation' or 'getting things done' are given to
them, they will respond with strong words – good, robust verbs that
are the very stuff of Western business proactivity: direct (on strategy), inform (on expectations), disseminate (instructions), allocate
(roles and responsibilities), setup accountability and timelines, implement (project management structures), create (reporting structures)
and report (on final outcomes) and justify (results).

Each of these brings into play the very active nature of the management and business skills profile that reassure us in the West that
things are 'being done' and makes business progress a matter of com-
forting visibility. Apply the same stimulus of 'getting things done' in
China, and the manner of approach would be entirely different. There
would be a completely new emphasis and the business 'action verbs'
would appear much later in the equation. First, there would be the
winning over of all team and project participants; there would be
strengthening of relationships to support the success of the 'carrying
through' stage; there would be the seeking of cooperation and team

support on the business goals; and there would be a quiet consensus on how joint resources could accomplish project goals while preserving harmony and face in the relationship, and accepting a joint responsibility for the project's success or failure.

Then come the action verbs: inform, disseminate, allocate, account for, report on – but in all cases the emphasis will be on maximum cooperation at relationship level and protecting the health of the relationships around the project. Moreover, the resources that are marshalled to ensure ultimate success often rest primarily on the human factor: networks of business contacts, business favours owed, business favours returned – especially at critical junctures, or moments of setback or adversity.

'Getting things done' or 'implementation' in China is much less a matter of 'powering through' towards all important deadlines than it is a matter of cooperation and the enthusiastic deploying of relationships and skills one trusts, because the relationships in question have primacy and enduring importance, way beyond the life of the project. Moreover, when relationships and public face have been jointly committed, the concept of not seeing the project through to the best of one's ability is unthinkable, because it would harm this joint face. You see the difference in emphasis and motivation. While, of course, it is important to succeed in the execution of business goals, it is the ultimate goal of successfully playing one's part in the critical landscape of trusted business relationships and shared public reputation that is the deeper motivator and reward.

So: Same goals, different paths for reaching them, in the case of China and the West. Or are they? We in the West seek to deploy our most talented managers in the implementation phase of our projects because they are needed in what we perceive as the 'make or break phase' of a project's life or a venture's potential success. Although we then seek to structure and control a great deal of this phase and feel reassured by creating a sustained feeling of activity including timelines navigated and forensic levels of progress analysis, we are at source, however, reliant on the talent of our people – and on their level of effective engagement with the project, our goals and their counterparts in our international ventures.

However, in harmonising our approach with that of China for the good of the project and the achievement of business goals, we simply need to rethink where we put the emphasis on skills sets and management prowess at the phase of implementation.

For the Chinese, the emphasis is on a manager's skilful handling of people and the relationship resources as well as the kind of technical brilliance they may show in bringing projects in on time, with flair, within budget or to specification.

To achieve the latter when partnering with the Chinese on the implementation of the project or strategy, it is the former skills set (skilful handling of people) that is required in abundance. In fact, it is a prerequisite to success. Given this, we need to have our most people-effective and inspirational managers or skills set (if we are a smaller company) to the fore at this stage of our business projects and ventures. This is because with China, truthfully, it is more about inspiring rather than powering through, keeping high levels of consensus rather than riding people hard for robust results and most certainly about being prepared to prioritise a strong unbroken flow of relationships around the project over a slavish dedication to specific timelines, exact budgets, a preset trajectory, or the project's progress.

So the skills needed are, of course, those for implementation: technical competence, fluent command of timelines, a commitment to delivering, and a proven track record of steering business projects to successful and timely completion.

But with China, more is required and the 'more' is the kind of fluid character, relationship focus, flexible people-handling style and an almost 'Chinese' level of skill in managing time without letting it bully or undermine the quality of business relationships.

Now the practical part. How do we as Western businesses combine these skills sets, particularly in the case of small companies where we cannot deploy different team members to exhibit and utilise particular strengths?

Firstly, we must think outside the box. Do we have a manager with particular people skills, are we free to deploy this manager and support the technical implementation skills ourselves? Or can we, as part of the China preparation phase documented elsewhere in this book, spend time focusing on the people skills and identifying which manager can take the lead, and how. Often, a firm commitment to managing the project on a 'relationship as priority' basis encourages the greatest 'in-company' champion to step forward. The person from whom you get the strongest buy-in for this approach represents your strongest suit in China. And if that happens to be you, or someone with little technical skill but a strong HR feel, then consider going yourself or sending them. Be bold. Remember what success means in China, remember the building blocks. Then find the right people, or aspects of your people, to pick them up.

It will make all the difference. And since projects, plans, carry through phases and implementation structures can be fallible or suffer in unforeseen conditions, choose a manager or fund a resource who is of the *nitor in adversum* (I strive against opposition) type. The Chinese, you will remember, relish the relationship-enhancing properties that come from jointly facing adversity. So a manager who knows that in the face of a setback, a bold, cheerful flexible disposition, a particular refocusing on relationships and a willingness to confidently rely on these relationships is a must, is a manager whom the Chinese can trust and 'grow' alongside.

Next, with the right champions, establish a China-friendly version of your implementation plans, beginning with your company's business champions achieving consensus – not just of goal, but of approach. Probe to find out if timelines are really realistic, ask if resources are sufficient, establish the most mutually effective way to document progress (the Chinese love voice communication – but not on video conferencing which places them on the spot and can compromise face) and make yourself part of the accountability process alongside those who are delivering for you. Once again, what we are really talking about here is the courage to profile our relationship and human engagement skills over a more predictable and controllable insistence on processes and structures.

Now, however, we know why we have to do this. We know the gains in our business friendship with China and mutual success generated by our endeavours. We have the rationale. As a final convincer on motivation, we might reflect on the fact that, if the Chinese family-based, relationship-driven business model which has ensured their economic ascendancy continues to impact and influence global styles of business, the skills we are deploying to bring our business projects to safe conclusion may well become the very skills that will ensure our business a leading edge place internationally in the new business order and style of operating.

PART II

PART II

Chapter Nine

ACCESSING BUSINESS SUPPORT

I hear, I know. I see, I remember. I do, I understand – Confucius

For the unprepared and unsupported, China can appear an unimaginably difficult market. Outside of China, culture shock as we know it has largely disappeared from our business trips, with the proliferation of recognised chains of hotels, restaurants, stores, coffee houses and the increased frequency of travel to remote places. There has been a steady erosion of the unfamiliarity or 'otherness' of many of the territories we choose to do business in. Cultural shock has been replaced by a more comfortable, even pleasant, 'cultural contrast' feeling – one we increasingly take in our stride and relish. However, in the case of China, achieving the same feeling of cultural comfort zone and a supportive, accessible environment in terms of business operations can still appear very elusive.

Some incredibly practical support systems need to be accessed if ease and a cultural comfort zone are to surround your business journey in China and become the norm for you there. First, because of a sense of cultural contrast you might experience a strong sense of disconnection in the early days of the trip. To counter this, elements of your business preparation for China, your communication style and the key strategies for connecting and communicating face are thoroughly covered elsewhere in this book and in good practical depth. Employed collectively, they act like a user's manual, especially given the deeper explanations to make the knowledge 'stick' and transform into real skills. The advice I will now give, though crucial, is more like wrapping a warm blanket around you so that you can see the more alien and apparently colder elements of

Chinese society through a positive lens. Hopefully this lens will enable you to relax, enjoy, expect the good, project a positive perception of China and find this coming back to you as reputation, business results and the Holy Grail – cherished business friendships.

So, irrespective of task or sector, let's look at what you might need to do in each of the phases of your business development and who, in each instance, you might draw on as your China support team.

Let's start at the beginning. You are travelling to China. There is a choice of hotel to make. This is an easy decision in most Westerners' eyes and one that can be described in simple, practical, commercially sound words in the Western business lexicon. Cost, value, comfort and expediency will usually be the deciding factors. The job may be delegated to a PA or an assistant with instructions on scheduling, indicating the very utilitarian way we view business travel and accommodation arrangements. It is somewhere to work and to settle into speedily, so that the 'real business' can begin. Really? Well, not in China. The success veterans of China know differently. Choosing a hotel that gives face can be a most incredibly potent tool in the early stages of making your mark, giving face to potential partners, signalling respect and communicating that you and your business are secure and financially underpinned, while lining up a day-to-day supportive environment.

The Chinese-owned chains in particular can be a great soft landing, allowing you to flex your cultural skills in a safe environment before facing the business world and to adjust to the manner and disposition of the people, particularly if these are your first forays into China.

But the hotel is more than that. Dedication to client service in China, particularly in Premier chains, can solve a whole host of problems and make you feel supported. You may frequently be collected or dropped off at your hotel and everything from the location to the calibre is important in Chinese eyes. If you are in China to signal respect and impress with the seriousness of your business proposition, and you must be – to be successful – then you must begin by communicating the financial health of your business. Assuming you are deploying reasonably senior staff on China trips, or undertaking them yourself as CEO or MD of a smaller company, then there is also an issue of status. While the Chinese expect government to conduct itself on a financial best-value model in order to show respect for the 'people's money', what they are seeking in private companies is proof of solid businesses that respect their senior managers and corporate leaders. Simultaneously giving face and proclaiming a company's sound financial status, the right hotel reassures beyond what we Westerners can imagine.

The Chinese need this reassurance. They have had less than wonderful results from what they call 'briefcase companies', i.e. Western companies who run from virtual premises and are fleeting in the benefit they bring. These are companies who are in China to exploit a burgeoning sector, attractive regional benefits and manufacturing subsidies, with no real thought for building longevity and loyalty with Chinese partners, suppliers, distributors or clients. In essence, they are businesses that have little interest in creating mutual benefit, contributing to China, building business friendships and operating with respect in creating a joint reputation with Chinese business people.

Yet these are the very things that China wants and which encourage it to select us in preference to others. And, quite frankly, now that it is courted heavily from many competitor countries in most business sectors, these are the things it expects.

This can be very tricky for us. Proving that we are a viable company is different in the modern Western business climate than in China.

In China, owning land is a sign of a solid commercial business. So as businesses grow and achieve financial health, this often involves owning the buildings they previously leased during the early stages of growth. Moreover, the ability to deploy a strong Human Resource figure, to have an abundance of talent and the sheer numbers to accomplish tasks, add weight through numbers at meetings, host events and banquets, and nurture the company's relationship base, is a sign of a solid financial framework. Those companies tend to rent premises and actually work from them so that their relationships are nurtured by a continuity of presence, locale and brand image. Even small companies try to make these hospitable and attractive and to see them as receiving centres for clients in order to add weight and respect to their client relations.

Within their medium- to long-term business plans, many will admit to the desire to own their premises as a sign of business solidity and the ever-cherished quality of continuity.

In the West, it has been quite a different story for some time now. Increasingly, in demonstrating our business viability and acumen, we have embraced a tough cost/effectiveness scale and a value for money, an 'as needed' approach to everything from human resources to business premises via public relations and client account management. This has meant the use of fewer people, deploying lighter manpower as we seek to win overseas markets, and back home relying more on virtual offices, outsourced company functions and our mobile and home offices.

Not all of this is reassuring to the Chinese. Not all of this sounds serious in business and cultural terms to them. And yet *we* know we are serious and productive – and in all those cases where 'leaner' has not meant 'meaner', we are committed to relationships and the development of our business in domestic and other markets.

So, how can we put this right and ensure that the perception we are creating of our business's financial health and resources is not harming our chances with prospective Chinese partners, particularly in the crucial early stages of relationship building? Simple. We address those things we can and make sure that other less 'China ready' aspects of our business development are minimised, presented aspirationally and without embellishment. So, let's return to somewhere we do have control: choice of hotel. Choose a good one. Send an image of seriousness and respect. At this point, business people usually explain the cost of the hotel, the travel, the huge outlay – and the often prolonged lead time China represents. Understood.

However, as previously advised, businesses which are not at least reasonably financially underpinned should rethink or delay their China plans. They are not ready. The extended conversion times alone make this non-viable and the financial tension will hamper the precious relationship-making that ensures success. I have seen this, it is poignant and uncomfortable to watch for all concerned, and it is not to be recommended.

However, for those companies that are relatively well underpinned but still balk at the 'higher cost' of a good hotel – I have enquired deeper, only to find that they have reserved generous budgets to consistently wine and dine Chinese partners, actual or potential. Do not do this. Whilst of course you wish to extend hospitality, it is unnecessary to budget large amounts for this. Plan to do it much less, but with care, style and respect. The truth is, when you are on their territory, the boundless hospitality of the Chinese takes over and you will be respectfully and thoughtfully received and banqueted.

So reserve the financial goodwill for the moment and mentally commit to reciprocating this wonderful lavish attention (which is never curtailed by time or convenience and is generously bestowed) in exactly the same way, when your turn comes in your country and culture. Stick to this plan. It will speak volumes to the Chinese.

In the meantime, spend on your hotel – it signals respect for them and starts your journey well. I have seen situations where difficulties arose in negotiations or where business dialogues were seriously compromised. In such situations, face was preserved in the moment, but later that day senior Chinese executives visited the British company and their hotel. The fact that it was elegant, discreet, uplifting and had wi-fi in all private meeting rooms and recesses turned a delicate situation into a successful one.

So, give yourself a China-friendly point of departure by making this choice well. It is quite simply the first element of your support team.

Next, do not stint on your people, and send them equipped. Whilst not wishing to duplicate the excellent advice on team readiness in the business preparation/due diligence chapter, it is crucial to drop any 'what can we get away with' approaches to deploying your team. While some companies simply do not have the manpower, others do, but feel that it should be sparingly deployed especially until there is proof of significant interest and realisable business opportunity with China counterparts. Unfortunately, this is not good logic for the Chinese. It is beginnings that matter in China. Deploy what you can afford in the beginning. If you are very small and can only send one or two managers, ask yourself if you can also spare an administrator or assistant to give them public respect and status. And if you have limited manpower to send, make a supreme effort to send them frequently until the relationship is built, then space the trips, making them longer, and keeping up excellent levels of communication in all forms – where possible one-to-one phone calls. In a universe of Skype, this is enormously possible without wasting precious financial resources.

And pay attention to how your team present themselves. At the risk of sounding like a wannabe business fashion guru, leave your least fashionable clothes at home, the ones that you got in a sale and bought four of, and the ones that promised to be crease-resistant and you can wear on the flight.

In a world of face, this seemingly superficial advice could be image making or breaking. The Chinese look up to us. They pay attention to image. They consider business prestigious. They do it with elegance and finesse. They aspire to communicate this in ways that match our Western-style preferences. So they are excited by our suits, our briefcases, our mobile phones, our non-business wear and our accessories, both business and professional.

They are excited by the way we marshal ideas, gather thoughts and make presentations. But in the relationship and face-style, they are interested not just in how we do what we do but the manner in which we do it. Let's show this excitement some respect. It is flattering. It helps us bond. Sharing Western and Chinese *art de vivre* and business styles makes connections. And once we try it, the Chinese reciprocate and the richness of what they share makes for great business friendships and fascinating exchanges.

So, in China, your business image is part of your support team. It is another critical communicator. It says, I am here, I take business seriously, I do it with care and style, I and my business make great 'face partners' and the minutiae of great reputation – and great self-presentation – matter to me and to my company. If previous chapters have done their job and convinced you of the value of a positive image and reputation in this culture, then I am sure you can imagine the Chinese response. I am equally sure that this is exactly the response you are seeking to create from your future Chinese partners, distributors and suppliers. And if it is not, it should be.

So, now you are in China, beautifully presented, staying in a hotel that signals the financial health of your company and respect for your prospective partners and clients and the true business dialogue is about to begin.

Where is the next part of your support team to be found? It is among your interpreting team. First of all get an interpreter – even if you use them sparingly. If correctly chosen, they are not just a wordsmith on your behalf, they are an intercultural resource, an advocate for your ideas, a facilitator and a wonderful addition to your efforts. They will, at times, steer you away from *faux pas* and deflect difficult questions. They will also help you to structure your ideas better, more soundly and in a way that makes sense in terms of how the Chinese approach ideas, marshal evidence, make arguments, conclude meetings and reach consensus. The best interpreter will journey with you, add weight to your team and do their work in the spirit of mutual benefit which you are attempting to communicate to your Chinese business hosts, as being your real intention and motivation.Well chosen, they are a critical part of your support team. But choosing well and making a relationship with them makes all the difference.

The following suggestions are based on working with a number of interpreters and then finding a really good one – and observing the critical difference in business results. Instead of giving general do's and don'ts, I would simply like to offer my experience as a working template and urge you to replicate it.

Firstly, the interpreter in question had both an academic and business background and was on the staff of a major university in the interpreting faculty. She was equally at home with government and private sector meetings, something that is very important in China where government, both local and regional, continues to play a strong, helpful role in facilitating business. She had visited the United Kingdom and had an excellent grasp of the way we live, organise thought and interpret ideas – and how we like to define and achieve business goals.

Critically, we spent time together in advance of any meetings analysing the latter. Her questions enabled me to refine business goals and their presentation, and to anticipate how these would be perceived and interrogated. It made me more culturally ready and more ready for a meeting Chinese-style. It made me confident.

As a linguist myself, I realised early on that she had a Mandarin that was of a very high quality, moved speedily across registers and was rich in communicating relatively complex ideas expressed in English in quite sophisticated language, without having to dumb down. Where something was too quick or complex, we worked out a speedy way of signalling alternatives without breaking the flow of the dialogue or losing joint face.

Most importantly, though, because we had discussed the key points and their context in ways where the end goal was clear, there were no major gaps or breaks. In a world of face, this is crucial. Equally, I was at pains to show my appreciation of her role and never to correct her publicly. Where an important point was coming across wrongly, I would simply rephrase it and repeat it until it made its mark.

Most of all, and this is really important, I got real buy-in from my interpreter for what I was trying to achieve. Like many other Chinese colleagues and associates, she wanted to know the nature of my character, the value of my work, its meaning for her people. My desire to understand and become a trusted business friend and express continuity and longevity in my dealings were major assets. They made her feel safe, reassured and proud as a Chinese person to be assisting in the business dialogue she was interpreting. This made all the difference. The Chinese, more than any other culture I have been privileged to work with, give their all when they believe in, respect and are totally engaged with a subject – providing the relationship has been made before proceeding to business.

Finally, we were both women and mothers who adored children and their families. Often our long, arduous days would be punctuated by swapping anecdotes about family. As stated elsewhere in this book, daring to show your commitment to your family and its primary importance to you places you on the Chinese wavelength. It is always valued.

Finally, my interpreter's help proved invaluable in tying up essential loose ends. This is crucial in China. While it must never be forced, diplomatically but firmly marking the stage business has reached is important in a culture with long exploratory business timelines, heavy reliance on oral exchanges and strong degrees of relationship reliance and expectation on qualities such as trust and friendship.

Where the letter of intent is often more important than the contract, it is the skills of the culturally informed, diplomatic interpreter that help you leave with the letter in your briefcase, and in good shape. In such moments, your Chinese aides are as pragmatic on your behalf, as they are on their own – once they have become your trusted and willing advocates.

Chapter Ten

LAW AND RELATIONSHIPS THAT WORK IN CHINA

The cautious seldom err; the expectations of life depend upon diligence – Confucius

In this section, and before moving on to specific advice about the law and its relationship to your China success,[1] it will be useful to look at the cultural and philosophical backgrounds, our own and China's, which have made this, at times, a problematical area. First, our respective attitudes to rules of every kind; next, the concepts of sharing versus ownership and territory; notions of agreement and finally attitudes to the legal profession and its role in underpinning business.

A lot has been said about how China reveres its past thinkers and antecedents. But what does this mean and why is this special, especially given the fact that we in the West also revere advanced thinking and established wisdom? What French businessman, for example, would dispute the contribution of Descartes and Cartesian logic to his business thinking? And whilst not wishing to emulate all that he represented, the world of Western strategic thinking would certainly acknowledge the value of Machiavelli's thought processes, if not their application or ethics.

---

[1] I would like to acknowledge the contribution of Chloe Lee, Partner, Intellectual Property, Stephenson Harwood & Lo, Hong Kong. I thank her for her expert insights, professional analysis and informed, yet accessible, updating of the prevailing legal climate in China around critical issues such as patenting and IPR, as well as her enlightened views on law and relationships in China.

However, it is different in China. Business thinkers of today literally rely on and incorporate the core precepts of revered thinkers like Confucius, Lao Tzu and Sun Tzu into the very fabric of their decision making and leadership. It is as relevant to them today as it was when first expounded by the sages they revere.

However, and this is crucial to issues such as intellectual property rights (IPR), it is the knowledge that they revere, not its 'ownership'. Confucius himself said, 'I transmit, rather than create'. Knowledge is seen as something to share, transfer willingly and for the good of the many. In keeping with the team approach and its role within the knowledge economy, China has been interested in and excited by the transmission of knowledge rather than concerned with individual attribution and the protection of the source of knowledge. This explains much, if we think about it. It negates the appearance of a China that is manipulatively lax about IPR and seeks to 'help itself' liberally to knowledge or skills which are the property of others.

In a culture where sharing is fundamental and knowledge a universal right and value, such concepts are alien. And China's exposure to them, compared to its 5000-year history, dates from only 100 years or so when Western commerce brought such concepts to China's door.

And what has China done since it realised the importance of attribution, ownership and source acknowledgement to the West? It has sought to understand this difference and the commercial implications of Western views of knowledge ownership, and to adjust. That is what China does and this is something that we can lose sight of in the often fraught atmosphere which surrounds IPR. China does what it needs to do diligently in matters of international trade and investment.

China has made drastic changes in its IP laws and practice in recent years. Over the past 10 years, numerous laws and regulations regarding the protection of different forms of IPRs have been passed. Some more significant examples are looked into in slightly greater detail below.

Trade Mark Law and Patent Law are being revamped. The current TM Law has been in effect since 27 October 2001. In order to keep up with the advancements to the protection of trade marks, draft amendments to the current Trade Marks Law have been proposed and are in discussion. The existing Patent Law has been in effect since 25 August 2000. The third amendment to the Patent Law was approved by the National People's Congress in December 2008 and took effect from 1 October 2009. Most changes when formally adopted and/or implemented will bring China's law more into line with the universal standards adopted by most Western countries.

The State Council's National IP Strategy announced in 2008 was further supported by various follow-up implementation plans both at national and local level. The key focuses of the strategy are on perfecting the IP system, promotion of IP creation, avoidance of IP abuse and nurturing respect for IP.

Various Supreme People's Court Opinions/Judicial Interpretations on different IPR-related issues were issued. An Opinion published on 30 March 2009 sets out more detailed plans for implementation of reforms under the National IPR Strategy such as (1) increasing deterrent penalties such as raising compensation awards; (2) imposing civil fines and confiscation of property and (3) encouraging preliminary injunctions. The setting up of a specialised IP court has already been put into practice in Shanghai and Chengdu, and both are proving successful precedents. The trend for specialist IP courts is set.

IP case law in China has also shown encouraging development. The number of IP cases brought to court in China has steadily risen over the years. In 2007, a total of around 17,000 IP cases were brought to court whereas in 2008, the total number of IP cases was around 24,000, marking a rate of increase of about 36%.

The scope of IP cases has also expanded in China. These are no longer restricted to infringement of trademarks, copyright and/or patent. IP cases involving franchising, domain names, trade names and antitrust issues have also been brought to court in China in recent years.

More high profile successful IP cases involving foreign companies are heard of and widely publicised from time to time. Various brand names have initiated and won IP cases in China, such as Starbucks, Yamaha, Harley-Davidson and Porsche for trade mark infringement and/or copyright infringement.

More importantly, and this is noteworthy, higher compensatory damages were awarded. The courts in China are more ready to award companies a higher amount of damages on finding of IP infringement to serve as a useful deterrent measure. The Chinese court awarded Yamaha a record high of US$1 million in damages against a Chinese company. In another case, a Chinese company as the plaintiff sued the French electronics group Schneider over infringement of its utility model registration for a miniature circuit breaker. The Chinese court found in favour of the Chinese company and ordered the French group to pay US$48 million as damages. That case was finally settled with the Schneider paying US$23 million instead of pursuing an appeal.

Availability of criminal sanction for IP infringement is now more evident. The courts are readier to consider sentencing masterminds of organised IP infringement to jail, which is more effective in eradicating the more sophisticated infringers.

The increasing number of Chinese Customs actions is also encouraging news for many Western IPR owners who often find their IPR hijacked in China even well before they themselves have made any plan for marketing there. It is more common for IPR owners to collaborate with Chinese Customs to combat IP infringement. The Chinese Customs seized about 17 million items of infringing goods over 2008–2009.

Returning now to the central theme of this book, we would like to suggest how IPR protection is assisted by soundly managed relationships and mutual respect. It is easiest to explore this question in the enforcement of IPR aspects as set out below.

China is a very much a document-based country; many authorities there require substantive documentation proving the IPR owner's existing IP rights before agreeing to take any form of enforcement action. However, if the IPR owner is familiar with the local authorities (i.e. the Administration of Industry and Commerce (AIC)), these authorities may be willing to take enforcement action such as raids at short notice. As a company becomes more familiar with the local AIC and more raid actions are taken in collaboration with them, the local AIC may have more flexibility in formalities required in contingent cases. Moreover, if the local AIC has greater familiarity with the IPR or its owner, this certainly facilitates it more easily in readily spotting and tackling infringement of their own volition. This applies *mutatis mutandis* to Customs seizure cases.

Experience also shows that companies that have put resources into and boosted/developed the economy in a particular region will find that the local authorities are naturally more willing to help guard their IP rights and take enforcement actions against infringers.

However, the speed of change needs to reflect that China is not so much merely altering laws, practice and implementation (though since WTO accession it has done this at a dizzying rate and tremendous scale as illustrated at some length above), it is endeavouring to shift a culture from knowledge share and collective ownership of ideas to a much more compartmentalised and selective ownership over ideas and the entire terrain of knowledge. This explains why China is so gratefully responsive to Western companies that are partnering her in making this cultural shift, such as Philips, with its programme of IP Academy projects in conjunction with Renmin, Tsinghua and Fudan universities and its seminars for Chinese companies on key IPR issues and topics, with support from the Shanghai Municipal Government and the Ministry of Economic Affairs of the Netherlands.[2] However, as Professor Ruth Soetendorp,[3] an expert and enlightened voice on IPR progress in China points out,[4] China needs to do more than train its next generation of elite business thinkers, critical though this is.

---

[2] https://www.ip.philips.com/articles/backgrounders/ips_in_china2006 1004.html.

[3] Professor Emerita, Associate Director, Centre for Intellectual Property Policy & Management, Bournemouth University.

[4] Ruth Soetendorp Intellectual Property Education in Jonathan Reuvid (ed.), *Business Insights: China*, (London: Kogan Page, 2008, 9780749450625).

China is making a cultural shift from unregulated knowledge share to attributed and documented knowledge ownership. To make this shift requires a deeper strategy and a wider application. Professor Soetendorp provides fascinating insights and examples of current Chinese initiatives to achieve this goal, such as the one in Foshan, Guangdong Province, where IPR education has been taken success-fully into primary and middle schools. As Professor Soetendorp explains, the theme of Foshan's IPR education programme is, 'teach one student, affect one family, influence the whole of society'. In her appraisal, such work is having a positive impact and effect, and the approach itself is summed up by her as a 'child, family, society' chain of influence, clearly indicating the ripple effect such initiatives are set to create.

While this is only one aspect of the IPR initiatives proliferating in today's China, it is a very logical and Chinese approach to the task of changing the culture of thinking 'about knowledge and wisdom' which has prevailed for centuries into a more internationally accept-able one. It shows enormous goodwill, whilst not hiding the extent of the task.

We too, however, in the West are making a journey on the philo-sophical and cultural aspects of knowledge and sharing. We recog-nise that what we consider to be 'careful' in the dissemination of ideas may to a more collectivist society appear more on the paranoid end of the scale. Of course, we want to 'protect what we know', but sometimes it is better to share, partner and continue to innovate for continued usefulness and market differentiation than to stagnate through territoriality or risk encouraging acquisition.

In many cases, it is better for Western companies to partner, share knowledge and risk positives like commercial success and being enriched by what China does with its knowledge, than for partner-ships to disappear into acquisition – unless these enrich the people and knowledge bases of both parties. Instead of 'knowledge and its source protection', 'knowledge and cooperation' is perhaps how we should be beginning to frame our joint philosophical and business aspirations in this area – or better still, 'knowledge and partnership'.

And it is crucial to remember two things to encourage us in this direction. One, that there are cultural roots to explain the contrast in the Chinese and Western views of knowledge and its sharing. This helps take the sensitivity out of the issue. Moreover, it helps to remember that, whilst China may not have always understood our Western sensitivity on issues of knowledge ownership and its protection, it has generally not sought, for the reasons explained, to protect its own IPR assiduously or comprehensively.

At a time when the West is finally acknowledging the huge creative R&D and innovation skills the Chinese possess, we can begin to wonder who is more at risk. And we can see more sympathetically that while Chinese cultural thinking may have made it, at times, an unconscious infringer, it was from a cultural base that also failed to encourage protection of its own powerhouse of knowledge and creativity. This makes it easier for us to address sympathetically and jointly the cultural shifts towards information and knowledge share that might assist us to 'meet in the middle'.

China is no longer the world's workshop. There is no need to fear that the West will have its ideas 'taken', only to have them turned into products in the manufacturing hubs of China.

China is more likely to be the provenance of the next generation of design in many of those areas – either on its own merits or in successful ventures of a business, science or technical nature with Western partners. According to the UK government IP Office's press release in February 2009, Chinese companies now file four times as many patents as five years ago, and by 2012 is forecast to become the largest patenting country in the world. It is time for a different spirit and approach to knowledge and information share with China. It really is. And hopefully, one which finally provides an antidote to the climate of paranoia, hostility and resentment that prevailed until recently. Perhaps, as this book has advocated, the real change is towards a relationship-based model of engagement where 'mine' and 'yours' yield to the notion and vocabulary of true partnership. To help us move to a greater understanding of the journey towards a middle ground, we are also interested in looking at contrasting perspectives between China and the West on subjects as diverse as the setting and maintaining of rules and the notions of agreement.

In other areas of this chapter, we will find the time to consider, more formally, the role of law in relation to the concept of rules and the creation and implementation of successful agreement. We hope this will be of considerable help and encouragement.

There is a story/joke which illustrates the Chinese attitudes to rules and how these tend to be flexible and fluid. Before quoting it, however, we need to consider generally the kind of cultural terrain which rules represent for the Chinese. This might be summed up as follows: they exist and they have to be taken account of, but they are seen more as something that holds the balance points in social and business contexts, and certainly something that needs to bend readily to the greater demands of relationships.

It is relationships which carry more distinct, accepted and fixed rules. And these are widely understood and comprehensively obeyed. They involve undertaking to protect joint face, reputation management, strategies for creating goodwill and maintaining of respect as well as a checks and balances system of favours and support rendered. This system of rules also relies on one prominent feature which might be encapsulated for our purpose in the French expression *chose promise, chose due (something promised, something owed).*

It is a critical, if not the primary, role of Chinese relationships that one keeps one's word. It engenders trust, maintains face and builds relationship. Say that you will do something and you must do it – no ifs, buts or 'well, the thing is'. The Chinese do not want to hear it. This can be perplexing, bewildering and anxiety-making for Western businesses; it looks to us remarkably like failure to understand contingencies, setbacks and reality checks.

Whilst keeping one's word is important to us, processes and rules, which we also consider to be of paramount importance, sometimes get in the way of doing that – and sometimes we can only bring a slightly modified or scaled-down version of the results promised. And since 'contingency' is an accepted concept and 'processes/rules' are highly respected and counted upon in Western business culture, we roll with the punches and, equally importantly, we understand each other.

In China, however, where rules are appreciated and worked out flexibly, it is above all in the area of 'relationship' that rules are mutually understood and agreed upon. It is this area which prevails. And if it is not to be damaged, creative and flexible ways of working with conditions and processes must be found to enable us to deliver what we promise. And so they are, consistently.

Here is the joke to illustrate the point. For this, I am indebted to Linda Lin and Ning Wright of KPMG China and HKSAR[5], and it shows the very idiosyncratic way in which the Chinese take rules and make them their own – and how, once understood, this unusual trajectory often works efficiently:

A tourist, having just landed at Shanghai airport, got into a taxi. The driver took off at such a speed that the tourist began to turn white. The driver turned around and said to the tourist that it was very safe driving around in Shanghai. His brother had been driving a taxi for 10 years and he hadn't had one single accident despite the fact that he never stopped at a red traffic light. Aghast, the tourist just wanted to get out of the taxi when the taxi approached a crossroads with traffic lights. Just as he dived down below the seat behind the driver, he noticed that the lights were green. To the tourist's surprise, the taxi driver slowed down to stop. Surprised, he asked the driver why he had stopped at a green light. The driver grinned and said you never knew when his brother was coming the other way!

Rules – as in processes, regulations and instructions – have their place but they can never be impediments or rationalisations for not keeping one's word. They cannot stand instead of the relationship, they have no power to intimidate in China, and they are never allowed to represent the kind of hurdle that might ultimately spell failure.

The Chinese do not like to fail, so if a promised goal cannot be reached in one way, then it will be reached in another. For this

---

[5] Linda Lin and Ning Wright Due Diligence and Integration in Jonathan Reuvid (ed.), *Business Insights: China*, (London: Kogan Page, 2008, 9780749450625).

reason, difficulties with processes are speedily and creatively accommodated so as to preserve cherished outcomes and the contribution that they make to the reputation and face of concerned parties. So when the Chinese give feedback on hurdles with processes, listen carefully for the 'outside the box' thinking that follows. And whilst maintaining proper respect for the law and probity in business conduct, do not miss the opportunity to learn. So often the very structures and processes our businesses have devised in the West to protect their smooth operation become cumbersome impediments to doing just that – especially for the small businessman and entrepreneur. And we can be too easily defeated by business prognoses, figures, trends, dips and forecasts. For the Chinese, with a 5000-year history of received business wisdom and problem solving, there is always an 'encouraging' precedent for any difficulty you may face, and a ready-made and often timelessly appropriate piece of wisdom and strategy to employ. And since the problem or some version of its root cause or symptoms has been faced and overcome already, why give up or let it harm relationships? This is Chinese logic and it is the opposite of defeatist. It refuses to be intimidated by events or pressures. So, as ever, relationships and robust attitudes prevail and processes and structures take their place behind them.

The lens through which the Chinese perceive 'agreement' is also one where relationship plays a major part in the definition, its continuum of expression and its timelines. Relationships even define the expression that an agreement is given and the way in which it is underpinned in written form.

It is useful to take a step back here and consider the implications of the term 'agreement'. In the West, this word has many core elements in its semantic field, including cooperation, collusion, complicity of goal and intention. But on a word association basis, we in the West are likely to hold a mental image of a written agreement – the documented formal and formulaic recording of mutual consent to a deal, a business venture, or a financial structure. Without wishing to play on words, 'mutual consent' is closer to our definition of agreement, and within our most conscientious and visionary moments, balanced mutual benefit. In China, this would be only one facet – perhaps the most obvious of what agreement means.

For the Chinese, it is the seeking of consent, cooperation, mutuality of interest and goal within the relationship which acts as a preface to and facilitator of the more formal business journey towards agreement. To quote verbatim from China's General Principles of Civil Law, which has been effective since 1986 in providing underlying principles to govern all civil activities, civil relations, civil rights and interests of citizens and legal persons, Article 4 states '[i]n civil activities, the principles of voluntariness, fairness, making compensation for equal value, honesty and credibility shall be observed'. Civil activities cover agreements between business parties and the heavily emphasised terms such as voluntariness, fairness, equality, honesty and credibility all point to the critical and important weight relationships are accorded. So the agreement must be sought within the different layers of the relationship and engagement between parties, making the formal contract simply a natural consequence and expression of relationship harmony. It means, in Chinese terms, that we have now reached a point where we can now proceed to an agreement on relationship consensus, wrapped in harmony, which is their true and full definition of agreement. This is so much more than mutual consent to a set of terms and conditions.

Moreover, at this moment, we become joint signatories to something infinitely more complex, deeper, and of fuller significance. We become joint agents in agreeing to the paradigm of helpful relationship parameters, rules and networks which will power business, build our joint reputation and protect our joint face.

This is the layer of meaning that is not iterated on the written pages but which will govern the maintenance of harmony and protect the level of consensus reached and the continuity of this precious accord.

This has important implications for the way in which the Chinese view the recording of agreement and the role of law in this framework. So how do the Chinese see the stage of committing to paper within a budding relationship, venture or deal? Quite simply as just that, a record of a developing relationship – like an audit trail of progress or, more aptly, a series of relationship markers. And within these relationship markers and the trail they form, there is an expectation of fluidity, since the progress of a relationship – which is essentially an organic thing – requires room to develop and grow and breathe and, importantly, change.

This is difficult rhetoric for a Western business ear to hear, with understandable and very real pressures, traditionally less cushioning from government sources and very high levels of stakeholder expectations as well as a deeper emphasis on timelines.

It is helpful to understand that the Chinese have their own pressures of face and reputation. This encourages us to work with something equally important and real in Chinese terms, the absolute imperative of cherishing relationships and their primacy at the very core of personal and organisational success and to acknowledge them as the dominant factor in any concept of true business performance, delivery or agreement. So working flexibly with the agreement framework and its recording, and allowing it to mirror the stages of a developing relationship is central to working with the consensus aspect as well as other cultural and philosophical aspects of the Chinese notions of agreement.

To work well with this, we need to monitor constantly how we are relating. We need to 'take the temperature' – often – and allow this to be mirrored in the increasingly solid way we record and write up levels of agreement, remembering that it is the relationship and its health that will tell you where you are in your deal or partnership. It is this which will guide the how and when of firm contracts. It is this which will dictate the pace and timing of letters of intent and contracts.

So, how do we accommodate our Western imperatives of early formal recording of mutual consent? By choosing to work with lawyers who are informed about and willing to work with the important, overarching framework that relationships represent in agreement and consensus, Chinese style. These are culturally-informed lawyers who can operate with empathy in both cultures. This is law that puts the preservation of the relationship at the head of the intervention and client representation, knowing that, if this is done, the deal will follow. It is also a sensitivity in a legal approach that is willing to guide clients to work with the timelines needed, to consult with their legal advocates on the building strength of their relationship with Chinese partners and to operate with tact and attentiveness in the timing and construction of legal contracts. It is a style of lawyer who is not afraid to explain to clients that, sometimes in China, it is the letter of intent that often carries deep significance, and that it is the successful evolution of the business relationship beyond this stage, rather than deal making pressure, incentives or bonuses for early conversion, which will ensure the smooth transition to a brilliant and harmoniously consensual formal contract.

So choose well. Look for intercultural and relationship skills rather than 'shiny' deal experience. See how much China is represented on your legal team – this speaks volumes.

Finally, assess whether the lawyers are 'walking the talk' as legal advisers to the Chinese system: cooperation, harmony, cultural sensitivity, and emphasis on relationships and an attitude of patient service. This is what you need in the legal advocates of today and tomorrow in China.

Chapter Eleven

ATTITUDES AS STRATEGY

To the mind that is still, the whole universe surrenders – Lao Tzu

Attitudes of respect for success

You may have noticed how, in situations where problems arise with China's business culture, the solution is often relationship-based rather than the process-based fix-it kit that we might expect in times of business crisis.

This book has helped us understand the reasons for this and, hopefully, to embrace them.

However, it also flags up the hugely important role in successful and culturally-adapted business behaviour played by our attitudes, and invites us to transform these into real contributors to the success of our businesses in China.

So, building on the breaking of stereotypes work we achieved earlier, this chapter invites us to formulate new business attitudes that will serve us well with China, rather than retaining those, usually based on misinformation, apprehension and a little false pride, that communicate a less-than-positive expectation of our dialogue with China and its potential to fulfil our business aspirations.

It may take courage and imagination to make this leap, but every business person and entrepreneur among you are already demonstrating these qualities on a daily basis in your professional life and it will be, I assure you, entirely worth the effort.

So let me guide you through what I believe to be the real success contributors with the Chinese in the attitude stakes.

The first of these is so important that it has been used as the title of this book: *Connection*. It seems like a truism but the truth is that it requires stating. We need to make this a sincere intention and mindset, not a business 'accessory' or an offshoot of profitable deals – this kind of definition has no power in the relationship-focused logic of China. The Chinese sense attitudinal truths with uncanny precision, so faking it does not work. Let us reflect on this for one moment from the perspective of attitude as strategy, from the perspective of facilitating our own success with China.

It is apposite to ask how one can hope to build the latter without approaching China from a desire for engagement and connection. Yet I have observed (mostly Western) businessmen who have asked me what it takes to 'get the job done' in China, and being offered the response 'a desire for connection', look bewildered and deterred from the task.

There is no need to be. In other more familiar cultures, we naturally seek connection, rapport and the engagement of our respective business approaches and propositions. But we find that easy to do with, say, France or the US or Spain because we have gathered sufficient emotional and cultural intelligence about them and have absorbed it to a significant degree so that we know the rules of connection and how to step onto a common terrain with relative ease. In reality, this is what the majority of the business people seeking to trade with China also want. But they feel that their perceived 'distance' from the Chinese would hamper their efforts. Most of all, they feel that they lack the tools and that if success in this market depend on what they perceive as inadequate tools and knowledge, they are doomed to failure.

For those intent on holding on to such polarised attitudes, this has been, sadly, at times a self-fulfilling prophecy. However, this was not the case for those who grasped that the sincere intention to connect backed by even the most rudimentary advice on demonstrating this successfully in their dealings with China was enough to engage with the Chinese, and lay powerful foundations for a relationship. These are exactly the clients who, having grasped this truth, immediately ask how this culture likes to receive gifts, how to communicate sincerity, how to have their company's people engage with those of their Chinese counterparts. These are the business people who prove to be winners in China.

And it helps that many of these very business people have sought to translate their interest and fascination for the Chinese into an active empathy and liking. This, not surprisingly, has helped their case enormously; imagine, if you will, the prospect of dealing with someone in business who finds you difficult to read, remote, diffident, formal, standoffish, disturbingly canny in business terms, unnervingly able and resourceful as negotiators, oh and who, by the way, is not at all sure they particularly like you or your culture both socially and in business. It would not exactly inspire you to trade long-term with this person, particularly with your reputation and success dependent upon it. Well, it does not exactly inspire China either, so let's do it differently for our own sake, for the sake of our business success and, dare I say, for the sake of really enjoying the work we choose to do in our business dealings over the next months and years.

Start by emulating the mindset of those winners by bringing your own brilliant ideas and instincts for connection to the task of making your dealings with China dynamic and real, person-to-person business. This is what the Chinese like. This is what we, in the West, excel at. Watch any networking event with entrepreneurs promoting their wares, and it is pure genius at work. The recent, scary climate might have tempted us to pack away these instincts and become 'serious business people facing tough times', but the Chinese are reminding all of us who know how to read the signs that the will to connect is a core success skill, not some tangential soft skill accessory. Let's listen. The success of our businesses depend upon it. So let your desire to connect permeate that email, whether it is the first or the thirty-first you have sent to China this month, speak directly more often and let your empathy and excitement play around the edges of your words. Let it develop uncensored until you realise one morning in Beijing or Guangzhou or Shenyang how much you like the Chinese people, how connected you feel to them and how much this feeling alone seems to open doors and call out the best levels of cooperation from them. And then you will have to schedule some time to think about what you will do with all the resultant success.

So, what other attitudes do these winning properties embody in our dealings with China? Once again, the ones we have chosen to profile in this title: mutual benefit and respect.

Mutual benefit first of all. What does this mean? Why is it so important to China, and how can this really be an attitude? Well, the dictionary definition of mutual benefit is as follows: reciprocal advantage. But without wishing to dissolve into semantics or philosophy, for the purpose of succeeding with the Chinese business culture, it is crucial for this to encompass a desire to see China benefit with and through you. The days are gone when China has allowed people to benefit and profit from her, as either a cut-price manufacturer or distributor, whilst failing to engage with Chinese society and regional and local communities, share skills and knowledge and, in many cases, systematically employ overseas managers in preference to local Chinese talent.

The omission of regular business contact or the non-deployment of a permanent business presence in the area are luxuries that businesses dealing with China can no longer afford. And it is to all our benefit. What appeared to the Chinese as a very one-sided and predatory approach to trade is not who we are as business people in the West, it is not how we wish to represent ourselves to China going forward – and, most importantly, it is not the best we are capable of.

So how can we, in terms of our individual business profiles, conduct ourselves differently and, significantly, start communicating our commitment to mutual benefit so that both we and China get to win and, in that joint winning, deepen the very bonds of connection that made this success possible?

We return, obligatorily, to attitudes and to their demonstration within our relationships with the Chinese. We need to ask ourselves two fundamental questions. What can we bring China? What do we seek from China? If the answers to these two questions fit satisfactorily with equal weight on a balance sheet of benefits gained, we are well on our way.

However, if the responses suggest that, whilst we desire profits and continuity of success in sourcing from or selling into China, we do not have a commitment to employing local, sharing skills, or looking for ways to contribute to our sector's development in China, to local communities, to Sino-Western relationships or to China's positive profile and perception internationally, then we might rightly ask why China should bother.

I can already hear dissenting business voices asserting that it is enough that we wish to trade with, manufacture in, or sell our excellent products/services into China. Surely positive benefits will follow naturally? Why do I have to subscribe so actively to the notion of mutual benefit to be successful in China? The truth is, you do not. And you may even experience success, for a while. However, it will not last. Why? Because as stated elsewhere in this text, China is now highly solicited and courted in the business sense by most nations on our planet. We are not alone in seeking to make our business relationship with China. We really are not. So imagine you are China and you have a choice between two companies of similar value, import and potential, both courting what you have. However, one of these companies genuinely seeks to prosper China as much as itself, is prudent but not territorial about its skills and knowledge, looks to connect with your city or region, and signals longevity of commitment in business dealings, while the other offers a much less committed picture. Which would you go for? Not a difficult answer to anticipate, is it? Moreover, if some of these companies come from countries where the governments are showing real desire to build commercial relations of mutual benefit and setting committed joint targets, wouldn't that option look infinitely more appealing?

So there are two things we as business people can do to influence our destiny here. One is to cultivate and communicate a real commitment to mutual benefit in our dealings with China. Once we have the business will, the means and strategies for communicating this to the Chinese will emerge. Our embassies can help, the CBBC can help, your research can help. But such an attitude, which is desirous of mutual benefit and firmly and resolutely held from the beginning, will draw to it opportunities to demonstrate your serious commitment to this ideal within your sector and your chosen region of China. The Chinese adore this kind of partnership. Once they know you are ready, they will prompt and inspire you and offer you the needed opportunities to express and develop mutual benefit. The result will be successful, long-term business relationships.

But there is something more we as business people can do. We can use the very powerful voice we have with our governments and our professional institutes to ask them to adopt more of this critical approach, seeking mutual benefit in our dealings with China, on our behalf. For this to become increasingly the tone and subject of the way they represent our trade aspirations and business dealings. And we can insist that this is more than rhetoric, that it is dynamic and real and begins to hallmark our dialogue with China and, above all, ensure that messages are backed up by action.

Ask them to think carefully about how businesses like yours that seek to create success with China through mutual benefit can be particularly lauded and supported. Ask them to encourage your business bankers to be more supportive of your efforts in China, the longer timelines needed for building relationships and mutual benefit in China and the time it takes to convert these into success for your business, for China and for your home economy. Ask them to praise and reward banks who do this.

Most of all, ask our institutes and governments to replace the unflattering and unhelpful attitudes and approaches to trading with China of recent years with the eminently more constructive concept of mutual benefit. Insist that this replace the former, unhelpful, attitudes that we in the intercultural industry have labelled respectively 'China cringe' and 'China scare'.

'China cringe' is the notion that in seeking to build deep engagement and connection in our business relations with China, we are attempting to integrate ourselves with the Chinese. This is offensive to us.

It is also highly offensive to the Chinese, for whom relationships are meant to be equal and equitable and above all harmonious. China does not like imbalance in anything – least of all the relationships that constitute the life-blood of its increasingly international business culture.

Let's be clear. China does not seek surrender of our identity or power, it seeks partnership. It would never encourage us to surrender ourselves or become servile or scraping in either our business or diplomatic profiles. Cultures with a strong emphasis on dignity, like China, tend to like this to be universally and consistently echoed in the partners they choose for long-term partnerships, commercial and otherwise.

Zhou Enlai, the first Premier of the People's Republic of China, said at the Bandung conference of 1955 that China wants both the West and its own culture to engage in sincerely 'seeking common ground, while preserving differences'. This is not a call for surrender, but for partnership. It is as true today as it was then, except that China's current administration have expressed a desire to put their relationships with the West on 'a higher plane' and to achieve together in a spirit of creating a 'harmonious society'. This is not mere rhetoric. In commercial terms, it means preserving core values that protect the business relationship model which China sees as the facilitator of true success. In commercial terms, it means seeking – and creating – and preserving mutual benefit as the cornerstone of our business aspirations and dealings with China.

Which takes us neatly to respect – the last of the primary winning success attitudes towards China that I am advocating.

At the core of all the unsatisfactory and unhappy aspects of our commercial dealings with China, whether the unacceptable and shameful disappointments of the 19th century or the equally poignant moments that I have witnessed where business dialogue goes astray and failure results, is a fundamental missed opportunity to give China what it most wants: respect.

This is critical to the success we can experience as individuals and individual companies. But it has a much greater significance, and here we can play our part in protecting the China we want to see in future years: in other words, in making social, relationship and business history with and on behalf of China. Just as we are at a crossroads with China, so China is at a seminal juncture and we in the West have a role to play in influencing that direction. A recent bestseller in China, *China Is Not Happy*,[1] written by a group of respected and learned intellectuals, presents the hypothesis that China is allowing itself to be dragged down by the West, and the influence of the latter has had a weakening and predatory effect. The book advocates, among other things, that China should carry out business 'sword in hand'. Despite the dissatisfied tone of these comments, the book struck a sufficiently strong resonance to have allegedly sold half a million copies within a few months of its launch. In spite of being countered by other reasonable Chinese voices advocating a more 'balanced view', this voice and the restriction of a strong continuing pace within the opening up of China's commercial landscape which it advocates, is a potential cause for concern.

At its core, though, both this book and its predecessor, *China Can Say No* – a bestseller in 1996 – are communicating something quite profound in respect of the West and the relationship prerequisite to the engagement Chinese yearns for, which is quite simply respect. Respect for its commercial acumen; for having transitioned from being the world's workshop to the world's design studio to one of the world's most astute, solicited and discerning consumers; for having had the courage and vision, not to mention tolerance in overcoming residual feelings towards certain Imperialistic aspects of the behaviour in China of 19th century Western powers, to engage in the wholesale opening up of its territories, opportunities and commercial landscape.

---

[1] Song Shaojun, Wang Xiaodong, Huang Jisu, Song Qiang and Liu Yang. Both the book and the controversy it created are analysed in a balanced and accessible article by Raymond Zhou which appeared in *China Daily*, 24 April 2009: http://www.chinadaily.net/opinion/2009-04-24/content_7710542.htm (accessed 19 January 2010).

China wants respect. And more than this, China needs it to form commercial relationships that work, ones which make them feel secure and have the possibility of lasting.

But, perhaps more than these pragmatic concerns, China needs to be able to answer the various voices within its own intellectual and business elite who fear the deep connections with the West at all levels of the social and commercial order, and to be empowered to respond, 'we were right to trust'. What an incredible opportunity for us in the West to support China in this way, and to reward the opportunities it is offering for commercial partnership with the kind of respect, striving for mutual benefit and 'giving something back' that gives public face to the braver, more open minded and visionary aspect of China's admirable search for international partnership and 'opening up'.

The other chapters of this book provide the minutiae of business protocol and behaviour that act as specific indicators of respect in China and which work well because they are culturally adapted.

But respect is first and foremost an attitude, a disposition.

A concern for mutual benefit, and a desire to support and applaud the brave and sustained opening up of China's commercial landscape is something we can all communicate if and when we feel it.

What has this to do with me and my individual business in China, you may ask? Everything. The Chinese proverb 'A journey of a thousand *li* (miles) begins with a single step'[2] is apposite here. Each of

---

[2] Lao Tzu, *Dao De Jing*, Chinese philosopher (604 BC – 531 BC). The Dao De Jing is a seminal work in Daoist philosophy and is generally attributed to Lao Tzu. It is an elegant treatise on morality and ethics, which seeks to allow man to express what Lao Tzu feels is his true perfection, not from concerns of orderly society or stable conformist hierarchies, as is largely the case with Confucius, but from the broader goal of spiritual self-fulfilment and harmony with fellow men.

us in China represents a crucial statistic in the checks and balances of how appropriate it is for that country to create the kind of active, fast-developing climate of commercial opportunity and partnership which allows our individual businesses to prosper there. We can each be a statistic that contributes to the 'rightness' of this kind of cooperation. In truth, China does not need our dollars or pounds or euros, but it does desire commercial partnership and, most of all, it wants to be given respect and to be vindicated in the respect it is seeking to give the West.

Participating in good outcomes here is not just an investment in positive returns for your company, it is a chance to have a dynamic role in one of the greatest commercial ascendancies of our time, and to support it through respect to feel happier and more secure in its choice of us in the West as partners. We can take this chance or we can provide evidence that feeds the malaise and self-doubt that have given rise to the 'China is not happy' syndrome.

In other words, we can be part of the problem or the solution.

Respect is a wonderful business virtue – for either the giver or the receiver. We have allowed it to be overshadowed by terms like 'delivery', 'professionalism' and 'due diligence', high-performing versions for tough times of something much more fundamental. Yet enduring success in business is based on respect and mutual benefit with our partners. With China as our partner, the giving of respect could turn out to be a trust builder, and the litmus test surrounding our intentions towards China and the appropriateness through its massive opening up of the trust China has placed in us. It cannot have been easy, based on historical experience, to find this trust. It wasn't – the dissenting voices prove that. But China did it. And we have responded by going in our thousands to offer our products, services and commercial wares. By putting respect at the heart of this exchange, we can enrich this process and guarantee its continuity.

Chapter Twelve

THE PRACTICALITIES OF CHINA SUCCESS

People in their handling of affairs often fail when they are about to succeed. If one remains as careful at the end as one was at the beginning, there will be no failure – Lao Tzu

This is the point in the building of your skills with China where we look at the very practical, concrete milestones that will line your path to success. This is a route map. In advising you at this juncture, you will hear not just my cultural experience of China, but specific business advice from planning to success and from voices expert in approaching China.

First, you will hear about the planning phase – often neglected in the 'gold rush' mentality created around China's meteoric economic rise, impressive reserves, GDP and spending power.

And yet, notwithstanding this growth context, China is risk averse – at least when potential risks have not been subjected to due diligence. China is also cautious and prudent. Moreover, it expects you to be – if you are to be successfully considered to partner China – in whatever denomination of business relationship you seek.

Dale Carnegie's words 'only the prepared deserve to be confident' (Carnegie, 1948) could not apply more than in China. Preparation needs to be thorough, astute and professionally supported to stand up to Chinese business scrutiny, as this is one of the most analytical and strategic business cultures in the world.

So, you will hear about preparing for China from excellent advisors tasked with helping businesses succeed in this market.

Moreover, you will hear from one expert in depth on preparing for success in China, through questioning and examining not just your business proposition but your business team, your relationship to and mandate from your shareholders, the cultural fluency of those you choose to plead your business case, the ability of your business proposition to cross cultural frontiers, and your knowledge of the psyche of your end user for your produce/services – both from an emotional and purchasing perspective.

In hearing from Robert Bentley and other business experts, you will also hear the importance of access to funding for your China effort. This support is important. Use it; here you will hear the why, the how and, equally importantly, the when of it.

Added to this practical cultural and business advice, you will hear the early stages of one company's China market entry. This will focus you on the preparation phase and on the critical need to bring your stakeholders with you, to clarify the China version of your proposition to formulate and accessorise it to become China effective, and to examine how your people will translate as commercial and cultural ambassadors for your products and services.

Next, you will hear of the amazing success that can be achieved by having a sound, China-solicited business proposition or service married to the deep relationship skills and communication techniques advocated in this book.

One company, whose success marked them out as winners against incredible competition for the 2008 Cathay Pacific China Business Awards,[1] will share their insights in support of this book's theme and your future success in China.

---

[1] The Cathay Pacific Business Awards attracted entries from a multitude of UK industries ranging from academia to engineering, manufacturing and retail. The Rising Stars Award was presented to Belfast based Andor Technology, a company that specialises in the development and production

We are privileged to have this topical, generously shared information. Much of what has been made available to exemplify techniques for success in China to date has been drawn from the experience of multinationals: AIG, Philips and Unilever. Whilst this provides amazing insights and, in the case of companies like Philips, demonstrates how to build strong enduring business partnerships with the Chinese, it has been reached via projects that have sought to create mutual benefit through generous support in training and knowledge share with China. With Philips, this has taken the form of strong initiatives with major Chinese universities to create awareness of intellectual property rights in the next generation of business leaders.

Such commitment has built a strong bond between these companies and China – and it is deserved. The majority of you are not IBM, Philips or AEG and yet your chances of success are no less tangible as long as you can access the skills and inspiration you need through the example of companies closer to your experience in size, spend and business objectives.

Finally, I will take the information provided by fellow experts and give you a practical distillation, a succinct route map, that will serve and protect your business objectives in China, even on those days,

------

of high performance digital camera and light measuring technology. This award acknowledges business dynamism and success by small and medium sized enterprises (SMEs) operating in Hong Kong and China. Andor Technology was one of the first Northern Irish companies to establish a direct presence in China. They then expanded their distribution network from a Beijing-centric base to nationwide, with the appointment of Titan Electro-Optics (TEO) as their exclusive representative in Hong Kong and China in May 2007. As a result sales in China and Hong Kong have more than trebled since 2006. The judging panel felt that for a UK company to achieve success in such a competitive field was testament to the very spirit of dynamism worthy of winning this award. Cathay Pacific http://www.cathaypacific. com/cpa/en_GB/7e6822a19ddcc010VgnVCM32000011d21c39RCRD?refID= 8200771f906fc010VgnVCM32000011d21c39 (accessed 19 January 2010).

or in those situations, where the correct business protocol eludes you or where cultural differences threaten to overwhelm you.

These are chapters of reassurance, very practical reassurance. Read them once to feel better. Read them often to perform well in China and to know, really know, that success is possible because others have done it – and because at this moment, more than any other to date, help is available to build your China success.

Chapter Thirteen

GETTING READY FOR CHINA

The journey of a thousand miles begins with one step – Lao Tzu

Developing a strategy for success in China[1]

Leading your company into new international markets is a challenging but stimulating role which calls for a wide range of professional and interpersonal skills and a measure of personal assertiveness. Some of the challenges include:

- having to negotiate between the different cultures, operating styles and expectations of the organisations and individuals from very different backgrounds;
- acting as a go-between for your own partners and stakeholders, who are used to calling the shots, and who can be reluctant to share power and responsibility in a joint venture;
- being expected to act with an air of relative impartiality to balance the needs and aspirations of both your own organisation and that of your potential international partners with which you are seeking to engage;
- having to work at the speed of both the fastest and the slowest players;
- sheer hard work over long periods of time in an environment in which it can sometimes appear that not all parties are signed up to the same agenda;

---

[1] I am indebted to Robert Bentley, Managing Director, Market Sector Research International, for the detailed advice he has provided as a template for migrating businesses to China and for creating and sustaining success there. Robert's contribution to providing a due diligence model for every stage of your company's journey cannot be underestimated. The book's theme is enriched by it.

- dealing with raised expectations and any anger and despair which well up when expectations are frustrated.

In order to best prepare yourself for a sustained process that will ultimately bring about effective cooperation with new partners in China, it is critical to be clear about;

- what you want to achieve;
- how you intend to achieve it;
- the benefits, costs and obstacles.

It will also require scrupulous project and stakeholder management.

The following headings, whilst generic to any significant new business undertaking, should give you some confidence that your 'China Project' can follow a quality process that your organisation will most probably have been through before. However, there is a particular emphasis here on the depth of stakeholder working and level of market research required to specifically prepare for a successful business strategy with China.

Throughout this section, we highlight why you need to get help within your home country and in China in order to fully research the likely opportunities and avoid potential pitfalls. We also want to ensure you have a good understanding of where to get help from.

Knowledge of the Chinese market in whichever region or sector you are in will be important to make your proposals strategically sound to stakeholders – they will need to understand what needs to be done and how it will work. This is critical to securing their buy-in to a project that will have a significant opportunity cost.

Management and accountability
The relationship between your organisation's board and the management team is the key to ensuring that intentions are turned into reality. It follows that issues relating to representation of the organisation and its accountability are discussed as part of the initial consultation. The broader initial discussion must consist of

seeking out, analysing and synthesising the views of stakeholders and making sure that these inform the governance and management functions. An example of a particular potential area of contention is the likely involvement of longer lead times in order to achieve success.

Where board and management work well together, they will be assisted in this task by the board. In more troubled circumstances, management can either try to enthuse and energise an apathetic board or become a peace-keeping force between two or more factions.

Effective stakeholder engagement

Developing successful relations in China takes effort; it is often complex, demanding, frustrating and challenging. At the same time, it can be immensely rewarding, inspiring and empowering. There will be barriers to overcome. It will require finding creative solutions to the unique circumstances of a coming together of people from a very different history, culture and values. A first important stage is to ensure that you have the full backing and commitment of your stakeholders – your board, owners/shareholders, key customers and employees. Consider also including your commercial bank among your stakeholders to ensure you have a financial mandate.

It is important to access the personality profiles of the various stakeholders. If this is left until the presentation stage it will be much more difficult to achieve.

The following is designed to act as a guide to provide ideas to develop a process that leads you towards a successful outcome in terms of gaining that commitment and backing. We suggest the following five-stage process to help to structure your initial thoughts and construct a successful strategy for doing business in China.

Consistency of purpose Ensure that there is an common vision of what is to be achieved, and that the business objectives, the measures, targets, activities, resources and reviews will all have been derived from the needs and expectations of the main stakeholders.

In order to achieve this, a useful approach is to undertake internal consultation with key stakeholders, preferably on an individual basis, listen to their individual aspirations and get a sense of the relative importance to them of engaging in a long-term campaign to achieve a significant market entry. This can be followed up with an initial scoping presentation back to the board and senior management staff highlighting the degree of consistency and any serious concerns in an objective, impartial fashion.

An exercise of this nature will help define your company's overall goals, setting out what it wants to achieve in the short and medium term and how it wants to be perceived. These goals are best formed by looking both inwards and outwards and expressed relative to the needs and expectations of stakeholders or benevolent interested parties.

Stakeholders will need to have identified the mutual advantage of working in China and understand that they may need to be prepared to make changes to how they currently operate as a result. There will need to be a firmly understood sharing of risks and rewards. The language needs to be characterised by 'we' as opposed to 'them and us'.

Clarity of purpose   Ensure that all stakeholders understand the scale of the venture that is being proposed.

There are four distinct steps to establishing clarity of purpose:

- clarify your organisation's purpose, mission and vision (goals) – this is what the organisation has been formed to do and the direction in which it is proceeding in the short and long term; it is the organisation's purpose;
- confirm the values and principles that will guide the organisation towards its goals;
- identify stakeholder needs relative to the purpose, mission and vision;
- identify stakeholder satisfaction measures relative to these needs.

To aid this process, which can run alongside the 'Consistency' stage, it will be important to prepare an internal audit of your own organisation's capabilities for export, international trade and business development. The aim here is to guide stakeholders' decision making on what proportion of current resources can be committed to this particular project. The report may require external experts to advise on where the focus needs to be in order to provide a sufficiently compelling document to support discussions with stakeholders. Do not be afraid to ask for handholding support from these external organisations. They expect this, given that it is a very specialist area, and if you trust their judgement, they will serve you well.

Connectivity with objectives Ensure that the actions and decisions that are undertaken will be only those necessary to achieve the objectives and hence there will be demonstrable connectivity between the two. Stakeholders will need to behave in an open manner, giving constructive feedback, avoiding defensive actions and seeking to develop and maintain trust.

This exercise will help to test the level of consensus across stakeholders and provide clear parameters for the group who will be meeting prospective Chinese partners. This will prove central to presenting a coherent, well-thought-out presentation and supporting discussion which will form the backbone of your future working relationship.

Competence and capability Ensure that the quality of service on offer genuinely reflects the competence of the people, including their behaviour, to produce the required results.

The SWOT (Strengths, Weaknesses, Opportunities and Threats) Analysis is akin to a capability assessment. Without a clear understanding of an organisation's strengths, weaknesses, opportunities and threats, plans may fail, roles will be missed and new products or services development programmes will fail to live up to their potential.

The result enables management to act in a manner that does not leave the organisation vulnerable. Strengths and weaknesses are internal to the organisation whereas opportunities and threats are external. The results are often very subjective and will vary depending on what or who does the analysis. SWOT should be used as a guide, but use of weighting factors can improve its validity.

Certainty of results   Ensure that the desired results are measurable and reviewed against the agreed targets. This could prove very expensive if it goes wrong, both financially and to your organisation's reputation.

You will need to give some thought to potential sources of help in carrying out additional research on your behalf. First port of call will be the China British Business Council (CBBC) and UK Trade and Investment (UKTI), but there are also many Chinese-approved agencies. The Chinese Association of International Trade (CAIT) can provide help and consultancy support to help with market entry, market strategy and market selection. We have included several useful addresses at the back of the book.

These five Cs, if approached, will add up to the single biggest **C** that you are seeking from stakeholders – **Commitment**. And commitment from your stakeholders is the biggest single asset you can take to China – you will need to draw on it often.

You may ask yourself at this stage – why is all of this so central to developing successful relationships in China? Like any major undertaking, it is vital to have the leadership and support of key stakeholders to ensure that the venture has sufficient resources in order to achieve the ultimate aim – to secure strong relationships with Chinese partner organisations as the basis for profitable international trade. These particularly apply to China because of the extent of the potential opportunity, the cultural contrast and the servicing that the venture will ultimately require both in terms of staffing and financial backing.

The benefits of adopting an overall approach along the lines suggested above are that you will have engaged your stakeholders in an analysis of the respective pros and cons of the venture. Any investment put forward has to be sensibly costed (time and people) and linked to a clear set of deliverables over a set timeframe. In practical terms, this process will aid the venture sticking to agreed timelines and providing a fast referral route for a ready response from stakeholders once you are out in the field.

You will be taking with you a well-thought-through proposal, you will have an advantage over other organisations that have not taken this approach and you will be able to show your Chinese counterparts that you are there to do serious business.

The result is the seventh **C – Confidence!** This will be evident to your Chinese hosts and will win you early respect, it is to be treasured.

Conversely, the consequence of not doing these correctly is that you will jeopardise the commitment you require from your stakeholders and, as a result, you will not have this commitment as a backbone for relationship building with your Chinese hosts. Going forward in a venture such as this without due diligence would be a fatal error; not only is it likely to cost your organisation time and money but it may also deflect focus away from your core business, with much graver consequences.

A key exercise is a robust risk/reward assessment for your planned venture with a specific focus on the costs to include cost of personnel away from the core business. If the potential benefit to your organisation of what will be a substantial investment of time and money is not sufficiently clear from the outset, then not only will success be difficult to measure but it may be that strategically investing in China is not right for you at this time. This is not an exercise that benefits from mere tinkering.

It will be important at this stage to identify an individual who can take a lead on the project internally. This may be someone from marketing, business development or sales, but needs to be someone equipped with their own research capabilities or who is able to tap into external agencies or providers in order to get the information that is required.

Whoever the tasks are delegated to, they will need to be seconded from their usual job in order to focus fully on this particular role.

Suggested key tasks will include an assessment of your business's existing products and services to ascertain which have a high demand in China. Ask yourself which of your existing projects would benefit from an international dimension, or where you can offer up elements of good practice. In addition, you will need to assess the competition for your products and services, and which other companies are likely to be trading in China.

In order to achieve this, it is recommended that you consult with organisations like CAIT (China Association of International Trade) or the British Embassy and Consulate General in the various regions who undertake sector research and have substantial local knowledge and contacts. Furthermore, you could enter into exploratory talks with businesses in sectors related to your own, and gain understanding of the places to go within the private sector. It is also well worth considering the idea of partnering with current competitors or complementary businesses in order to gain collective access to new markets.

A key question in the preparation phase is whether Chinese organisations and businesses will work with your organisation. This will draw significantly on your language and cultural skills. You may not know the true answer at the initial stage and may benefit from the input of an external advisor who can offer a cultural perspective.

It is worth identifying the back office services that could be delivered in China by a supplier company. Outsourcing services such as database management, opportunities for e-business and website development could help your organisation save money as well as gain support from your Chinese hosts.

If you are planning to work with brokers or local agencies operating in China, it will pay dividends later to understand their capabilities/quality of work, especially in terms of language skills.

The prospect of working in China can generate a range of emotions among personnel involved or potentially affected by the venture. It is usual for those directly involved to feel nervous yet excited about the prospect of new challenges. Other colleagues may feel more wary or even quite sceptical about the loss of control and dependence on others to deliver.

Feelings associated with these pioneering activities will need to be managed carefully. Good management of the process will recognise the need to strike a balance between guarded optimism and the acknowledgement of uncertainty. It will be important to hold a briefing event within the early development stages to listen to any apprehension and temper initial excitement. The event should aim to provide clarity to key personnel (who are also key stakeholders in the venture) and respond to any objections. Successful internal consultation and briefing will help ensure that there is clarity over the purpose of the endeavour, and an appreciation of the financial risks as well as the risks to the reputation of the company.

It is wise to ask yourself a number of questions that help to add a note of caution to the process. This would be the responsibility of the lead stakeholders or for those acting on their behalf. Suggested questions follow:

- Are there any gaps in the offer/service presented?
- Is there sufficient internal investment to help our business/organisation develop and maintain support?
- Will we be resourced sufficiently to do the project/venture justice?
- Have we costed the benefits of the venture to our business/organisation for international growth?
- Are there staff issues which would contribute to or jeopardise the success of the venture, e.g. insecurity, pace of change, lack of experience?
- How can we gain experience given that we are unfamiliar with the territory?
- How will we address the language problem?
- How can we best deal with issues of cultural understanding?
- What is the current level of competition in the area(s) we are planning to target?

- To what extent and for how long can we operate a loss leader?
- Do we understand the Chinese approach to pricing and contractual issues (the Chinese are very price sensitive)?
- Can we adapt delivery to the Chinese way of doing things?
- How confident are we of our abilities to succeed?
- Will there be a short-term detriment impact on our core business?
- Do we have sufficient knowledge of the Chinese legal system?
- How can we reassure existing clients of our commitment to them?

A place for creativity

Notwithstanding the above, like all other aspects of business development, working in China will benefit from an entrepreneurial, creative approach. Useful approaches to consider here include learning the basics of Mandarin or Cantonese – this can have a transforming effect on early relationship building. If possible, spend some time in the region of interest and build a business and social network, starting with a few Chinese nationals who can help navigate the early stages.

It will be important to learn from other companies, UKTI and certainly business associations such as the China-Britain Business Council (CBBC). Advice given by these organisations may help you review the way you plan to deliver your products and services. Given the size of the country, plan to deliver in one region well.

In addition to joint working with other Western companies and consultants, there is a wealth of Chinese businesses that can be used to source further expertise by way of seasoned traders. Working with agents or companies with established links in your field of operation will help to reduce the initial risk of time and effort.

Early marketing activities would include developing a Chinese version of your website, if only a few pages.

Market and sector research

Naturally, well before you leave for your planned visit to China, you will need to have undertaken some solid market research with particular respect to the region you will be travelling to and the sector in which you operate.

A classic PEST analysis is a sensible start to gain an initial overview of financial and trading conditions, which can then be enhanced to examine specific sectoral market trends. Selected topic areas are listed below:

Political
Legal, ethical and law enforcement issues
Local, national and international pressure groups
Prevailing government values and stability
Regulation and deregulation trends, levels of bureaucracy
Social and employment legislation, minimum wage
Strength and credibility of opposition parties
Tax policy, trade and tariff controls, regional issues
Funding grants and initiatives

Developing an understanding of China's political system covers political structure, fundamental laws, rules, regulations and practices that are implemented in China's mainland and regulate the state power in government. Knowledge of the multi-party cooperation and political consultation under the leadership of the Communist Party of China (CPC) helps Westerners to understand the relationships between the state and society.

China's political system means that the CPC is the only party in power in the People's Republic of China. Under the precondition of accepting the leadership of the CPC, the eight other political parties participate in the discussion and management of state affairs in cooperation with the CPC.

Political consultation means that under the leadership of the CPC, all parties, mass organizations and representatives from all walks of life take part in consultations about the country's basic policies and important issues in political, economic, cultural and social affairs before a decision is adopted and in the discussion of major issues in the implementation of these decisions.

Political consultation is the most important aspect of the multi-party system.

There is great internal respect for the political system within the Chinese business community and it is therefore wise to refrain from direct commentary or criticism, which may prove detrimental to your business prospects.

Economic
Exchange rates
Impact of globalisation
Inflation, interest rates, unemployment, immigration and GDP
Labour availability movement, costs and trends
Levels of disposable income and income distribution
Local and global climatic changes
Market and trade circles, distribution trends
Raw material availability, costs and trends
Specific industry factors

The Chinese government remains upfront with a guiding role on commerce, in contrast to the free market economy familiar to Westerners. Until just recently, public and private were one and the same in a political and economic sense.

China commerce and industry work cheek by jowl with its political system. It is a marriage that works and is an interesting differential that you will need to readily appreciate.

At regional level, there are permits/levies/duties that involve working with local and regional government. To further their business case, Chinese entrepreneurs need to work with senior officials to make connections and navigate the state bureaucracy.

All Chinese CEOs court regional officials and consider themselves lucky to be associated with government. Connection to government at a macro and regional level is highly germane to business success in China and is a significant achievement to aspire to during your business journey.

Social

Brand, company, technology image, preferences

Buying access, patterns and trends, advertising and publicity

Consumer attitudes and opinions, language differences and preferences, environmental influences

Demographics, age, sex, wealth, marriage, children, location, profiles and trends

Ethnic and religious influences, attitudes to work, employment patterns

Fashion and role models, roles of men and women within society

Law changes affecting social factors

Lifestyle choices, leisure time breaks, mobility, health and education

Major events and influences (natural and man-made disasters)

Media views, attitudes and influences, public opinion, social attitudes and social taboos

It is well understood that China is undergoing great historical changes in the shifting process from a traditional to a modern society. This cultural transition has shaken the underlying establishment of traditional social values. Along with the development of a market economy system, notably the entry into the World Trade Organisation, cultural values based on a long history of self-enclosed small peasant farming have seen challenges from a newborn social consciousness, different behaviour patterns and codes of conduct.

China has irreversibly stepped into the global process of modernisation. Just like Western nations, China will enjoy its fruits, with its vitality and competitiveness, and face the need to adapt to meet the challenges posed by entering this new age. The globalisation of the world economy will invariably lead to changes within Chinese civil society.

It is important, therefore, to balance an appreciation of 'old China' traditional values that displays an attitude which is respectful towards the Chinese cultural heritage with the knowledge that Chinese people, and particularly the new wave of young entrepreneurs, are also being confronted with values from a very different and contrasting, modern social frame of reference.

Technological
Associated/dependent technologies
Consumer buying mechanisms and distribution channels
Development of competing and replacement technologies
Impact and maturing of existing and emerging technologies
Information and communications and security
Intellectual property issues
Process maturity, capability and capacity
Research and development funding
Sustainability issues and emerging technological solutions
Technology access transfer, licensing, patents

China is investing heavily in technology, nanotechnology and bio-technology in particular, and offers Western companies plenty of involvement. Companies in these and other high-tech sectors seeking to maximise these opportunities will require a good intellectual property portfolio, an effective management team and clear consumer demand. When coupled with strong corporate partnerships, this offers the best combination for success in obtaining funding and government contracts for research and development.

Depending on the nature of your business, and to an extent the region of interest, the PEST provides a very worthy model to consider for China. It is important to select some of the above areas and research in some depth in order to provide a stronger rationale for your business venture. There are many sources of useful information that can give you some confidence to examine the cultural, social and economic issues and look at various patterns as they have been changing. As well as UKTI and CBBC who offer these services there is CAIT, the Consulate General and a host of websites (please refer to Appendix for list of websites) that offer relevant information and guidance.

Take a 'total team' approach to building relationships

It should go without saying that the more bonded the team, the better. This is the model that is understood in China, yet in our experience has so often been overlooked, much to the detriment of the visit.

There are three principles that need to be borne in mind:

- your internal team needs to be harmonious with your stakeholders;
- there needs to be evidence of good practice in selecting, preparing and inducting the team;
- competencies and capabilities need to be assessed within the team and place junior partners with senior associates.

Role of team leader

Since the team relationships will be tested when working in China, it is important to hone the skills of the team members and ensure that they integrate well. As it is critical to ensure a consistent approach to business accountability and stakeholder commitment, team working can be structured based around the competencies of the team leader.

The team leader will need to be adept at people handling. A good Western strategy will need to be adapted to accommodate the different types of personalities of the team members. It may be appropriate to undertake some role play before setting off on the visit in order to work through areas such as business ethics and general behaviour as well as rehearsing the presentations.

Staff on the team cannot be preoccupied with other tasks; they need to be mentally freed up. A preoccupied manager is not a highly effective manager. The role of the team leader is to inform, mentor and reassure, and make the process sound easy. Key to success will be their relationship with staff, other employees and stakeholders.

Preparation is critical for all attendees. All of the participants in the visiting team need to prepare thoroughly in advance for their part of the meeting agenda. This should be planned a few days before the planned itinerary. Ideally, the presentations and key points should be rehearsed from a business proposition perspective, a team perspective and a cultural perspective:

- Business perspective – so that the stakeholders can clearly hear and comment on the clarity of the business offer and business proposal.
- Team perspective – because at the end of the day the potential Chinese partners will be looking to do work with you as individuals. They may well have come to a decision about your offer before you arrive. What they are looking to establish is whether they can do business with you. They will be scrutinising the way that you conduct yourselves, your body language and what you choose to say.
- Cultural perspective – to ensure that you work hard to acknowledge Chinese boundaries and know how to show an appropriate level of respect for your hosts and their country. In the Western world, it is typical for meetings to begin with an amiable, almost light-hearted ambience and each party often settles themselves down with some small talk and perhaps a joke or two. It is important during your China meetings to be somewhat more guarded and reverential and to acknowledge the hospitality of your hosts.

Planning meetings

When planning the logistics of your itinerary, it is wise to give yourself a buffer of time before your first commitments in order that you arrive for what might be a very long day, on time and fully refreshed. It is not advisable, for instance, to travel on the day for an afternoon meeting as it is likely that you will be travelling east and will most likely suffer from considerable jet lag, if not at that time then certainly at the customary banquet later in the day.

In terms of scheduling the meetings, allow for plenty of time, especially for meetings which start early in the morning. Do not assume that you will have finished by lunch time. For the Chinese, especially those who have had less exposure to Western ways, the prospect of greeting a party from Europe, the United States or elsewhere, is a particular honour and the duration of the meeting may be affected accordingly as the Chinese engage at length with honoured guests. It might therefore be advisable for you to set out a clear list of agenda items you wish to discuss and allow a sufficient buffer for each of these. It is often wise to effectively double the time allotted to such meetings.

Prepare visuals for the meeting, and when doing so ensure that you do not fill in all the details of any project if you expect to get group, and ultimately, customer buy-in. Let them help shape the decisions and be part of the success of the group decision, assuming it is a partnership item.

It may be useful to despatch literature and promotional material about your company in advance of your visit – preferably in Mandarin or Cantonese, but only where it is possible to guarantee the quality of the translation. In this way they will be particularly impressed that you have sought to translate material into a language that they can easily understand. It will also help reinforce the general understanding of your organisation and what it undertakes, which will save time and help aid clarification.

Meeting etiquette

At the outset of the meeting, after introductions, it is important simply to pave the way for discussions on the purpose of your attendance, recapping on previous conversations and email correspondence and to communicate gently and respectfully your meeting objectives. Following this, it would be wise to check for understanding from your Chinese hosts.

The use of translators and interpreters is to be treated with care, and for this reason we have covered this area extensively in Chapter 9. It is wise to pick an interpreter you have used before, or who has been recommended to you by, for instance, the British Embassy. Once into the meeting you will need to judge the pace and the amount that you say at any one stage. You will need to give the translator sufficient time to faithfully relate what you have just said to your Chinese counterparts.

It is recommended that you talk in very straightforward language that is not open to misinterpretation – this is an easy trap to fall into. Do avoid Western or local colloquialisms, check clarification with your Chinese hosts and watch their body language as they react to how the interpreter relates your message. If you are able to, and depending on the importance and size of the meeting, bring two interpreters to work in tandem.

Generally in the West, if a meeting is important enough, everyone switches off their mobile phones in order to warrant their full attention. This is not necessarily the case when conducting meetings in China. Here it will be common for individuals to take calls and discuss them whilst at the table. It is suggested, though, that the team leader and his or her team do not follow this same practice, as they all need to apply their fullest concentration.

Be wary of any other items that are introduced to the agenda. If you are not prepared for these you may not be in a position to give a good response and you may be responding without the knowledge or backing of your stakeholders at home. In this instance, it is best to suggest that the item, if a significant one, is deferred until the team can have some internal discussion about it.

It is important to assign someone to record the main discussion topics and the outcomes of the meeting. This will help to make sure that everyone who attended the meeting came away with the same understanding.

Sustaining relationships

Having done all this wonderful preparatory work and achieved a successful mission to China, you may be tempted to kick back thinking 'that was job well done'. Whilst this is hopefully true, it is when you are home that you need to begin the cycle again and work at maximising the value gained from your relationship building thus far.

Serious attention will be required to both follow up and reflect after your visit. Following up on a visit will require providing feedback both to your Chinese hosts and internal/external stakeholders.

Reporting to stakeholders
On your return from China, especially if it is your first visit, the question you will get from stakeholders and colleagues will be

whether the intention or purpose of the visit has been met. It is sometimes possible to achieve several aims and outcomes from a single visit, but the relationship-building process has only just begun.

Your priority is to link back with your various stakeholders, consider the outcomes of your mission in relation to the thinking process and discussions in the first stage 'Developing a Strategy for Success'. The follow-up model below needs to stress the stakeholders' need for business accountability and will require a plan similar to the earlier consultation phase in order to communicate effectively within a large structured organisation. This rarely depends on just one person to follow up with stakeholders.

Feedback is very important in ventures as significant as this, to include all relevant stakeholders. Effective feedback:

- provides the main headlines, with the option of further detail as appropriate;
- explains why certain behaviours/approaches were effective/ineffective on the visit;
- quotes specific examples to illustrate the above;
- allows stakeholders to comment/question;
- maintains esteem for all those involved in the team;
- focuses on the changes/outcomes that will have the most impact.

It is likely that stakeholders will be interested in:

- reviewing strategic added value to other internal development projects or existing operations;
- clarifying customer needs through various follow-up customer and stakeholder communications;
- any personality problems that came to light.

It is critical that all the investment in time and money is not eroded or allowed to deteriorate over the future weeks due to lack of sensitivity and attentiveness. It becomes important for stakeholders to ask:

How are we doing?
Is the relationship improving or deteriorating?

Are our promises being fulfilled?
Are we neglecting anything?
Have the needs and concerns of our Chinese partners changed?
How would we know if they had?
When did we last check our perceptions with our partners?

The modelling of this process has been designed to show that much of this important work can be carried out internally. This tends to have the effect of consolidating stakeholder understanding without the use of expensive external agencies. The benefit of structuring feedback in this way is that stakeholders will feel sufficiently informed to make a judgement on the next stage of the China journey. This then rejoins the beginning of the cycle of briefing and gaining stakeholder understanding, so that the venture may proceed to the next stage.

Follow-up with Chinese hosts

Equally important is dedicated follow-up with your Chinese hosts. Whilst a period of time between meeting and follow-up is more acceptable in Western cultures, as people appreciate that everyone is busy, the Chinese need early, thorough and frequent follow-up – they need to know that you care.

The key to developing the relationship is to acknowledge what might be conflicting pressures of time and resources and agree to work together on a clearly defined set of tasks. The agreed items need to be reported and focused on in order to share a timeline with the Chinese partners. Given that the issue of accountability on deadlines is a matter of strong cultural contrast with the Chinese, we recommend that you assimilate and employ the relationship strategies contained elsewhere in this book, to overcome this potentially challenging issue.

Listed below are some generic examples of good and bad practice that influence sustaining relationships of all natures but are of particular relevance in consolidating relationships with your Chinese partners.

Recommended	Not Recommended
Initiating positive phone calls	Simply returning calls
Suggesting recommendations based on further reflections on the visit	Making justifications at each stage
Using candour in language	Using accommodative language
Being concise, to the point	Using longwinded correspondence
Making appreciative comments	Waiting for misunderstandings to occur
Making suggestions for future contact	Waiting for requests for future contact
Using 'we' problem-solving language	Using legal language (e.g. as a representative of 'so-and-so')
Getting to problems early	Only responding to problems
Talking of 'our future together'	Dwelling on the past
Making responses routine	Having only irregular, diminishing contact

Learning points

Now that you have made your leap of faith and have sampled the Chinese experience, you will have absorbed considerable wisdom with regard to China which you can now relate to your original business objectives. The following guidelines will assist you in getting the best out of this exercise:

- review potential mutual benefits and contribution towards both business and cultural priorities;
- reconsider project management, planning and timing implications;
- review transport and infrastructure requirements, including future access to customers and logistics;
- reassess alternatives based on financial assessment of the options available;
- review forecast operational income and expenditure and break-even analysis;
- consider sustainability and viability over the medium to long term;

- understand the boundaries of possible activity;
- clarification of the necessary operational ways of working and staff skills/expertise needed;
- review the potential organisational and governance arrangements (legal structure, management arrangements, accountability, etc);
- identification of key partners and stakeholders that would need to be included in any board or steering group once operational;
- identification of the obstacles and proposed risk mitigations;
- awareness of any financial risks and proposed solutions.

Cultural rationale for a sound China preparation

Preparing the migration of your business offer to another culture inevitably requires the kind of business due diligence you have just seen described, if true and lasting success is to be achieved.

However, in China, the well-prepared are among the only businesses or partnership supplicants who prove to be truly surefooted in their endeavours, and elicit from the beginning the kind of respect which builds continuity of trade and success. This is where good business preparation becomes sound relationship building, and this pattern will be echoed repeatedly now, as we look at the positive effects in both relationship and reputation – the key drivers of success in China – of a thoughtful and committed preparation for China entry.

Let's look broadly at the cultural motivation and 'China implications' of each phase of the business due diligence preparation and market analysis, with which we have suggested you preface your entry into the Chinese market.

First, consistency of purpose, ensuring that the business objectives, the measures, targets, activities, resources and reviews are all derived from the needs and expectations of the main stakeholders.

This is essential for China. Firstly, they will want to know who your stakeholders are, and the exact extent of the mandate you have from them. China now has some considerable track record with Western companies as well as some less than happy experiences with companies who were not as wholeheartedly mandated or resourced to build their China business as they gave potential China partners to believe. These have made a significant impact on Chinese trust levels and are very fresh in Chinese memory. The longer lead-in times on conversion of sales, partnership, contracts and implementation that prevail in China found them out. This is damaging behaviour. It strikes a blow at the very heart of the relationship-building process so crucial for success with China. No one likes to think that they are having business information, such as the financial mandate behind projects, misrepresented or exaggerated and this is how inconsistent stakeholder backing appears to the Chinese. It also makes you, as the public face of the company, look inadequate in your management and negotiating skills. It is your responsibility, as the Chinese see it, to have anticipated the needs and timelines of a project and to have secured the backing of stakeholders. In Chinese relationship terms, this includes the skills to create a sufficiently strong relationship with stakeholders to weather delays, setbacks or project modifications. It also violates the most important norm that the Chinese insist upon within their business culture: the pursuit of balance and harmony.

If the company cannot hold successful internal dialogue with its stakeholders and agree on critical areas, from resources and investment to timelines for market return, as well as the criteria for assessment and review, then, in Chinese eyes, there is little hope of creating a harmonious, respectful and mutually accountable business partnership with them. And since business is an extension of the family model, inconsistency or disharmony are not seen as conducive to joint reputation. Rather, they are viewed as the worst kind of conflicted behaviour and internal squabbling. For the sake of early reputation building, and signalling the respect and concern for mutual benefit that encourages potential Chinese partners, it is important to get this phase right.

If we do not, we risk appearing to the supreme business strategists represented by the Chinese as though we are 'fighting with ourselves'. Consensus with stakeholders which is comprehensive and demonstrable, spells a business entity that is at peace with itself and harmonious. Clarity of purpose has a similar effect on the health or otherwise of our perceived relationship skills in China.

Do we know our 'subject' as the Chinese refer to it – and do those whom we deem as stakeholders? And if, like Andor whose China journey we will share with you later in this work, and other successful companies I have observed, you wish to extend the term 'stakeholder' in a meaningful way to the Chinese partners that you are recruiting, then you need to be clear that you have communicated your capabilities and goals and the exact parameters around the service being proposed, as well as the responsibilities of the partnership to take this to the Chinese market.

This can be an area of confusion. A diffuse business offer, poorly communicated, with multiple selling points, does not guarantee success in the Chinese market, it merely confuses it. It is better to promote one aspect or recruit one partner well and at a time, and do so with cultural sensitivity and relationship finesse, than to present a confused business offer on products or services, or create multiple partnership openings simultaneously.

On the basis that we cannot present subjects or persuade effectively on business topics that we are unclear about, it is critical to know our offer, goals, field of operation, and commitment before briefing a demanding market or potential partners about it. In examining Andor's journey, you will see how much an insistence on clarity and defining parameters of cooperation transparently with Chinese partners promotes respect and deepening commercial partnership. For Andor, it did just that. And it will for your business too. The Chinese value clarity. So make things clear in your own preparations and, when you have satisfied the need for clarity for your internal stakeholders, assess how you might need to do this differently to communicate clarity of purpose to Chinese partners.

Next, connectivity with objectives: the core of this issue is simple, but critical for the Chinese market. Are our goals and means in harmony? Is the route to our goals a perceivably efficient one, and how will we deploy our relationship base to reach these business goals?

This is a key area and our handling of it is of great interest to the Chinese who value intelligent routes to goal implementation, and who equally value the careful handling of relationships as an effective implementer and *modus operandi* for achieving these goals. The Chinese look for evidence, culturally, of excellent research and preparation, China-friendly strategy, well understood relationship models, and an ability to choose and manage people well. They will also be looking for our ability to get to our goals in a way that does not waste resources, energy and time. The Chinese promote intelligent effort and the kind of business activity and decision that follow research and mature reflection. They dislike knee jerks or activity for the sake of it. They look for partners who can display this approach. Conversely, activity in the Western business culture is, at times, confused with progress. Not so in China. The Chinese value informed action and advocate inaction when an immediate business decision or direction needs further clarity or elucidation.

More importantly, from their perspective, they will be looking at actions and decisions that build essential relationships – the ones which will carry forward strategies and business goals. And, here, they will be looking for us to make the *critical connection* that time invested in building the relationship is central, because 'relationship *is* strategy' in Chinese business culture. Skills, finesse and commitment in this area are the real 'activity' in the Chinese business culture – it is they that truly carry the success gene.

So, when we focus on actions and decisions to ensure connectivity with our business goals and see these through in China, we need to ensure that a focus on network creation, reputation creation and management, and people facilitating, in all its aspects, is at the core of our 'actions and decisions'. We need to further ensure that this is where we put our resources of time, money and energy, for relationships will be the true workhorses of any success plan we create.

Finally, in terms of objectives, it is important to remember time within this framework, and equally critically, beneficiaries of results achieved.

Objectives need to take account of, and demonstrably possess, an element of creating mutual benefit if they are to entice the much solicited Chinese business market – heavily laden with opportunities, but equally heavily courted.

The Chinese, as stated elsewhere, respond more to the notion of mutual benefit and relationships that exhibit respect, than to offers of partnership which focus exclusively on 'bigger and better' profits and gains.

China wants more. It wants real partnership and respect, because these secure the continuity of the most precious Chinese business collateral: relationships and people.

So ensure that your objectives are framed in terms of mutual benefit and are further framed in terms of gains and enhancement for both partners, not just in the area of financial reward, but in the enhancement of people, relationships, reputation and skills building.

And above all, remember to frame and communicate your objectives in ways which imply longevity and continuity – and mean it.

Short-termism is over as a strategy for the Chinese market. In a culture which values relationships and emphasises trust, it was always a flawed and unhelpful strategy. Now, however, the Chinese insist on a more committed approach and longer-term objectives as a prerequisite to selecting a Western business as partner. And they can afford to do so. They have the choice. Moreover, while this may require more effort and vision on your part and that of your business stakeholders, it is more likely to gain you success and recognition in China, than any 'quick fix' approach.

In straitened business climates, it is natural for us to want to demonstrate speedy returns and high yields. In China, however, this smacks of opportunism and desperation.

Conversely, if you use the skills advocated here by making sound relationship creation a key objective, you may well find yourself reporting higher yields and returns than you hoped, by deploying a more 'Chinese' logic and method to do so.

This brings us neatly to the area of 'competence and capability' and the contribution to success which 'doing what you say you do, with people who are sufficiently skilled to do it', makes in our business engagement with China. Two things are central here, and they have been mentioned earlier. The Chinese do not like surprises and have high perfectionistic tendencies and standards. They look to the West for the kind of quality standards they want to make universal, in time, across their entire product base and service offer as a business culture. They expect it. We have told them that we can offer it.

It is crucial that we deliver, because inferior results, poor quality, shoddy deadlines and mismatched promise and outcome, tend to do more than simply hamper business efficiency and progress. They damage trust, which compromises face, which harms – sometimes irreparably in China – a business reputation.

This is also the case with choosing to deploy the right team. I have observed senior personnel, carrying titles that implied a knowledge of, say, finance or research and development, who, when asked highly piercing questions by the Chinese, were unable to field questions in the detail required. At such moments, there was a loss of face for all the team members and the business itself. Competencies must be clearly matched to skills areas and the critical ability to communicate these effectively, fluently and in a way that is inducive of trust on the part of the Chinese partners – and which can withstand scrutiny.

Apart from the area of competence, however, there is also the area of cultural fluency. What does this mean, and how does it affect your performance in China and your choice of people to deploy?

Frequently, on overseas work, people tend to deploy their most results-based high performer – a kind of 'can-do' person who has high stakeholder credibility and can implement speedily while being focused on the bottom line.

Everything you have read so far in this book has hopefully encouraged you to look for a different profile when choosing your team. Product knowledge, management competency, technical expertise – these are all assumed in China. What is required within the team – ideally prominently – is someone who creates and maintains relationships well, is flexible, has excellent stamina and patience and likes the fact that people do business with people – in fact gets out of bed because of their belief in this fact. And if this kind of champion of relationship skills (who will become your strongest advocate and asset in China) is you, then get involved, however long you have owned the company or sat on the board. It will truly make your business in China. Because nowhere does China dislike and fear disappointment more than in the area of people.

Remembering that what is inferior in people or products is a relationship breaker and that relationships are the true drivers of business success in China, will make you more intent and resolute in your competence and capability review to the long-term gain and credit of your businesses.

Certainty of results, and ensuring that desired results are measurable and reviewed against the agreed targets, brings in these people skills.

First, identifying partners who are willing and able to work to desired results levels and be accountable against targets set can be a challenge. It is worth taking your time and spelling it out. Spelling it out, China style, means that after all the explanations, preamble and rationalisations we Westerners offer before giving instructions, we then remember to actively give the instructions and give them clearly: the when, where and how of what we expect. The Chinese are pragmatists and embrace hierarchy. They like clarity. And they like to be motivated to consult on issues that affect their business destiny and likelihood of success. So do not be afraid to set robust targets, but do it jointly and get buy-in for any accountability structures you set up. Providing that your need is clear and providing the resources to reach the targets are made available, your Chinese partner will seek to reach these goals – not least because bigger things depend upon it: the health of the business relationship and its growth.

You will also note that in an effort to prepare your business Chinese style, a fairly exhaustive PEST model has been advocated to avoid pitfalls and ensure a surefooted market performance.

It is important to know your market and your partners. A business truism, one would think. However, with countries like China where there is a perceived sense of cultural distance, huge levels of internal diversity, and a rapidly changing socio-economic and socio-cultural framework, it is mandatory.

China is diverse. China is changing. Your sector, irrespective of its nature, needs to take account of new factors, expanded disposable income levels, increased partnering opportunities and high levels of recent influence from other cultures around the globe on everything from China's workstyle to its earning expectations and consumer preferences.

To gain a solid anchor, use the research tools you have available to look at social, political and economic trends as well as technological advances and consumer preferences. Not only will it inform your business strategy in a helpful way, but it will give you an addition-ally informed business 'face' in China. And since you are your busi-ness in this market ... you see the implications. Do not wait for your first hotel room or your 40th visit to begin regularly reading a repu-table English version of a Chinese broadsheet. Know the political leaders, understand the forces that are currently shaping change in China, see what is influencing them from our world, and take account of it in your business. It will make all the difference. It signals respect. Moreover, it is hard to create mutual benefit as an objective if you do not understand where and why it is solicited.

And finally, take a 'total team' approach to presentations and negotiations.

In embracing this concept and putting it at the heart of your China success, it is crucial to understand how this affects the way your business is perceived in China. This is the true motivator for adapting some of our more individualistic business behaviour and signals.

China respects team players, not personalities. While they admire firm character and clear leadership, they see the team as central to business endeavour and cooperation. They trust team players because, with them, they understand the rules of engagement and can proceed to build relationships from a shared basis, intent and objective. This is what China wants. And where team spirit prevails, objectives are generally achieved without conflicts of interest, loss of face, disruption, disharmony or conflicted relationships and interests.

This is business Nirvana for the Chinese. This is their world.

So brief staff, encourage sharing, be clear on hierarchy, 'read' your audience all day, all the time, with the most intense attentiveness and concentration you can muster. Never 'wing it'; this implies disrespect and insults the intelligence of a race who value and prepare for opportunity. Above all, give time to your Chinese business partners or potential partners.

More importantly, and ensure that this is true for your people as well, give them the gift of 'you'. Invest yourself, not just your business, find aspects to relish and enjoy and communicate these enthusiastically, do not count problems if they occur, first strengthen the relationship and then, with the help of the relationship, move gracefully and, if possible, without complaining, to their resolution.

Finally, because relationships matter, follow up!

When you plan and engage in follow-up activities, remember to base them not just on the business communication models you use with other cultures, but on the kind of follow-up you might deploy after an agreeable time with friends or family.

Chinese sensibilities are tender. They respond to nurturing, respect and – the lifeblood of good relationship management – higher and more consistent levels of communication than we would normally muster in the West.

Remember that 'not keeping in touch' for the Chinese does not mean you are too busy, it means you do not care enough. If like them, relationships are your priority, then communication would take precedence over other demands. Use the phone, be flexible in changing what does not work, but do so with the consensus of Chinese partners and as non-judgementally as possible. Keep close to customers, partners, associates, agents and distributors – geographically, if possible – if not by phone, then by email. Approach the use of video conferencing with care, always give preparation time and avoid putting individuals on the spot or asking overly direct questions. An inadequate answer can cost 'face' in a Chinese team, especially if recorded and played into the board meeting.

Do not be afraid to ask for accountability, but be part of it and remember that this accountability is team-wide in China, not focused on individuals – a preference which it is wise to work with, and not against.

The Chinese expect you to be anticipating success for your business partnership with them and, as long as you respect the methods they deploy to reach this goal and for you, they will never shy away from results reviews or frank discussions on what will achieve success.

Relationships well made facilitate such a dialogue, even in adverse moments, and call out the strategic excellence of this race in the pursuit of success for you and your business, providing the goal is that of mutual benefit, the effort is joint and the business is conducted with respect.

A successful China market entry is within your grasp. All that is required beyond having the sound products and services that China desires, is a thorough business preparation, a well-selected team and a true commitment to relationship as a means to success. The skills that make you successful in your domestic markets are the exact same skills which will help you continue this success with China. However, they will need to be honed and developed to become real assets in a market defined by high strategic quality, intensely valued relationship networks and a commitment to the long term. In the end, however, it is the opinion that China forms of us as (business) people which is the ultimate decider of our business destiny. Thorough preparation, however, allows us to influence China's perception in our favour. This is its true value.

Chapter Fourteen

SUSTAINING SUCCESS IN CHINA THROUGH RELATIONSHIPS: ANDOR – A CASE STUDY

From caring comes courage – Lao Tzu

It is hoped that the theme of this book has ably demonstrated the importance of relationships to success in China. However, in the pragmatic core of all of us who are versed in international business is the rogue belief that good products, services, business propositions and ideas speak for themselves, the globe over – and that attention to relationships or cultural norms is far from mandatory.

This, as far as China is concerned, is misplaced and erroneous.

The Chinese assume that those who court the increasingly crowded arena of their key business sectors have come with good business propositions, services and offers, and that these correspond to an identifiable need within China's ever developing consumer landscape.

What China further seeks, however, is reassurance from its international partners, suppliers and associates in the form of highly developed finesse in the business of relationship and reputation building – and dedication to the many forums of building the only business collateral that matters: relationships networks.

For our business to migrate well, it will ideally: meet a topical and identifiable need; be introduced with strong attention, from the off, to relationship creation; and take time to allow the relationship to dictate the nature and pace of the business dialogue. It will involve signs of good faith such as local presence, and it will hold the seeds of longevity in the way the business is introduced.

In charting the journey made by Andor[1] in China, we will be looking at the unmistakably winning formula that is a sound proposition or business product underpinned by a solid and committed approach to relationship and real connection with China and its business culture. We will not codify the methods used. Other chapters will help you understand how to apply the wisdom in your own culturally-adapted relationship building with China, but you will find elements and advice that will coalesce into a template for success – echoed and elaborated on by the cultural comments we offer around Andor's experience.

What they have done, you too can do. There are tips and practical strategies and techniques but, as Andor's experience exemplifies, it is truly our winning disposition and intention to build strong relationships, acknowledge and reciprocate commitment and hospitality, and be open to real connection that differentiates us from others in our sector and marks us out for trust and success.

This is the truly winning formula in China.

Andor Technology case study

Introduction
Andor Technology plc is a Northern Irish company based in Belfast and operates at the high-value end of the global scientific digital camera market. It is also a major category winner of the prestigious Cathay Pacific China Business Awards, in recognition of the substantial success which the company has built with China – as well as the ability it has exhibited to sustain this success.

---

[1] I am indebted to the management of Andor for their kind permission to narrate their company's development and success in China. I am particularly grateful to Philip Moore, Asia-Pacific Sales Manager, for his detailed insights and explanations which illuminated the Andor journey and helped to distil its wisdom into this chapter.

Moreover, they have chosen to share generously with us their particular commitment to prioritising relationship-building strategies with their Chinese clients and partners, which they believe is central to success.

But first, the Andor profile. We would like to share the highly successful research, design innovation and client focus that hallmark Andor and, more specifically, in setting the scene for its success in China, the company's commitment to teamwork, to people and to a wide and comprehensive definition of stakeholders. We will highlight its core values and how, in a demanding sector such as scientific cameras and in a demanding market such as China, it has achieved and managed such distinction, achievements and brand profile.

Andor Technology plc is a highly successful and rapidly developing company that aims to become a global leader in pioneering and manufacturing high-performance light measuring solutions. Andor's impressive business journey to date has seen it grow from its genesis in Queen's University Belfast Physics Department, to becoming an employer of 200 people in its 15 offices worldwide and distributing its products to 10,000 customers in 55 countries.

And what products! Andor's brilliant and sustained innovation has made a significant contribution to the world of scientific research as well as the medical and industrial communities.

All of this was born from a desire for excellence: the company's founders, realised that the cameras available in the Physics Department were inadequate for their demanding applications, and set about developing their own. When these had been used in various imaging and spectroscopic applications, researchers in other departments of Queen's as well as in other major universities began to solicit their use.

Andor's inception in 1989 was a response to the emerging needs of the research and scientific communities. So, a desire for excellence, a penchant for innovation and an 'if it does not exist and it is needed, let's make it' philosophy has been present since the company's early days.

Such values, amongst others, have ensured that Andor is today the fastest-growing company manufacturing high-performance digital cameras, having been the pioneers of this particular technology within their industry.

Andor Technology plc was admitted to AIM (the London Stock Exchange's Alternative Investment Market, a global market for smaller, growing companies) on Friday 3 December 2004 when dealings in its ordinary shares commenced.

Andor's dedication to, and exceptional track record in, innovation makes inspiring reading – but there have been specific highlights in innovation worth citing for the Andor range and product dedication which they exemplify:

- 1989, first non-controller based scientific camera
- 1991, first permanent vacuum sealed spectroscopy camera
- 1994, first fully integrated ICCD (Intensified Charge Coupled Device)
- 2001, first EMCCD (Electron Multiplying Charge Coupled Device)
- 2009, Scientific CMOS Technology launch.

Andor ascribes its success to being a result of maintaining a closer, unbroken focus on certain key facets of the company's values and business code.

Developing a strategy for success in China

Upon launching the brand, China was seen as a substantial market and plans were put in place to appoint representatives as soon as possible. This was crucial for retaining a strong profile in this major sector.

Andor's clients come from within the faculties of science in universities across China as well as the various branches of the Chinese Academy of Science. In addition, they have an OEM customer base in analytical instrument manufacturers for a wide range of applications. Selling to a demanding market with clearly defined needs and standards, Andor was keen to build its market intelligently. As such, tracking the important growth in funding and investment in scientific research in China – and following the areas and projects to which these funds were being allocated – was an important key in identifying the market parameters and identifying an expanding needs base in Chinese clients.

In terms of getting established and building profile, Andor instinctively developed a very people-focused, visible approach to cultivating relationship at the heart of their success formula.

Initial profile was established by looking to install Andor systems with key researchers who could become 'reference sites' for Andor products. As well as local references, the reputation of both products and company was enhanced by the placing at customers' disposal a healthy portfolio of references from international customers testifying to the capabilities of Andor products on offer.

Keeping abreast of funding and development strategies towards the scientific community by the Chinese government was important to Andor; for example, the Chinese government policy for growing basic research capability has been to encourage overseas-based researchers to return to China, with funds allocated for the setup of key state laboratories in various disciplines.

Pre-market entry: building relationships

The early stages of Andor's preparation for their Chinese market entry were hallmarked by a number of supporting visits to build relations with partners and distributors. Detailed research into key industry players and their channels was undertaken. At this point, just as Andor decided to launch into the market under its own brand, a realignment of rival distribution channels allowed the opportunity to work with experienced personnel who had previously worked with rival products. This was fortunate for Andor and would have been so in any market. However, this was particularly the case for the Chinese market, because it allowed Andor to tap into this network of customers and influences and gave acceleration to gaining market penetration.

In China, to be wealthy in a business or personal sense is not necessarily to be in possession of massive financial assets; rather it is described as 'mankeep' or being well-connected. Identifying partners and representatives with strong reputations and helpful business relationships over a wide contact base is a huge asset in China, and a great accelerator of market penetration and the building of relationship.

But as has already been stated, it is the way we handle such vital resources that marks us out as winners in China. Much of the excellent way Andor built relationships was covered by their core company value – teamwork – but it is worth adding in and demonstrating the value of a few of their most successful strategies in relationship management skills.

Where researchers had previous exposure to Andor products, usually based in overseas institutes, they looked to Andor as a supplier when equipping their facilities in China. High satisfaction levels and familiarity with products often guarantee repeat sales from the Chinese, who revere excellence, dislike change for change's sake, and are keen to express loyalty. Moreover, Andor has sought to further its brand awareness and reputation by working with distributors in trade shows, marketing shows, academic meetings and by showing a strong, united face with Andor representatives on the ground in China. They went further, by organising specific seminars at key locations, inviting local customers and their students to hear talks from existing users, and regularly bringing technical experts to China for face-to-face meetings with clients.

In terms of proof of good faith, Andor acknowledged that demonstrating the capability of its systems was a key factor in allowing their expansion within the market. Given that their products are at the higher value end of goods available to the scientific community, they represented a relatively large commitment by the researchers purchasing. Therefore, the provision by Andor of generous levels of time for people to test out and work with the machines on sale was crucial. To this end, Andor very wisely invested in demonstration equipment held specifically for use in China.

Finally, the establishing of a direct representative office in 2006 allowed the Andor brand to be even better known. In incorporating the office, Andor engaged fully with their local distributors and gave them the opportunity of working with the company. This ensured that Andor was able to maintain its links to its existing customer base whilst also allowing it the opportunity to build its brand partners. At that time, Andor's distributor was based in Beijing, but as the business was about to expand nationally, Andor took the decision – jointly with its representative – to properly resource the support and sales infrastructure. The most prudent method, it was decided, was through establishing a direct presence.

In creating such a positive impact for its brand, sustaining success and building relationships with distributors, and by creating an effective sales and support infrastructure, Andor progressed in a very surefooted, China-aware way. It did this by intelligently using the resources available to it to support its China entry and development. For example, it wisely sought to draw on the expert trade missions, research contacts and local footprint offered by Invest Northern Ireland and United Kingdom Trade and Invest as well as the British and Irish embassies in China, the CBBC (China Britain Business Council). Sir William Ehrman, the British Ambassador, opened the Andor office in December 2006, and to ensure their brand's incorporation in China was carried out smoothly in a way that built reputation, Andor used PWC as the local consultants to guide them through the registration process for the office setup.

In short, Andor did a great deal in a short time with prudence, care and effectiveness. What is important to understand is how the steps that Andor took intuitively were such culturally adapted, positive strategies in building success, trust and mutual benefit with China: in other words creating the kind of partnership that China requires from us for enduring success as suppliers, purchasers or advisers. What we might call the People Success Template – one amply demonstrated by Andor's journey.

Consolidating business

By this stage Andor had an established presence in China and its aim was to develop a larger geographic footprint for sales across the country. Now adaptability and flexibility – two key skills in China – were needed and proved to be Andor's strong suit as the company was now offered an opportunity to work with Titan Electro-Optics,

one of the largest channels in their industry with regional representation across China. As a consequence, the company had to revise
sales strategy to take advantage of the new opportunity. This meant
that Andor could now work in the geographical areas that they had
targeted in shorter time frames while, in turn, their product innovation offered new potential to their Chinese channel.

Being adaptable to the changing market dynamics was key to developing business, but the local presence also came into its own now,
allowing Andor to provide stronger channel support.

As sales increased, China gained a more pronounced profile within
the company and Andor quickly saw the need to augment its investment in sales and support infrastructures. The larger growth brought
demands on internal structures that also required suitable resourcing.
To ensure success, the company had to invest proportionally to
develop the internal structures to match these external demands.

Andor also placed an even greater focus on the quality and internal
support they were creating to meet this larger growth, and were
quick and flexible in addressing any issues or requirements here.
And in a spirit that China would appreciate, Andor did not allow
their business to go forward without a clear long-term strategy to
help focus and inspire its business and partners.

China always thinks long-term while engaging in business and
expects its partners to do so also. And yet they rely on the sort of
relationship skills they advocate so passionately, and Andor has
embodied so well, to ensure the success of long-term strategy and
provide flexibility and solidarity if plans alter.

Market and sector research

Andor began with a very well understood need and the skills to
interrogate its potential client base, the scientific and industrial community, in depth about the nature of this need. This resulted in
consultation being at the very root of Andor's product research and
gave birth to a desire to innovate, in order to anticipate the needs
of this market and to avoid the kind of gaps in provision of research
tools it had experienced prior to the company's birth. The magic
word here is not merely innovation, but consultation.

Andor has continued to consult heavily with those university departments in China that form a section of its client base with the skills to elicit and respond to emerging or changing needs. This kind of consultation is crucial. It involves real partnership. It makes the client a stakeholder in the development of the tools that serve its needs and it involves China's scientific elite in Andor's success. Moreover, it allows a dialogue of respect and knowledge share between customer and supplier. This dialogue is just as fundamental to success in China as is the mutual benefit which results.

In Andor's case, they had the intelligence and consideration to consult Chinese policy in science and research investment, and to treat as a priority those areas and institutions to which funding was flowing. It was customer identification through showing interest in China's development and priorities. This is the kind of customer identification that China likes: intelligent strategy implemented with great care and attention to China's wellbeing and the health of the building commercial partnership and to relationships in general. Staying in close consultation with one's clients is fundamental in China, because relationships power the helpful transfer of information and vital customer research, as they do everything else. There is an old Chinese aphorism relating to the accountability of its historical emperors and leaders which states: 'who loses the will of the people, loses everything'. Consultation, consensus, involvement and buy-in are the keys to success in China. The Chinese do business with people they trust, and seek to have a major say in, and understanding of, anything they purchase to enhance their work or life.

As we said earlier, since its 'opening up' China is now exposed to huge external influences. Staying close to your customers allows you to update their customer profile and preferences, so central to gathering real business intelligence and so important in staying linked to your market. Andor also generously shared marketing costs with its distributors and was happy to exhibit under a joint name banner at local exhibitions and trade shows.

This is people management, China style. Do not quibble about small costs or pride of place with Chinese partners' brands, it is not considered business astuteness in China, it is considered poor form and it does not make sense. The Chinese partner's brand has a wealth

of local contacts and knows the promotional costs involved in courting clients Chinese style and in presenting a 'good face' for your
business. Of course there is always financial accountability and
brand protection to consider, but the Chinese will not risk harming
these if the relationship is correctly made and you are heavily
engaged in shoulder to shoulder partnering. Conversely, I have seen
the kind of 'false pride' over brand protectionism and an inexplicable
tightfistedness over shared costs – resulting in business inquisitions
over relatively small amounts of marketing or operational costs –
ruin relationships with promising Chinese partners and dispatch
amazing business opportunities into the arms of waiting competitor
companies, simply because they had a better understanding of partnership and the relationship support in China.

Building relationships

Developing relationships into business

Firstly, although Andor sought high levels of technical and language
competence in its partners, as well as proofs of business and financial stability, they were not afraid to take risks in working with small
companies that could demonstrate their capabilities in these areas.
Moreover, they nurtured them in precisely the right way to fan their
partners' pride in working with Andor, and to enhance the 'public
face' that is so important to the local Chinese partner when carrying
through their belief in Andor's product to bottom-line sales
conversion.

They supported in the Chinese style with resources, and presence
alongside partners at key events, roadshows and trade fairs. But
support Chinese style is also about knowing when to bring out the
'big guns', and nothing impresses like knowledge and credentials. So
Andor was not afraid to deploy technical specialists to support partners at critical roadshows, seminars and exhibitions. This was not
merely about supporting the technical skills of the Chinese partners
– these were already a prerequisite for selection – it was part of building the partners' public face, so in turn building their business offer.

Generosity in deploying the resources to succeed is a very Chinese
phenomenon. Consider the most humble SME fair in the most

remote region and you will see real resource deployment, fanfare, people presence and effort. Deploy your best demonstration equipment, as Andor did, be so confident in your product and humble in proving their effectiveness that you are willing to loan equipment to your potential customers. Andor did this and it impressed China and helped sales. So it should, for it involves a degree of trust and humility. As Andor saw it, the burden of proving product effectiveness fell to them and since trust and relationships figured large throughout their China dealings, it was to the benefit of all that the equipment be loaned to potential customers for the time needed to prove its effectiveness – and this included allowing their clients to be the judge of that process and its duration. And, of course, having made the relationship with their distributors and their distributors with Andor's clients and in many cases with the clients themselves, solidly and well, it is much easier to extend that trust and to operate with humility. This is the positive cycle generated by businesses that operate with a commitment to relationships and people at their core. This is why China loves this business model. This is why those who do commit to it find themselves enjoying success in China, and building exponentially on early successes as they remain committed to those principles.

Moreover, the support was not just given at the technical resources and co-presenting level. Andor regularly undertook training sessions regionally as well as at their factory. Giving training in China is seen as a mark of respect. All Chinese seek growth in their personal skills and prospects; this is fundamental to their psyche and work ethic. It is important to feed this; skills transfer, training, cascading achieve this goal in a way that spells commitment and longevity.

Andor further supported their partners by investing in resources to match the growth that they hoped to see. Thus they simultaneously demonstrated their faith in the partners they were working with, and gave them a strong boost to the particular reputation resources needed to persuade and sell well in the Chinese market.

They backed this by excellent levels of communication, by phone as well as email, and by partnering them in the highest levels of customer care, including after-sales, well met delivery deadlines, personal visits to clients to assess satisfaction levels, and a dedicated resource to look after customers and partners in the market.

Moreover, they enlisted the help of their partners in understanding cultural issues which affected their joint business success, and responded in ways that built reputation.

They took time to understand the requirement of the Chinese market – not relying on email alone, but having regular phone conversations as well. They were careful not to ship deliveries in the run-up to holidays in China (it helps to know these in-depth), and they were at pains to demonstrate the highest levels of engagement with their market. To quote Asia-Pacific Sales Manager, Philip Moore:

> **There is a need to demonstrate commitment over and above the norm in China – go the extra yard in terms of support and requests from customers.**

In Andor's case, it also involved treating Chinese partners as if they were part of the organisation – a winning combo in China. This further included the brave but important decision taken by the company to be flexible on prices and conditions that they offered and to share the pain of price alterations, where required, with their local partners. The Chinese have an amazing intuition for the kind of financial adapting needed for a company to flow well in the Chinese business climate, and if they are a trusted partner they also have a committed interest in achieving profitability for you. So it is wise to listen to their feedback and roll with it, including taking on board the kind of marketing and sales resources they need. Your job is to vet them, make them feel truly part of your organisation and a valued partner; their job is to tell you what really works in China. At this point, your job is to listen – Andor clearly did, while meeting the very high value the Chinese place on quality. Quality matters to them. They choose to partner us because they believe we can bring it to them. This is their aspiration. As Philip Moore counsels, 'Live up to it'.

Andor ascribes much of the success the business has achieved or continues to achieve to the primary importance that its customers hold for the company. It actively stimulates dialogue and feedback with its customers and, given the importance of its product quality to the scientific and industrial sectors which it services, seeks to constantly review and improve the product it offers.

Interestingly and importantly, Andor views the team as being the key stakeholders of Andor, and their definition encompasses customers, staff, distributors and suppliers. As if exemplifying the point, staff loyalty and retention is high and length of service impressive. Longer-serving employees have genuine pleasure in the growth of the company, pride in its innovation, achievements and in the company's largest facility in Belfast, a purpose-built 50,000 sq ft premises.

Andor has also sought to create a sales and sales support facility throughout the world and in close proximity to its customers. In terms of their China presence, in the early 1990s they were represented through a previous venture partner, Oriel Instruments' sales catalogue and representative. When, after an acquisition of Oriel by a large corporation, Andor had the opportunity to buy out the shares and to launch as an independent brand globally, it enthusiastically seized the chance.

However, and significantly, Andor opted for continuity in both relationships and dealings with the China market, by returning to the Oriel representatives and deploying them as Andor distributors. This was a brilliant move and one with multilayered significance, which we shall examine later.

If yours is a more exclusively commercial or managing skills set, ally yourself with the knowledge base behind your products and services and equip yourself with a greater level of communicable expertise on the science, logistics and innovation behind your products than you would do for other markets. Remember the scholar administrator. China likes its business leaders and partnership advocates to be men of knowledge as well as commerce.

Maintaining relationships
The fact that founding employees are still the driving force behind the company reassures beyond words. Continuity, as we have

stressed elsewhere, is the lifeblood of solid commercial relationships in China. Where change occurs or is forced on a business from outside, the Chinese always look for at least one stable element: and the preferred area of stability is people. Business circumstances alter, and the Chinese are pragmatic masters of moving fluidly with conditions, but people and relationships are the reference point in a sea of change and need to remain as stable and constant as is realistically possible in order to do sound, lasting business with China.

Andor's relationship with its founding employees fits the bill and this approach is further demonstrated by Andor's China-sensitive and committed approach to its clients and distributors in China; in other words, to its relationship management.

As we will see, it was also the way in which Andor established and migrated its core values as a company which attracted much of its success. And this is an important lesson. As with individuals, the Chinese are keen to see the 'character' of your company: its identity, ambitions and values.

Andor's bold, but clearly achievable, mission statement – 'to become the global leader in pioneering and manufacturing high-performance light measuring solutions' – immediately communicates its scientific and commercial aspirations, its dedication to excellence, its prominence in its chosen market, and its commitment to innovation. More importantly, Andor then went on to live these elements of its mission statement in adapting its core values and people-management style to the Chinese market. This is vital. Without the determination to be and live a mission statement, and translate it into the 'commercial' behaviour of the company, a business will not thrive in China. Misrepresentation in a world of reputation and face is inadvisable, as is exaggeration. But daring to communicate your company's identity, its strengths, values and policies is critical in order that China can assess your business and allow it access to opportunity and success. Think of your company in this light. Review your presentations. Define your identity – before approaching China!

So how did Andor communicate its profile successfully in China beyond a clear communication of its company identity? Through bringing its four key values to play in the way it developed its China business.

Firstly, innovation. Having created the early products in response to their own research and scientific needs, the research and development teams sought to keep innovation high on the Andor agenda. This wins respect in China. I have often reflected on the poor logic of those businesses I saw operating in China that had almost paranoid levels of vigilance in protecting IPR on products for which China was already looking to find newer and better alternatives. Whilst prudent measures to protect IPR are always commercial common sense, I could not help thinking that part of this energy could usefully be directed at innovating in order to partner China more dynamically and proactively, consulting on China's rapidly changing and emerging needs and keeping pace with its staggeringly impressive levels of dedication to innovation and development.

Andor has done that and, coincidentally, during my research with them I have not been exposed to the anxiety-ridden discussions other companies have held with me on IPR protection. I will leave you to make the connection, and refer you to Chapter 10 for deeper reflection.

When you bring China the best, it is less tempted to go elsewhere and more inclined to respect not just the product, but the partnership. It values excellence. If we continue to stand for this value, as Andor has, we predispose ourselves to smoother relations and mutual respect. Reserve your best products, your best teams and your best business thinking for China. It requires no less.

Following on from this point is the commitment Andor has shown to client focus as its core value and one which it committed to, extensively, in China. 'Client focus' is a term much bandied about. All businesses claim they have it. Few businesses can produce demonstrable evidence of it in the full spectrum of business dealings, fewer still understand how this value could or should migrate and be communicated in a culture like China. We are not at fault here; it is a genuine business aspiration, but it is also an abstract –

difficult at times to implement in the day-to-day challenges of achieving profitable business results. However, we must be seen to achieve this authentically, as Andor did, in order to succeed in China.

Client focus, Andor's second business core value, leads neatly to their third core value: the sense of team as a business priority and a stated commitment to people and relationships at the core of their business behaviour. This is the one to emulate in your business. So let's look in some depth at the elements of this value and how it specifically worked for Andor in China. It started with Andor's definition of stakeholders which, significantly, they saw as including distributors and clients. Seeing your clients and distributors in a culture like China as having 'ownership' of the company's success is exactly the kind of trust-building signal the Chinese like to receive. It suggests 'partnership thinking' from the off. And Andor's stakeholder definition was not mere marketing copy. They lived it. Here are some of the very people-based ways Andor sought to build and consolidate its business in China, which harmonised beautifully with the latter's emphasis on relationships as success builders.

Andor originally worked with two distributors in China, using a geographic divide – north–south of the Yangtze River – to organise their territories. The company was at great pains to make clear divisions when working with multiple channels so that no loss of face or reputation-sapping confusion could arise. This in itself would already have established them as face conscious and possessing relationship finesse – an important business criterion in China for cooperation or partnership. And they consolidated this impression in the way they chose to expand their partner base, researching the industry and looking at suppliers of complementary products and their distributors as being one of the potential options they could use.

They also, and this is very significant, worked with their existing distributors as a way of sourcing new distributors in different areas. This sent powerful messages to existing partners and potential partners. The message which China hears in such instances is loyalty to the relationship first, business expansion next, and business expansion through relationship. It evokes great cooperation, it makes China feel safe, it makes everyone winners. Conversely, 'playing people off', 'hiding' aspects of business relationships from potential partners and playing clever left-hand/right-hand games with people resources never achieves lasting results in this market. And if small gains are made, bigger things are lost – not least face, reputation and trust – so success is inevitably shortlived if companies use the cruder, profit-driven type of strategies, as I have unhappily seen deployed at times. It does not work. Relationship skills, transparency, consultation and consensus on the other hand, as Andor proved, work spectacularly. And Andor maintained this tack as it continued to grow. They were not afraid to look at the people their competitors were using and to meet with them, so as to get to know their industry. Since in China, people sometimes set up their own business, and it is the relationship not the structure which primarily matters, you have the opportunity to follow personnel into ventures of their own and work profitably with them in their new business structures. But this presupposes that, like Andor, you take the time to make the relationship work and never sacrifice it to short-term gains in the business or let it be compromised by business pressures. Not always easy to do, but look at the respect and mutual benefit it engenders.

Andor made sure that they personally visited all the potential companies they could have worked with. Of course, it would have been easy to rely on email, but Andor rightly assumed that this would compromise their ability to source the right partners and to send the correct signals in China about the seriousness of their commitment to partnership. Quite right. China does not do virtual, remote, hands-off or diffident. You have to want China and be prepared to invest yourself deeply to achieve success for your business in this market. So emulate Andor, signal your seriousness by visiting and visiting often: you are building relationships, and in this area, China never responds to 'virtual efforts' or 'helicopter commerce'.

And support the relationships you have made. Andor did this. They made sure that, just as they were available to share the benefits and profits with their China partners, they were equally willing to share the pain if things went wrong.

You will remember the uniquely Chinese characteristics of teamwork being joint responsibility for success and failure, absence of blame and strong mutual support in times of adversity, and the notion of 'no scapegoating' for failures or setbacks. Speaking honestly, this is a tough one for us Western business and professional people. We think that blame, accountability, reprimand are the stuff of business discipline, as referred to elsewhere. Resist the instinct to do this in China. It costs you the business relationship. Instead of taking away the face of an individual or a team that have done their best, show your understanding of the deeper relationship value of solidarity and back them, as Andor did, in good times or bad. It will make for brilliant partnerships with China around your business.

And give the support you are giving locally, publicly and in person. Andor found that placing staff locally showed the kind of relationship-strengthening commitment to their Chinese partners and the particular geographical region of China in which they were operating. This commitment to the personal and to the local profile was enough to tip opportunities, at times, in Andor's favour. Consider this example well and think through a very 'on the ground' strategy and presence for your business in China. Even a 'brief but often' approach to your on-the-ground visits to China is infinitely preferable, particularly in the building stages, to a massive investment in marketing accessories and company profiling tools deployed on rare visits or virtually from the safety of your London, Paris or New York offices. China does not do virtual – make this your success mantra.

Andor's counsel is to never underestimate the power of having real-time support with an 'inward facing' champion to the factories you use. It ensures that any issues are dealt with promptly – a big factor in maintaining harmony and face, with and for the Chinese. Having staff deployed locally also allows very regular distributor contact and shows of support. In addition, it allows a representative of the company to visit clients with the local distributor. This is so important. In China, numbers count, as does solidarity, and so does the weight of senior international management partnering their local distributor publicly, in a show of well-built relationships, commitment to China sales and the business's China profile. This works well. Consider it carefully as strategy and remember the high relationship spin-off when considering costs involved. By showing confidence in your distributors publicly, you validate your Chinese client's choice of your company. And, like Andor, a local presence allows you to build up customers of your own and get to know them personally. This is invaluable.

Finally, Andor's strong suit was in the choice of its own internal champions. When asked to begin illuminating the Andor China success path for the purposes of this chapter, Philip Moore, Andor's key resource in Asia said, and I quote: 'If working in China has taught me anything, it is that patience, common sense, good manners and a sense of humility go a long way. Sometimes the most effective things are the easiest to show.' At that point, and without hearing the many things Philip and his colleagues did brilliantly in China to build Andor's client and distributor base, I knew the real key to Andor's success: their people and the commitment of their people to the concept of 'team', 'the collective we' that we have described which removes ego-driven approaches to business and replaces them with a fundamental person-centred, collective view of success. This attitude breeds cultural sensitivity and the humility to relate well to business cultures whose characteristics differ from our own. And these, in turn, are the two most enduring aspects of a good inter-cultural manager.

Andor is proud of its achievements whilst generously crediting all those who made this success possible. Its office in China was opened by the British ambassador, Sir William Ehrman, thus giving its Chinese partners public recognition and reputation for their contri-bution. And other aspects of their profile reinforce credibility in Chinese eyes. They have international offices in four major territo-ries. They own a brand-new, substantial purpose-built facility. Given the relationship the Chinese see between businesses that own land and their solidity as partners, this is a great source of business reas-surance and inspiration for Andor clients and partners in China. They win prestigious awards for their continuing dedication to people, innovation and excellence – a very Chinese business wish list in the performance stakes. Not least, they are at pains to credit those who built their success, from the CBBC to UKTI and Invest NI for their generous research funds and mission opportunities, to the wonderful work of British and Irish embassies in China with their excellent local contacts and generosity in sharing local knowledge and regional business insights.

Andor has maintained excellent on-the-ground relationships in China, from its early stage market entry up to and through the establishing of a direct presence and Andor office.

A great deal of this success maintenance is attributable to the way Andor handled relationships. They went to China very often. They appointed a dedicated resource and team within the company to Asia Pacific. They ensured that, however busy, regular phone and email communications occurred. They were always available to address issues which arose. They were open and honest with partners as to future plans and expectations. And they showed a willingness, as mentioned, to share the pain as well as the benefits in areas such as pricing requirements.

Sustaining relationships and Andor's development in China

Andor's relationship handling proved particularly important in its development and expansion in China, for example in handling changes to strategies which were not working as well as expected. In Andor's case, this was needed when they became aware that the geographical split was not bringing the desired results, and a decision was taken to remove the representative in Southern China.

Although Andor's other partner was mainly focused in the Northern Territories, Andor decided to show faith in their ability and judgement, based on the results delivered, and consulted with them as to developing the southern China business. They then offered the partner this market but with very clear guidance on Andor's expectations for the market and sales therein.

This process showed Andor's relationship management skills at their best.

First, consulting an existing partner showed faith and commitment to the partner and, in Chinese terms, would have been a strong giver of validation and reputation. Second, by increasing this partner's territorial remit and responsibilities, having accepted his counsel (another important respect and face builder), Andor provided precise parameters for their expectations in terms of business performance and profits. This is essential. The Chinese value this. You have already, as they see it, honoured them in extending the business remit, but by providing them with clear guidelines and parameters you prevent the kind of potential overwhelm and inferior results through loss of direction that could result in damaging face and harm to the relationship.

And, as it transpired, showing this level of respect for and faith in their Chinese partner was an important step in building the business. The Chinese like to sense that they are trusted and guided simultaneously. It builds reputation and results, in their eyes. This was the case for Andor, and they continued with this winning combination of transparency and respect in their approach to relationships, as they developed their business. They carried out research to identify other potential partnerships in niche areas and were clear with channels on the parameters for their work. As a result, they began to register results and growth.

When they were approached by other potential partners, they were willing to consider the opportunities but, wherever possible, they looked for collaboration with the channels already in place. Not only did this avoid market confusion, but it avoided the kind of conflict-generating approach to relationship management in the pursuit of profits which has been the demise of many Western businesses in China. Poor approaches to relationships in China is poor business. Inescapable fact.

The company continued to attend with great care to its relationship base and approach by consulting with its existing partners when long-term plans for Andor's China growth suggested the desirability of an Andor office within China. Handled well, this is a mark of respect and a consolidation of local partnerships. Handled badly, it is seen as local relationships and skills being supplanted or overridden.

By involving local partners, it showed Andor's dedication to them and commitment to the Chinese market. The process was carried out efficiently and effectively by the dedicated team at PWC, and the representative office for Andor China was born. Whilst there is a cost involved to sourcing expert advice from global consultants, Andor is adamant about its value.

Whilst all companies will want to ensure the most cost-effective way to establish a presence, it is important to remember that the ultimate goal is to develop your business. The costs incurred in ensuring the correct advice is received and acted upon could save much greater cost further down the line. And the extra costs incurred should be more than repaid if the entity is established properly. The importance of having an expert team that have experience in establishing entities cannot be underestimated. The rules and regulations can be daunting and having expert advice to guide you through them is a must.

I would also add, that any job that might affect public face, presence and reputation in China simply has to be done well, or relationships suffer and, if they do, so will your business.

Lessons learned

So, from a cultural point of view, what did Andor do so well? Many things, is the answer. For reasons we will now analyse, there was much within Andor's identity, their genesis as a company, their value system and their business growth that would impress the Chinese, open doors and facilitate partnership. Beginning with Andor's origins, the business was born out of a venture company its founder employees created with, amongst others, Queen's University Belfast, a highly respected and high-ranking university within Ireland's hierarchy of tertiary institutions, from both teaching and research perspectives. China values cooperation between the academic institutions and its private sector, and indeed senior personnel often hold positions in both.

Moreover, where there is a scientific or technical basis to the product portfolio, the Chinese find the presence of this kind of alliance, at some point in the company's development, highly reassuring. Similarly, the notion that its founders created the early products from their own personal needs as scientists for higher-performing equipment, implies the kind of hands-on, empirical knowledge China values in its company leaders. There is a great and highly respected tradition of multifunctionalism in China – what we refer to as Renaissance Man, and what China describes, in its version, as the scholar administrator of Confucian times. In other words, principals in business who have knowledge of, or links to, the roots of their products and access to a fluent ability to demonstrate their credentials, as leaders of thought as well as commerce.

Andor's founding employees had all of the above, and their university research departments backing their commercial endeavours would have been a model which China favoured, appreciated and trusted from the outset. So this was the initial latent asset Andor possessed. In terms of your business, how would this apply? Well, first, remember to profile (with humility), the range of talents you bring to your business partnership, as well as, and in particular, any knowledge connection you have to your products. If your business offers consulting services and you were once a consultant to brands the Chinese would recognise, this is as important as your current status as managing director or your proven track record in your current remit.

How can you incorporate this into your business? Many of the required skills for taking into account China's needs, opinions and requirements are covered in Chapter 6. However, one much overlooked area is China's actual changing social and consumer climate, the demographics of need and the complex layering of consumer profiles that is emerging as China's continuing affluence creates new appetites for consuming and distinctly Chinese preferences. Try to incorporate this kind of research into your investigations of market potential. Look at what China is reading. It is just as easy to subscribe to a Chinese newspaper such as *China Daily* as it is to an English one and to look out for journalists who have a kind of multigenerational radar and a balanced, wise view of China's developing tastes, younger journalists like Raymond Zhou. Know your customers and, like Andor, consult at all stages, make them feel involved intellectually as well as commercially, and be as passionate about innovation as you are about sales or protecting your existing IP.

Most of all, however, it is a commitment to people and partnership that has won China success for Andor. One look at their corporate video was sufficient for me to know that people were at the heart of this company's success and that teamwork was their identity and not mere corporate rhetoric. This was the key to their success in China; this was their real asset base.

It is yours also. Find the commitment to relationships and to honing and deploying your skills in this area, and your business too will enjoy the success I have described. Andor has given us the template. The rest, as ever, is up to us as business managers and as people.

Chapter Fifteen

CHINA – YOUR ESSENTIAL REPAIR KIT

Anticipate the difficult by managing the easy – Lao Tzu

Despite having a firm template for success such as the one described in the previous chapters, things do go wrong in business. It's no one's fault, business is fallible because people are fallible and, despite the high standards, mistakes happen, contingences occur. So, you deal with it. If you are from a Western business culture, this will typically mean applying all your acumen and skills, calling out the nature of the mistake, subjecting it to robust debate, legislating against it reoccurring, and informing all concerned that you have solved the problem. This, typically, is how it is done. But not in China.

In a relationship-based culture, where the health of the business relationship is everything and the joint face it presents primordial, it is important to remember what the primary overarching value and goal is for the Chinese: harmony. When I was first presented with the starkness of this fact, I was incredulous – then I read an anec-dote[1] which brought the point home convincingly. The son of a major Chinese tycoon said that if he wanted to make a major busi-ness acquisition, he would not have to gain approval from his father, whereas the decision to sue someone, however apparently unim-portant, would require consultation with him.

What this story illustrates is the need to be screened by new priori-ties and values in our mind in order to capture the mood of our

---

[1]Ming Jer Chen, *Inside Chinese Business*, (Boston MA: Harvard Business School Press, 2001), 91–2.

Chinese business associates in moments of business slowdown, problems or difficulty. We too need to be thinking 'harmony' and, consequently, of the relationship opportunity we have been presented with, at times where difficulty, error, slowdown or inferior results feature in our business dialogue.

The second we do this, we find that we apply different strategies and are filled with new instincts and abilities; ones that will place us on the Chinese wavelength.

So the typical Western crisis management timeline might look something like this: identify the problem – allocate responsibility – call to account – debate solutions – fix the problem. In China, this would look more like: constructively and non-judgementally identify the problem – recommit firmly and publicly to the importance and strength of the business relationship – enthusiastically assume joint responsibility for solving the problem – use out of boardroom time to sort out strategies – return to the meeting/boardroom to celebrate solutions – recommit to the primacy of the relationship and to harmony and mutual benefit. This is crisis management and conflict resolution Chinese style.

Our priorities alter our conduct. Inexorably. Continually. So bringing our priorities closer to those valued by our business partners and their culture is a demonstration of business acumen. More than that, it is the ultimate tool in our repair kit when things go wrong and guarantor for not recreating the business difficulty.

This takes humility and courage. We in the West like to apportion responsibility. We like to remonstrate with those who fail us or when mistakes are serious. We like to publicly hold to account if only, as the French would say 'pour encourager les autres' – to set an example, deter unprofessional behaviour and stimulate productivity and discipline.

These things matter in our business culture, as does specific responsibility allocation. We feel they are an important part of maintaining the discipline of our business processes, learning from our mistakes and being seen to strive for best practice in every area of our business and professional life. And so they should. They matter to China, too – though less than the health of the relationship, collective support and partnership. So China is happy to address problems with you, but differently, discreetly, with consummate attention to face and specific attention to 'off message' and confidential resolution of things which are difficult. Cooperating with this Chinese spirit of problem solving and conflict resolution is very positive. In response to such adaptability from Western partners, I have seen the Chinese gratefully deploy all their incredible strategic abilities, their resourcefulness, and above all their ingenuity, to solving stalemates and overcoming disappointment.

The Chinese do not like to disappoint. It is poor face and even poorer relationship management, so they work hard to counteract this. To observe the Chinese work hard with goodwill to solve a problem or curtail a crisis is something to behold, and the results are often amazing. And most of all, the Chinese value these moments to see how we respond under adversity.

Deploy sensitivity, understanding and be ready to be the first to forgive. Minimise the problem and the Chinese will bring their formidable talents to solving it and things will be even better than they were before. Why? Because by demonstrating sensitivity, resilience and above all perseverance in adversity, you will have used the exact 'repair kit' the Chinese have historically used to solve business problems and crises, from resolving the Asian financial crisis to more recent, less dramatic problems in learning to partner internationally on a massive scale, to navigating multiple problems in cooperating with Western cultures and infrastructuring those cooperations smoothly.

So far so good. But what if it is you who has caused the problem for which our repair kit is needed? What if it is as a direct result of your interaction that problems arise and not that of a subordinate or intermediary? This is possible. Culture is a learning process – a lot of what we do is unconscious, almost a reflex action, which is why much of this book has focused on 'reprogramming' our attitudes to relationship because this acts as an insurance against mistakes and as compensation when it occurs. The Chinese are very forgiving, even indulgent to those for whom committed business relationships matter. As additional insurance, it is helpful to look at some of the common areas where mistakes may occur and how these can be repaired.

Again, it is impossible to legislate for practical business eventualities and problems – these are simply too potentially vast, varied and sector-specific. But a thorough, culturally informed due diligence like the one we have offered in Chapter 13 'Getting Ready for China', should anticipate and see off most of these issues. What I would like to give you now, are some of the more common interpersonal mistakes of a cultural nature and their solutions, remembering that 'interpersonal' is Chinese subtext for business success and therefore real bottom line stuff for you, your business and your profits.

'Interpersonal' errors of a cultural nature usually fall into five categories and the repair kit varies for each. These are by no means exhaustive, but they are indicative and will throw light on major potential pitfalls and their solutions.

You will detect the common denominator: that all the mistakes we are about to examine threaten the sense of the collective, which in turn threatens face, reputation and harmony. When this occurs, business progress is always on some level threatened, compromised and undermined. You will remember the crucial phrase in an earlier chapter which establishes the importance of the collective and of relationships in the Chinese business culture: 'the most important word in the Chinese (business) lexicon is we'. In the case of mistakes for which we need a repair kit, rather than mere procedural or administrative errors, it is always the sense of the collective that has been offended and the strength of the relationship that has inadvertently been bruised.

The first of these errors comes from understandable, but highly troublesome, differences in our need for space. This is very real and causes significant strain and forced errors in China.

Business in China entails exceptionally long days, and the movement from formal meetings and work situations to banqueting and back. This, combined with dealing with larger numbers of people than we are used to handling, can be exhausting. It might seem as though the Chinese require less space and fewer breaks, where we need more, if not much more. They seem to navigate the transition from formal to informal more easily, irrespective of the length of the day, intensity of the negotiations or size of the deal on the table.

And, to a large extent, this is true and there are important cultural reasons for this. The Chinese are natural hosts; they relish even the most formal banquets and food is a source of real pleasure and replenishment. However, although much of the relationship building continues and the scrutiny of partners and associates occurs through this business social ritual, banquets are nonetheless social occasions for the Chinese; they are never tense or stressful, nor do the Chinese see these moments as a PR exercise or a business task to be endured. Dining is real engagement for the Chinese and, as such, however serious, the dialogue is to be relished.

Nonetheless, I have seen Western business people so desperate for personal space that they have curtailed precious meal times because of fatigue and feeling 'peopled out'. Prospective clients, agents, interpreters or distributors, all of who are an equally critical part of your people collateral, view this badly – what one Chinese colleague described as 'a slap in the face'. Remembering what face means in China, this is more than a metaphor.

So, avoid delaying banquets or evening meals. A pause at the hotel to freshen up and shower will not be denied to you by your Chinese hosts, but it will preclude them from fitting the evening meal in as a continuation of the already long working day so that they can go home.

Do not refuse opportunities to banquet because of tiredness or overexposure. Do not send agents or support staff away because they work for you. Keep the dinner engagements, even if this means scheduling some of them at your hotel. Skip the refresher and show your host's family commitments consideration. This guarantees you an evening that can end at ten or twelve.

My experience, however, is that it is not the continuous days which prove difficult, but something more fundamental. And here, there is a new attitude to learn from the Chinese that can make us resilient, tiredness-proof and at ease with the kind of people-filled, lengthy days that China uniquely specialises in.

The secret is not to tense up. We in the West seem to confuse focused mental performance with being 'on guard', and important discussions or negotiations as requiring a kind of tense, unrelenting attentiveness. The Chinese have developed what we might call 'relaxed concentration' which permits them to focus without straining. Since work and private life boundaries are fluid and minimal, and business relationships have to be nurtured and maintained, irrespective of constraints of time and space, this has been an essential disposition to adopt.

The repair kit for the weariness of a people-filled China business agenda which allows for limited personal time and space to 'regroup' in our Western parlance, is to adopt a more relaxed concentration. 'Hard to do,' I can hear you say. If huge amounts of money or significant gains are on the table, understood. But if we remember that the relationship is the key underlying driver for success in this culture, and that tension is always self-defeating in the building and developing of great business relationships, then we may be more encouraged to develop and deploy more of this 'relaxed concentration'. The Chinese like people who have the confidence to be focused but natural, and not so rigidly intent on agendas that they miss business signals or that they show poor 'people stamina' or empathy of a sustained kind with the collective.

But all of us from Western cultures will have had moments when we crave inner space – a breather, to think and feel. This is true of the Chinese also, but they are pragmatic in how they achieve this. When there are no face issues and people are travelling from one place to another, they discreetly rest, withdraw, catnap. This works. It is a small but invaluable way to connect with resources and recharge. This avoids us having to use the repair kit. It also avoids the reputation-damaging behaviour I have observed from business people desperate for time and space in China: gaining space at the cost of arriving late; creating freshening-up time while their Chinese hosts waited accommodatingly; at the expense of crucial support staff in their China employ; or by abdicating important 'bonding' meals at the end of a day with the China staff who had contributed much to the day's business progress.

You will not always hear protest or complaint from the Chinese at this moment, so read the subtler signs: fidgeting, silence, discomfort, embarrassed laughter or smiles (it is easy to tell the difference if you look carefully). If this happens, review your plans: cut your freshening-up time short or, better still, jettison it and try to re-approach the business in hand with relaxed concentration, remembering that tasks require engagement and that true business success in China is always a matter of relational success. The latter is best ensured by a cooperative, fluid, easy manner and one firmly fixed on the collective.

Other pitfalls also centre on the collective and on boundaries. Here again, there is an interesting contrast with the potential for error. When we think of a boundary infringement in Western business cultures, we would immediately think in terms of what might infringe an individual colleague's or associate's boundaries. In China, this is more likely to focus on overstepping collective boundaries in ways that harm face.

An example I observed was of a Western manager praising a Chinese team member to his CEO, emphasising the tertiary level qualifications this person possessed, his superior command of English and his prestigious bicultural education.

In the West, this is acceptable, even welcome, flattery. Western leaders like to be told that they have chosen well and that their ability to nurture rising stars has been noticed and vindicated. In China, this is unhelpful and embarrassing. Chinese teams exist as a team, to be mentored by a very committed leader and to reflect back the positive results of his leadership and their development under his monitoring. The elegant response was, of course, to talk about the committed mentoring development and leadership that his leader had provided. This is complimentary to both CEO and rising star. It does not offend the sense of collective or the respect due to hierarchical order.

The Western manager sensitively regrouped, echoed the sentiments of the team member, and restored face to all.

The single biggest repair technique is to be sensitive for responses – particularly across an hierarchy – from Chinese managers/team members which deflect a compliment or pass emphasis to a superior. These are excellent indications that a boundary difficulty has arisen. Refocus on the most senior person, and pick up the last positive thread whilst remembering to signal respect and particular sensitivity to the relationship for the remainder of the session. In other words, try to look for balance and harmony.

This is one example. There are others. Respect for information, and the freedom with which we impart it, is not always uniform or compatible across Western and Chinese cultures. There is often a more open and discursive approach to business topics across teams and departments in Western cultures. In Chinese business culture, with clear demarcation lines between decision-makers and those they direct, it is not always appropriate to discuss all aspects of the project with those who have limited decision-making power; it compromises face if they cannot guide you because the dialogue goes beyond their power level or remit.

Similarly, I have seen Western executives express sensitivity over information they have asked a Chinese manager to gather in order to create the profile that the Chinese like to build with potential partners and associates. In this case, the information related to age and other important elements – in Chinese terms – for building a picture of maturity and experience. Always ask yourself if the relationship is more important than the detail of what appears to us to be of a slightly personal or social nature.

As for general discussions across teams, guarded and prudent communication will undo any misplaced talk. Repair kits here centre on listening intently, using silence for mature reflection and remembering to use your support team discreetly when judgement calls prove difficult.

Finally, there are what we might call the 'mistakes by omission': the venial sins of imperfect relating skills. These centre loosely on what might be called the 'protocol of giving and receiving'.

It starts with things as simple as the exchange of cards. An obvious point, given that most people are sufficiently savvy to know that cards are exchanged with both hands, is to have them ready. There are countless examples of Chinese CEOs and government officials waiting in cold lobbies while people struggled to retrieve business cards and then present them with both hands, while holding bags, briefcases, etc. Have them ready. Carry a simple cardholder in your pocket. Make sure it is attractive, and be prepared.

And when you receive the card, treat it with respect; study it – both sides, as cards are usually double sided – and be interested. Don't forget it is titles that matter in China and, unlike recent years in the West, they mean what they say and designate the person's actual status, power and remit.

Participate willingly in the important protocol of giving and receiving of gifts. These have real meaning. Their monetary value is irrelevant, but they mark occasions, situations and phases of business cooperation. Have some with you, and make them meaningful either about you, your company, city, etc, or if you have relevant information, make them pertinent to your guests.

Similarly, a photographic record of meetings and business cooperation means a great deal to the Chinese. So, participate generously, allow yourself to be guided on protocol, and have one of your team ready to photograph the meeting/event. This adds a sense of your company's enthusiasm. But always check with the Chinese team that it is acceptable. Do not make assumptions.

Take the time to complete meetings slowly. Refrain from immediately putting on outer garments before a photo opportunity occurs. As your business hosts walk you to the front of the building or your car, refrain from saying goodbye too early as this breaks the flow and makes you repeat yourself. It also suggests that you assume that hospitality ends at the meeting room door, which is rarely the case in China.

If you find yourself making mistakes in these small but important details, the repair kit is to observe your hosts, wait to take a lead from them, move slowly, be guided by your Chinese support team or alternatively follow the movements of the Chinese team leaders.

Finally, and this is extremely important, pay attention. I once had the entire preliminary elements of a Western and Chinese meeting go brilliantly only for the head of the delegation to be shown down-stairs to a sumptuous banquet and walk past the CEO, so modest and unassuming was the Chinese CEO in question.

Often speed, haste and an excessive preoccupation with the busi-ness at hand can be our real enemy in China. A preoccupation with the 'business of relationship' can be our most sustained ally and one which, when in evidence, will be gratefully acknowledged by the Chinese.

Chapter Sixteen

THE POWER OF CONNECTION FOR SUCCESS

He who does not trust enough, will not be trusted – Lao Tzu

With regard to China, much of the relationship advice given to Western companies over the last eight years has focused on everything but relating. It has emphasised controlling, managing, directing investments, getting the best out of China, implementing accountability with Chinese partners and deriving financial benefit. The advice has been detailed and comprehensive in seeking to provide pragmatic structures for controlling our business dialogue with China. Two things have been repeatedly inferred from this advice that they have now become wrongly accepted business truisms in the West: (a) China is hard to relate to, and (b) there is a widespread acceptance that we should settle for the different and much inferior goal of 'controlling' China.

Moreover, it is suggested that this goal needs to be achieved through the use of control, as defined within the tighter aspects of Western business practices of leadership, minimal delegation, high accountability and rigorous monitoring of returns. What we feel is difficult to understand and relate to, we tend to control relentlessly. And control in Western terms is a very proactive process, reliant on much exchange and dialogue, measures and processes, rather than inaction, patient waiting or asking for assistance from those we deal with.

Thus the perceived assumption is that we do not need to relate, we can simply choose to manage or control. Therein lies one of the most corrosive and self-defeating approaches of the Sino–Western dialogue: the loss of intention to connect, and the belief that we can achieve successful sustained business outcomes with China, and longevity in our cooperation, without finding a means to connect well, meaningfully and deeply. To create business relationships which are personal and are built on a positive will to engage dynamically with China, to reflect an interest in the business and cultural profile of the Chinese as well as an affinity for the same, is a much more 'winning' attitude than control based on fear of what we perceive as overly challenging levels of cultural distance and 'otherness'. One has antipathy and fear at its basis; the other has sincere intention to connect, and the sustained motivation to relate, at its core. These are not abstractions. These are the real differentiators and makers of success in China, and these are why one Western company achieves reputation, prestige, contracts and respect in China, and others do not. This is the ultimate selection process.

Moreover, the selection process applies very early on in our dialogue. No phase of our business journey is exempt. At every stage, we will have multiple opportunities to show the true nature of our disposition towards those we seek to do business with. If it is to control, the Chinese will sense and dislike it; for both historical reasons and endemic preferences, they will resist 'being controlled' by outsiders, and the dialogue will deteriorate or abort.

Additionally, the will to dominate in a business dialogue, rather than achieve common goals through 'mature flourishing relationships', suggests that we are fundamentally misguided about key aspects of Chinese business preferences in the areas of cooperation and partnership.

A desire to control, rather than relate, represents a failure to provide familiar landmarks to the Chinese: respect, warmth, connection and the creation of a common set of goals, framework and benefits. The Chinese do business with those they respect. If we offer inferior approaches and intention in the area of relationships to a culture that is fundamentally relationship-centric, then we are being disrespectful to our Chinese business interlocutors and disrespectful to ourselves. This provides no basis for engagement, reputation or achievement, the three pillars of enduring broad-based success with China.

At this point business pragmatists will assert that, fundamentally, the Chinese are realists who are quintessentially practical and commercially astute and therefore willing to accept a very broad church of business associates and partners, providing there is proof of business acumen and a guarantee of profits.

In truth, only the more complimentary elements of this assertion are correct. The Chinese are fundamentally commercial, value acumen, cherish achievement and relish demonstrations of well-managed business in the form of sustained and substantial profits. However, and this is important, the Chinese will not sustain the above in the absence of well-made partnerships and business relationships that create reputation, are based on a solid feeling of connection and cemented by strong engagement between partners.

It is never just about the deal for the Chinese and, minus a relationship, it is never about the deal. For them, this quite simply does not compute.

At this juncture, those who have advocated a functional attitude to building a business dialogue with China will quote the success of the deals and business dialogue undertaken by Western multinationals and suggest that, here, strength of product, brand and proposition was enough. However, this is not the full picture. The greatest success stories in China, even by multinational firms, are those where investment, sound business offering and efficient service are allied with a clear desire to connect with China and to make a relationship-based contribution to its wellbeing.

This has variously taken the form of knowledge share, sponsorship, training, skills cascading and joint research projects. It has often involved strong cooperation between multinational leaders and local/national Chinese government, participation in civic initiatives, and contributions, overt or covert, to specific aspects of the socio-economic climate of China, resulting in the enhancement of its citizens' wellbeing.

More than simply the contribution itself, what matters is the dedication to medium- and long-term contributions displayed by such multinationals. The desire is not just to build relationship and display a genuine interest in enhancing China's talent pool, knowledge base and quality of life, but it is also about doing this for upcoming as well as existing generations, by gravitating towards projects and skills transfer requiring long-term input and commitment.

So, in the end, obligatorily, we return to the enormous importance of relationships and the requirement that they constitute in China for success in business and society. If major brand multinationals with long-standing success records in China concede the importance of relationships and make concerted, strategic gestures of great merit (such as investment in training, partnering or sponsoring the development of talent), then we have a clear example for other smaller enterprises wishing to court China as partner, supplier or customer.

In view of this evidence in favour of prioritising relationships within our business armoury for China, we must question the reticence of some Western companies to acknowledge this critical area as more than a mere business accessory and their lack of commitment to demonstrating the kind of disposition and attitudes that would create real connection and engagement.

We return to our earlier point. Fear of China's perceived cultural distance, apparent formality and its reputation as a business culture which is 'difficult to read', has encouraged a kind of passivity. Really, it is merely a form of fear, which has had the effect of allowing the 'intimidating', formal differences in business culture to make us wary of seeking real connection and valued engagement rather than merely lucrative business.

There may also be a deeper reason. We talked earlier about the Chinese approach to relationships in business and life as fundamentally collective in nature, intense, comprehensive and outside time and convenience-based rationale. This model is characterised by people-oriented teams, in which mutual allegiance to colleagues is naturally given and respected. Equally respected is a contribution to making others look and feel comfortable. Everything in this paradigm flows on the basis of an unbroken thread, running through business and professional relationships, of commitment to other's wellbeing, reputation and the notion of shared face, achievement and benefit.

The concept of 'for me to win, you must also win' is a particularly powerful lubricant to business dealings and the creation of success in ways that create mutual benefit. It permeates Chinese thinking and behaviour once – and this is crucial – a solid, meaningful relationship has been built, and is rigorously applied. And with the privileges (shared responsibility for achieving business goals, unparalleled levels of support, even, and especially in the presence of contingencies or adversities) comes the requirement to commit to a fundamentally intense, shared approach. Not just to business gains but to the kind of relationship bonding that allows such gains to be reached.

This requires a readjustment of the balance of time and individual/company investment, and a rebalancing of what we give to the business process on the one hand and the collective collateral of business relationships we are building on the other.

However, it further requires that we overcome a much more basic kind of resistance: to commit wholeheartedly to relationships and allow them to become highly personal and intense without labelling this as intrusive and predatory. It challenges us in the West in two ways, and constitutes a real opportunity for us to re-evaluate our attitudes to key aspects of our business behaviour for its effectiveness and humanity.

Why are relationships, character and supportive people-dynamics no longer quite so central to our business vision and behaviour? Why, increasingly in the West, are relationships considered as assets to be controlled and, at times, expendable assets at that, to be relinquished under business strain and adversity, constantly checked for returns, and restricted in the resources of time, energy and enthusiasm we allocate to them?

Why has our departure from the former importance given to character and solid client and colleague relationships blinded us to the deep and profound skills that we, in the West, spent time building over the last decades? Why are we now choosing to ignore the huge collateral base of skills these constitute for China? Powerful, business-enhancing, deal-making, profit-attracting skills. These are the very stuff that success in China is made of.

The problem is that these very business values – integrity, character-based dealings, committed relationships of loyal nature in good and bad business times – have been left to erode in the increasingly challenging and 'under siege' atmosphere of the current Western business and economic climate. We have run for cover, replacing commitment to people and relationships by commitment to processes and tough sounding rhetoric to appease the all-pervading anxiety over financial conditions and what we perceive as restricted opportunities for success.

Not only is this ethically unsound, with regard to our own business culture, but certainly in respect of the massive opportunity China represents, we have killed the 'golden goose'.

Reflect for a moment on the sheer commitment we in the West have shown to personal growth and professional development, the hundreds of man hours that we have devoted to motivational courses, leadership, corporate governance or the ethics of due diligence, or the hundreds of additional hours we spent in the 1980s and 1990s learning, with almost Orwellian fervour, that there is no 'I' in team. In other words, how to bond, support, motivate and facilitate better business relationships and, more importantly, how to live them within our business culture and that of our partners and clients.

And what does China ask of us? What is the key to unlocking and realising the huge potential that its culture holds for our business? The resuscitation of these skills and their enthusiastic, wholehearted application in all our business dealings with China.

It will mean digging deep, initially, for these resources and applying them with courage and intelligence. But this book will guide you on how to deploy these as a sincere but effective business and personal asset, and on how to adapt these skills to the Chinese relationship model.

In truth, though, once we find and dare to use these skills, their cultural adaptation becomes a less intimidating and daunting prospect. Once the Chinese sense these skills and our commitment to bringing them into our business life, they will instantly feel safer, on more familiar ground, and more open to partnership success and long-term friendship with you, to the benefit of your company, stakeholders, profits, brand, image and standing.

This is a huge trade-off, considering that all that is required on our part is a commitment to skills we already have and which, if we choose to reapply them and trust them, will make us more effective, happier and more successful in all business cultures, not just in China. Moreover, it will go a long way to negating old, clichéd and obsolete differences about East–West business models and relationships, and will truly allow the birth of a new landscape of success through connection, one that will profoundly benefit our own businesses and the businesses that follow. China will reciprocate, and the dream of comfortable, effective, successful business relationships of mutual benefit becoming the norm will come one step closer – because of you and your business. It may even have the effect of sending our own business culture back to an appreciation of what makes it work and succeed – its people and their efforts – and we will remember, in that moment, to be grateful to China for reminding us of a great business truth which we had, to our cost, temporarily forgotten.

Let's do this!

Success through connection, mutual benefit and respect: A summary

When I realised what the real ingredients for success were in China, and I determined that I should write a book calling for the vision, courage, self-awareness and influence to implement the strategies needed for success with that country, I wondered momentarily if the business world was the right audience for the kind of innovative, passionate approach needed to remake our destiny in China. And then I thought of the respect I hold for this community; for the many business people, owners, managers, entrepreneurs and captains of industry I have worked with and of how, in order to do what they do, they have to take a vision and implement it with courage and audacity, often in the teeth of reason, sometimes in climates of adversity and translate their original vision into success. And I realised that the international business community, both in China and the West, is exactly those with the passion and vision to lead the way in redefining our commercial and other relationships with China. They are also the most stalwart allies in the achievement of this new direction, and therefore, deservedly, the most worthy beneficiaries of the success which will inevitably attend these better directions.

What makes the business world the natural ally and supporter of this new approach to China? The fact that it is this section that in the West has engendered and maintained a strong dynamic movement over the last decades towards awareness in business relationships which took us from basic definitions of 'personnel' to the more comprehensive 'human resources', via 'teambuilding', 'leadership' and 'human dynamics'. These have become regular features of the way we tried to understand ourselves at work and our efforts to create structure and science around a more capable distribution and allocation of human resources in our organisations and institutions.

We encapsulated much of this knowledge into the approaches to teams, understanding that greater bonding here could be stimulated and promoted. We created leadership programmes so that the principles behind our most iconic, charismatic leaders could cascade for the benefit of middle management.

All of this was the direct result of the skills the Western business world sought to develop and refine into a form of practical science, and which the Chinese would describe with one word: relationship.

The Chinese themselves were busy applying the collective principles of relationship and skills derived from a fundamentally we-based model, practised in Chinese family life, to the creation of equally intense relationships in their business and social life. While not so heavily or frequently demonstrated, analysed or wrapped up in the language of management science, it was the same core priorities and skills at play.

Now these skills need to come together again, because these are the ones which can mediate, uplift and bridge our cultures into joint business success. They are our true common denominators. The Western business world committed significant time to the application of these skills in the world of work, and understandably so. Though it has not been of late particularly fashionable to admit it, if we take care of people first, business tends to follow. The Chinese have always considered this to be an immutable truth and lived it in the way they cultivate skills in life and in business, adhering to the principle that relationship equals business equals success, in all climates and in all situations.

The West is remembering this, and with it the many man hours of committed time we gave to understanding the importance of relationships to our business, and to infrastructuring this with the skills to partner, manage and team build with people across an increasingly international range of cultures and business contexts.

We have the skills. In abundance. We may need to re-flex our muscles but the business community is able to call on wonderful latent stores of relationship abilities to meet China on a level it trusts and appreciates and to use this terrain as the favoured basis for strong commercial engagement and success. Moreover, we have the sphere of influence and the weight needed to underpin this approach – and make it universal.

When the business world legitimises the notion of relationships of mutual benefit, connection and respect with China being fundamental to our success, others will listen. The principle will gain acceptance. It will be adhered to. Since this approach will in turn breed success, and the gains of business success will be demonstrable and visible, the cycle will perpetuate itself positively.

However, in remembering the importance of relationship and the human dynamic in business, we do not only vastly increase, nay guarantee, our chance of success with China, we enrich the value and content of business within our own culture. It is a return to what we in the West have always known, and China has never forgotten. It is a call to return to the value of 'we' versus 'I'.

It has served China brilliantly in its economic ascendancy, in overcoming financial crises, adversity and contingencies. It will cement the future of our commercial relationships and bring a great sense of shared pride in our achievements. These are not just the skills for building success with China, these are the skills for our time. In applying them, our businesses will 'score' more than profits, they will have a chance to become a voice in the most dynamic chapter of China's relations with its Western commercial partners. And, finally, the practical motivation to support their relationship efforts – China partners, supports and remains loyal to those with whom it truly bonds in business on an amazing level. It courts loyalty and continuity and values commitment. When we share these, the foundation is solid.

Moreover, we in the business world will be the first to anticipate and work with the huge power China will wield now in every part of our lives. Imagine a scenario where China plays a major part in or influences the employment of your children, the banking style you experience, the person you work or study beside, the film you watch, the business you are involved with, the media project you are involved in, the style of architecture you live or work in. If you think that this scenario is entirely fictional or at a considerable distance from reality, then you have not understood the strength of China's economic rise, cultural influence or wide-ranging emerging profile in a vast array of prominent fields of human endeavour.

In leading a business vanguard, in learning to relate to China through connection, respect and mutual benefit, you are simultaneously making not just a business contribution but a social one. You are placing business back where it belongs in the realm of engagement, in the hands of people, and you are jointly embracing with China new definitions of respect and commercial cooperation for our time.

Chapter Seventeen

CHINA SPEAKS

A leader is best when people barely know he exists, when his work is done, his aim fulfilled, they will say: we did it ourselves
– Lao Tzu

This is perhaps the most important chapter in this book for you and your business. At first, I considered calling it 'Listening to China', but this seemed to presuppose that we are not already engaged in this vital exercise. The reality is, however, that businesses across the West have looked to cultural experts in both the public and private sector to guide them, and the latter have done so, often in highly astute and comprehensive ways. However, despite the sincere and, at times, brilliant cultural commentary, at some point it is highly necessary and reassuring that Western businesses confirm those experts' understandings and perceptions of China, and more specifically of Chinese business.

There are two reasons to do this and both are vital to the success of your business. The first is to confirm the topical nature of the insights, given the pace of change in China, and also to confirm that the advice given tallies precisely with what China needs, wants and appreciates in terms of expected business behaviour and cooperation, as this is the bedrock of your joint success. Second, it is crucial to ensure that the experts' own 'cultural filter' has not influenced their perception or the quality of the advice they offer.

When you seek success with a culture or organisation, no one is better placed than your prospective partners to inform you about what will create this success. In our case, it is China and Chinese business culture.

So, on your behalf, I questioned a number of Chinese CEOs[1] about what we, as prospective business partners to the Chinese, could do to ensure success and what areas of our current business approach, methods and behaviour could be improved in order to eradicate barriers or impediments to success.

With the assistance of my Chinese colleagues in Shenyang, I chose to reflect the opinions of 15 separate business voices ranging from CEOs of companies in both the service and manufacturing industries, to an interpreter to the higher echelons of Chinese business, and a Chinese national and business facilitator who has participated for three years in research and market entry in the north-east of China for a range of companies.

Although the individuals and organisations are based in north-east China, their operations are international, and in certain cases their domestic operations, manufacturing centres or outlets are China-wide and are therefore representative of business opinions across China itself.

I have also chosen to use only a limited number of responses. First, because the quality of these was excellent and intensive. Second, because casting the net wider on such an exercise can be counter-productive, partly because giving opinions and appearing to 'tell others what to do' is a matter of great delicacy and reticence in China. Contrary to some unflattering China reporting in recent years,

---

[1]The intensive interviewing was carried out in the city of Shenyang in the province of Liaoning between July and September 2009 and reflects opinions at the level of Managing Director, CEO and Vice Director within a Chinese focus group of companies representing a range of business activities, including import/export, automotive, technology, property development, trade promotion, the management of business showrooms, trade displays and foreign business consultants. Answers were acquired in both Mandarin and English and cross-referenced with a senior certified interpreter in the region to ensure true and accurate reflection of opinions given. I would like to express my grateful acknowledgement for these contributions.

the Chinese do not like telling people what to do. On the contrary, they are very modest, contained and prudent in the giving of opinion and instruction.

In the case of those who generously provided the information which follows, it was specifically their relationship with the questioner – and the trust involved – that evoked such careful, enlightening and diligent responses. Moreover, and this was most encouraging, it was in a spirit of helpfulness to those Western businesses which, like yours, seek to build exciting and profitable ventures with China for mutual benefit and long-term business friendship. It was also the kind belief that this book is sincerely intentioned and will add value to China. Finally, it is important to explain that the Chinese reticence in releasing information about themselves is well founded. When the Chinese nation last 'opened themselves up' in knowledge, culture and skills to Western powers, it was neither respected nor valued. On the contrary, it was greatly misused.

I would like to salute China and its businessmen and women for having the courage to 'open up again' and, on behalf of a new generation of Western businessmen and women, I would like to assure you that this time we will cherish and respect what you share, that we will look to share back and that we will create mutual benefit and respect to chase away past disappointments. I now invite you, my business reader, to be part of the vanguard of businesses to make relationship history with China, to show our renewed level of respect, and to honour the courage it took to reopen its business and cultural borders and boundaries to us.

In this spirit, let us analyse the wonderful guidance provided by this representative tranche of Chinese business thinking.

Initially, we asked if all the companies surveyed already had relationships with Western companies and traded internationally. This included checking whether they had current experience of dealing with Western employees, agents, partners and board members. All the companies had experience of the above and regularly received Westerners into business meetings, for collaboration on projects and to inspect/visit their companies and/or manufacturing sites.

In other words, and this is crucial to the relevance of your business and of the material being gathered, they all (with minor exceptions) had recent, topical and consistent empirical knowledge and experience of working with Western companies. As such they represented the very people you will meet, befriend and build business success with, in China.

Having established this credential, we first asked them to state in frank detail what their perception was of the different ways in which Western and Chinese businesses approach relationships.

The first, and most critical, perceived difference was that the Western company is typically focused on the business-to-business relationship. In many ways, it is the two businesses' functions and profiles which are relating. So that if, for example, hiring or firing of key personnel takes place, this does not change the nature of the business. Business performance and function continue largely unaltered by this event and relationships between the two businesses also continue unchanged.

Chinese business, however, is considerably more focused on business relationships and their dynamics. These matter intensely. Chinese companies do business much more on a person-to-person basis, and if key people leave, the Chinese will follow that person into a new company and withdraw from doing business with the former company. Whilst there may be exceptions to this, it is generally true, and a critical fact of Chinese business culture, that the business will follow the relationship, not the reverse, and therein lies the first level of confirmation and reward for the motivation you have shown in reading this book and embracing the emphasis on relationship skills which it advocates.

So Chinese business will follow a trusted relationship into a new company and be willing to sign a contract with the key executive's new company in order to preserve the relationship and have this person as their continued interface and valued business friend. This is paramount. It amounts to business policy; a human-based strategy for the why and how of doing business in China and creating success.

And what kind of business contact would merit such loyalty? Essentially, those who fit into the category of 'Pengyou' – a good business friend with a valuable and sincerely developed network of business friendships. The Chinese consider such relationships as priceless. In Chinese eyes, Western businesses appear to take little account of the skills, relationships and human loyalties and, as such, they exhibit what appears to be a much less committed approach to people and relationships, which they deem 'unkind'. On the other hand, the Chinese are also aware that their intense commitment to relationships and their primacy may make them appear to us in the West as though they have no policy or serious commitment to business strategy and procedures.

Leading on from the contrasting approach to relationships, the Chinese CEOs felt that these were often affected by existing attitudes to timescales. This constituted a major difference in Chinese and Western business styles. The Chinese approach is always to take the 'long view' and this has implications for how they conduct business in the now. In general, a Chinese company will give up much in the short term, including early yields or quick returns, in order to gain in the longer term. This, in turn, informs their strategy towards the market and market share and has implications for both pricing policy and profit margin. It also demands considerable faith, patience and trust on behalf of partners with regard to profit levels and ROI.

On the other hand, Western companies appear to the Chinese to have a much more short-term approach and to be interested in setting targets and meeting them in what appeared to the Chinese to be 'the very near future'.

One CEO provided an excellent example of where contrasts in attitudes to market and to relationship practice converge: a Chinese company provides some goods or business services to a Western business which have disappointed in quality or contain imperfections. Typically, the Western company would expect a penalty to be imposed and honoured immediately, as well as wanting the problem corrected. The Chinese company, however, would want to be permitted to pay the loss gradually, either by ongoing incremental penalty payments or sustained discount over the requisite period for goods charged. You see the contrast here.

The Chinese company appears not to have solved the immediate problem, either in terms of rectifying the fault or making good by means of a penalty payment. However, it believes that by paying gradually, it is committing to the continuing relationship, acquiring time to rectify the problem, and giving a space for the relationship to become stronger through solving these problems together. Thus the relationship is preserved and guaranteed, penalties (a concept the Chinese find harsh if delivered in a strong manner) are agreed mutually through harmonious compromise, and a greater incentive is created to improving the end quality of goods and services provided: something which China is genuinely addressing.

You can see the possible challenges in rectifying the contrasting approaches to issues such as quality standards, compensation and conflict resolution – yet we can defuse the complexity of such situations and the potential for damaging the business relationship or terminating it, by asking a critical relationship-based question. Which course of action will gain my business real success in the longer term: **either** preserving the relationship, incentivising my Chinese partners to solve the quality problem and accepting gradual compensation to secure the relationship; **or** putting into place the full enforcement of immediate compensation, conflict-inducing and hostile accountability exercises with the early risk of relationship termination and loss of investment?

What we can see here is also a preview of the kind of contrasting attitudes from the cultural perspective inherent in our approach to products/objects – their quality, standards, usage and preservation.

The Chinese expect relationships to last and symbols of their culture and heritage to endure. However, they have a very different attitude to the everyday objects they use to clean a kitchen, boil water or store utensils. They do not expect to be using the same model in five years, or in some cases one year. This would frustrate the desire for innovation as well as their love for what is efficient and contemporary in terms of objects for pragmatic use, rather than ones that celebrate their cultural heritage. So massive investment in quality is seen more as stagnation than preservation. We will return to this point shortly when we examine Chinese and Western attitudes to manufacturing standards, market profile and pricing strategies.

Meanwhile, our next set of questions was aimed at identifying how Westerners can signal their understanding of Chinese business behaviour across key areas of relationship building.

We began with observing protocol, and how thoughtful behaviour in this area could ensure success. Something which the Chinese CEOs stressed here is that it is both customary and important to go outside their company building to meet and greet Western guests and to 'welcome and bring them in'. Equally, it is important to 'see them out', taking them right to their car, station, and in some cases with visitors from nearby cities, to their city of provenance. The Chinese consider this level of civility extremely important. Since this is their country, they are living here, so they should extend hospitality along the lines described above. So although it is often more convenient to allow departing business guests to take the train or a taxi, it is quite simply not the Chinese way.

Also, no matter how busy or intensive the work schedule, you must organise meals thoughtfully as well as scheduling generous time for these occasions. And at the first meeting, it is important to mark the promising beginnings of the relationship you are building with a gift exchange (guidance on this important area is dealt with elsewhere in this book).

The Chinese expect similar levels of care and civility when they are received by their Western business associates and hosts, particularly in the quality of the welcome and the manner in which they are received.

More commonly, however, they find that a map of the Western company's location is provided in advance of their visit by email. Whilst they acknowledge that this is largely explained by the greater independence Westerners exhibit in their professional itineraries, they are often disappointed and disorientated by simply being provided with a map rather than receiving a more hands-on welcome. On arrival, it is also often the case that there is poor meal provision – something which is tantamount to incivility towards cherished business guests in China. They describe the feeling they have in such moments as one of 'neglect'. They even construe this 'neglect' as a sign that the Western company is unhappy with them and is signalling its disapproval to them or, even more damaging, that it is showing that it does not want to work with them.

Of course, this is not the case. It is much more likely that these Western companies are expecting high levels of independence in their visitors and are saving their energy and civility for inside the meeting room when the 'real business' begins. Except that we now know from our relationship work that the 'real business' begins with the relationship. And for Chinese business people, particularly those who are unfamiliar with Western business culture, the CEOs pointed out such behaviour would produce a 'gulf' where 'mistakes' will proliferate and where the likely outcome is 'estrangement'.

All of this spells disaster for building any kind of business relationship. The Chinese need to feel safe and taken care of in order to consider building partnership and cooperation; when questioned how maps to their prospective partner's offices and the absence of meal provision and hospitality left them feeling, the response was quite an emotive one: 'unsafe'. Civility, care, attention to detail, hospitality and respect are all prerequisites for partnering China. You will recall Andor's advice to 'go the extra mile'. And yet, when considered in the light of relationships and their importance, the concept of meeting and greeting well, providing business meals with grace and attentiveness and extending a meaningful welcome to those with whom we have to do business is scarcely an imposition or an exaggerated request.

Perhaps in reflecting on this, we have the opportunity to resuscitate some of the wonderful levels of business courtesy and civility that used to hallmark Western business and which, more recently, we have allowed to be eroded under pressures of time, profitability and expediency.

The Chinese are not any less busy than we are, yet they make the time to ensure that partners, associates and suppliers who visit them from the West are met well and given respectful and generous hospitality. They too have families and private lives. Yet they prioritise time to receive and accommodate overseas business visitors. It is a prerequisite to our success with China that we reciprocate. It is also a chance to reflect on who we are as business people and to review how we intend to behave when partnering China.

Having assimilated this helpful information on protocol, we moved our questioning to the critical area of negotiation, and sought advice on Chinese preferences, approaches and views on the negotiating process – and how we, as Westerners, could relate to it.

The major contrast identified here was the difference in operating and cooperating. In the case of Western companies negotiating in China, the head of the company takes the negotiation forward and in the process goes through a significant amount of the negotiation detail. In China, however, the company leader usually provides the direction, lead and policy. Once these have been given, the people under him or her flesh out the details needed for the body of the negotiation and for its progress. The leader does not engage in or oversee this detail personally.

So the result is that Western companies feel that within the negotiating forum there is a lack of professionalism and detailed knowledge of operating at company leader level in China, while the Chinese feel that the Western people waste their most senior personnel's time on small numbers and details, instead of allowing them to stay focused on the 'bigger picture' and to steer the negotiations to success.

The solution to this 'mismatch' of status and roles in negotiation was suggested by one CEO as follows: allocate different personnel and divide the groups at different stages of negotiations.

In this model, the Chinese and Western heads of company would meet to set policy, define objectives and steer the negotiations, and hand over to their respective teams to develop the detail of the negotiation. The teams should then report to the company heads, providing them with a full portfolio of the information required to continue and resolve the negotiation with their opposite number. This way, each leadership team reports to its head and the heads – who, importantly, are matched in status – can proceed in dignity and awareness to advance the discussion.

This would avoid the very embarrassing phenomenon for the Chinese business mind of the mismatching of personnel and status or failure to 'mesh' at appropriate levels, thereby resulting in what they described as 'awkwardness'.

It is difficult to overemphasise this point, once you understand its importance to the Chinese business world. 'Leader' is the word used for people who head up companies and business in China and for good reason. Such titles denote a progression through advancing skills in thought and people leadership to a position of important status and 'face'. For this to be matched with a person who has not made this progression strikes the Chinese as undignified, puzzling and downright wrong. It is worth reflecting on the guidance provided elsewhere in this book on this element of 'getting it right'.

Interestingly, I have seen many Western companies exhibit anxiety about this issue of matching status – not as they should do in regard to the boardroom and negotiating table but in terms of the banquet. On one level, it is excellent observance of protocol that they should do so. Matching status and seating arrangements is important as a reflection of parity and as a mark of respect. But the implications of getting it wrong in the negotiating mix is an infinitely greater generator of awkwardness than any unconscious mistake in the banqueting arrangements, which is much easier to rectify.

Indeed, our anxiety about protocol in the banquet situation will be much allayed by what the CEOs had to say. First, they did not feel the need to give any special directions, commenting that most Westerners had good table manners. One thing they pointed out which I wish to echo is that the Chinese are very relaxed when they eat, so there are no huge protocol boundaries. What the Chinese want most in the banquet is to see that business guests are relaxed and taking pleasure in the meal and their company. In other words, they are looking for evidence of real enjoyment on the part of their business guests. This is because, in their eyes, you are then confirming that their hosting is successful. This means they have made an excellent contribution to building or making the relationship with the civility and hospitality which, in Chinese eyes, encourages business relationships to flourish.

Our next set of questions to our selected Chinese businessmen and women centred on something which will be very important for all of your business: the creation of successful joint ventures or partnerships of other denominations; EJVs (Equity Joint Ventures) or WOFEs (Wholly-Owned Foreign Enterprises).

Interestingly, the responses moved immediately to situations in these partnerships that involved the handling of difficulties when they arise, and how Western companies communicated with Chinese companies at such moments. This is clearly a sensitive issue. First, the Chinese pointed out a major difference at the time of entering into agreements. Here, they mentioned, it was important to consider how contract provision for areas of problems or future difficulty should be made and carried out. Heavy emphasis on negative issues such as compensation and penalties prior to the signing of a contract sounds very hostile and like a mild threat, which in turn betokens less than solid faith in the flourishing of the business relationship.

They advocated that, when speaking of these issues (which they appreciate must be addressed), it is important for the Western company to deliver such discussions in a 'mild' manner and with gentleness. The firm or strong language should be reserved for the paper. Indeed, one CEO remarked that the terms 'penalties', 'compensation' and 'dispute' feel so negative and difficult for the Chinese that they can barely pronounce them out of 'shyness'.

To grasp this fully, we obligatorily turn to relationships and to the area of public face and reputation. While provision must always be made for the negative and for contingencies in business, the Chinese like to feel that relationships which are well built will sustain the businesses behind them in times of adversity. It is also their hope that in times of difficulty, setback or dissatisfaction, problem solving will be jointly undertaken in a spirit of harmony and that, beyond acknowledgement of responsibility, there will be no sense of witch-hunting or relationship-busting sanctions which are unilaterally decided and imposed, punitive in nature and reputation-breaking in effect.

You will remember the illustration of how a Chinese CEO wished to handle the issue of compensation in the event of quality issues on services/goods provided to Western companies. They wanted to offer staggered compensation to preserve the relationship long-term, jointly agree this with the Western company, and then proceed, in consultation, to satisfy the quality standards and rectify the problems at their end.

This all makes perfect sense in a world where relationships and their care are the primary drivers of success. It is the overridingly important factor in any business action including, and especially, conflict and business issue resolution and the way in which legal provision is discussed verbally with potential Chinese partners. We need to train ourselves to approach such issues with relationships as our guide. This is paramount. If you are maintaining a mindset and a behaviour paradigm where successful, healthy business relationships are your core business objective, you will react much better and deliver your terms with more mildness and civility than if you are driven by watertight provision for the 'what if' moments which you are then at pains to communicate 'firmly'.

Firmness is usual with us, coming as we do from a process- and function-driven business model, but it can sound like insensitivity and threats to the more relationship-centric Chinese business model.

You will remember the emotive choice of the word 'cruel' used earlier by a CEO when communicating his view of those business models where processes dominate and relationships are seen as secondary, with key personnel being viewed as dispensable and important relationships, in the Chinese view, being sacrificed to expediency. 'Value relationships, civility and respect,' the Chinese CEOs told us, 'and we will value your business.'

They were very specific in response to our next set of questions, which focused on what criteria are of interest to a Chinese business when considering a potential partner from the West.

First, they emphasised how important it was for the Western company to communicate their growth as a company, particularly their rate of development, size and market share. The Chinese put huge store by this. This will become clearer as we examine the Chinese approach to market strategy but, initially, what it is critical to understand are Chinese ambitions. They like to see boldness in our goals because they believe that the key to business success lies in the ability of a business to expand its branches, holdings and interests to go more speedily in the direction of cornering the market, gaining monopoly and eventually dominating the market and sector. For this reason, they are not so worried about high margins, early yields and establishing brand reputation and market position by high-end quality.

The Chinese CEOs pointed out that in exploratory discussions there was a feeling from their Western counterparts that unless one was looking at significant margins, which they considered healthy and which had been achieved elsewhere, there was little point in continuing. In other words, they perceived their potential Western business partners as exclusively focused on margins, so much so that if these margins could not be agreed upon, the Western business managers declared the business nonviable.

This is a distinct difference and a potentially troublesome one, and the contrasts continue in this area. Before talking about solutions, which happily there are, it is helpful to look at some other fundamental contrasts in business approach highlighted by the CEOs.

The Chinese felt that (a) Western businesses were very heavily focused on forecasting, and (b) Western businesses suggested that the Chinese do not invest sufficiently well in research.

In reality, there is a difference in the amount of time devoted to research and forecasting between Chinese and Western business. And the reason is simple and, as is often the case, refers more to the philosophical and cultural roots of Chinese business thinking.

The Chinese believe that since 'the plan cannot chase change', focusing all our efforts on one set of forecasts or one specific time-bound piece of business research will not protect the business against the many variables that may besiege its potential success. Because, therefore, we are always somewhat 'in the dark' in terms of what may happen next or what factors may affect our business destinies, it is eminently more useful and appropriate to learn to 'climb in the dark', to 'touch the stones to guide you across the river' or 'ride the donkey to catch the horse'. So use the strategy of growing your business and expanding its place in the market through humble margins. Then, by means of these 'stones' or this 'donkey', you will grow to dominate your sector and be capable of riding out any market changes or adversities because you will be the market leader in good times and bad.

Preferring to keep costs down and maximise market expansion, the Chinese do not like to overinvest in their buildings, training or factories. They do not want to put all of their resources into things which may alter and would inflate the price and the potential for rapid movement to high market profile and eventual market domination. In this context, it is also useful to remember that, whilst the Chinese diligently and with reverence cherish heirlooms and family memorabilia and examples of their culture, their attitudes to and expectations of everyday objects that serve the practical functions of life are quite different and entirely pragmatic. They are much more interested in what is efficient, practical and well priced – given that, in time, they will look to change it for something which is equally affordable but reflects the latest design, improved efficiency and additional features. So this influences them towards a more 'disposable' culture in purchasing – where look, price, affordability and contemporary nature are eminently more important than durability and high, enduring, market-leading quality.

In the West, however, we build to last, buy for quality – by which we often mean durability and the length of return on money spent on an object. It is often on quality that Western companies build their sector profile, and by holding high standards, they expect to corner the market, gain an important profit margin and expand through the positioning of their sales around their product's quality.

The CEOs saw these areas as being the ones most in need of communication and mutual understanding between Chinese and Western companies, believing that there is much to learn from a cooperative strategy around these contrasting business approaches. In the short term, they recommend increased cooperation on matters of pricing and market strategy, more frequent face-to-face discussions and compromise from both parties, with China attempting, as it has done now for 30 years, to look at quality improvements and Western companies trying to accommodate the sense of security a Chinese company gains through rapid expansion towards market dominance.

These contrasts, which we will now further define, were identified as major difficulties in undertaking business ventures with Western companies. On the one hand, the low pricing policy engaged in by the Chinese requires hefty year-on-year increases in sales, and particularly sales volume, to assist its viability as a strategy for rapid expansion and sector dominance. And cooperating with Western companies often fuels the achievement of this sales volume specifically desired by Chinese companies. However, Western companies, it seems to the Chinese, are often more focused on quality, high early profit margin and sustained, organic growth as their business strategy.

The Chinese, while fully understanding this philosophy and wishing to benefit from the increased sales volume the venture brings, feel anxious about losing the competitive advantage produced by low pricing, modest margins and high volume and, simultaneously, losing the prospect of sector domination that offers security and protection against adversity and market changes, thus allowing them to compensate for changes in forecasting due to market factors. This represents for them a secure island in an ever-changing business reality and a 30-year transformation, and a more viable strategy than 'fixing' ideas, quality or locations in a culture which knows that the 'plan cannot chase change'.

Accommodating different ambitions, policies and approaches is never easy. But it is what business excels at. In the case of China, however, there are additional critical tools that will prove invaluable: the reliance on relationships to achieve much of the middle ground we seek; an attitude of civility and respect in the handling of differences, particularly around ambitions; the skills to create a sense of safety in business dealings; and an attentive and sensitive listening ear.

The next questions we asked of our Chinese business panel were the most crucial and practical type of questions you will ever need to ask in order to get started in China and, once there, to continue effectively. I framed these questions because my business experience has told me over and over that what the Chinese seek from those who are new to them are strong proofs of solidity and good faith. In essence, to do good business, we need to make China feel safe. And this was indeed confirmed by the answers given by the CEOs. Whilst not requesting huge disclosures from potential Western partners, the Chinese want, and need, proof of solid credentials in the financial and commercial management of your business, and solid track records in your sector, secure people handling skills (crucial) and, finally, proof of reputation and prestige.

Let's look at this in more detail. First, the Chinese requested that, from the beginning, we are transparent about the numbers. This is a crucial trust builder and an equally powerful trust breaker if we fudge or otherwise misreport in this area. Critically, they want to know exactly how long a business has existed as a trading entity. They understand brand modifications or changes in companies; what they are trying to ascertain is the continuity of the trading history. Annual sales and profit margins as well as breadth of sales and sales portfolio need to be reported on in depth.

Equally important is the nature of the product base, manufacturing capability, facilities and equipment provision. If yours is a plc company, it is crucial to display the share variation and to evaluate current share levels in a way that is meaningful to China. Their preferred model spans six levels and tracks share movement very seriously. Investigate this and report in terms that prospective partners in China recognise and appreciate.

Be transparent and comprehensive in describing cooperation or joint ventures that you have already put in place, particularly if these are with big companies. This communicates credibility and prior experience of international cooperation.

They also advocated providing details of employee numbers and staff retention levels as this reassures China on our commitment to staff, business relationships and networks.

The CEOs further pointed out that, for Chinese business, the credibility which you hold within the business community is highly important and relevant. And this is not just in terms of awards, honours and industry achievements, although these count for much in China and are immensely valued. They are also referring specifically to any regular showroom slots you may have at sector-specific international fairs, shows or exhibitions, and what high-quality manpower (in volume and seniority) you choose to deploy at these events. This is very important to the Chinese, as it is a public statement of credibility, reputation and status within one's chosen sector.

Similarly, they advocate ensuring that your website is of the highest quality, contains a high level of information, introduces products comprehensively but above all compellingly, has plenty of sector-related information and reflects the dynamics of your chosen sector. For China, they emphasise, it is also important that you put at the head of your website any technical and scientific information pertaining to your products and expertise. China relishes such detail and appreciates the seriousness and commitment of websites that lead with such context. It is a differentiator.

As you can see from this guidance, what the Chinese want, what makes them feel safe, is excellent company information shared in a spirit of clarity and willing transparency. What they also want to see is evidence that you have built a respected profile through the achievements of your company and the reputation of your managers within the marketplace and your own sector's evaluation.

Next, it is in the area of handling finances that the Chinese suggest that we, as a prospective Western partner, have the opportunity to demonstrate our solidity. In China, to prove good financial status and secure underpinning, a company is at pains when selling products or services to give evidence of not being precipitous or desperate in clawing in money against recent invoices. Conversely, when buying from suppliers, they will pay quickly to demonstrate that they can (face, credibility and reputation) and that they want to (goodwill, relationship building and network management).

This, of course, is in contrast to the 'cash is king', 'cash flow is everything' style of financial management prevalent in the West and well known, for serious self-preservation reasons, to many medium- and smaller-sized businesses. The reality is, however, that China esteems companies which are sufficiently well underpinned and managed that they can take their time in financial matters. This includes having sufficient clout with their bankers and other stakeholders to weather any periods of cash flow strain. It is a sign of a business which is solidly viable and prosperous. This makes China feel safe and enthusiastic in matters of business partnering.

Conversely, in a world of face and reputation, being seen to aggressively chase payments, grab profits or display desperation in respect of cash earned, is a trust breaker and compromises face.

Continuing on 'what makes Western companies look solid', the next body of detailed advice from our Chinese businessmen and women centred on what could loosely be grouped as Preparation and Information Management. Here, once again, and very helpfully, they were very specific.

In presenting with a view to partnering Chinese companies, it was critical to be prepared and for the degree of preparation to be visible.

First, it was important to have very specific and comprehensive information about one's industry. This included the newest technology, market trends and directions and preferences. This would also include competitors' product portfolio and status and refer to changes in pricing levels relevant to materials and products and technical expertise. It would also be important to give full details of product specification guidelines, capability, technical expertise and price.

The Chinese CEOs further advised that Western businesses came with specific negotiating aims and objectives and that we are prepared for, and capable of, discussion about all the above issues in depth.

In response to the question 'what quality would you most like us to display when negotiating effectively but harmoniously with the Chinese', the answers ranged from 'passion' to 'discipline' via 'civility' and 'understanding'.

Reflecting on these qualities made me understand how, for the Chinese, as stated elsewhere in this book, negotiation is actually a continuation of a business discussion and dialogue and needs to be approached accordingly if success with mutual benefit is to be achieved.

My final question and one which I know to be at the hub of success with China was: 'How can a Western company demonstrate its trustworthiness as a commercial partner?'

A similar question posed to Western business would have drawn answers of a technical and process-based character via lots of references to accountability, professionalism and due diligence. In China, the response given was one part technical and six parts character and relationship skills orientated. Perhaps at this juncture in our exploration of the importance of relationship skills, you would have expected no less. In any event, they stressed the importance of what we Westerners familiarly call 'knowing our stuff'. An ability to demonstrate through knowledge, particularly an abundance of academic knowledge, is not merely a mark of competence, but of respect. The Chinese feel enriched and honoured by the sharing of academic/ business knowledge of high calibre and respect those who possess it. More, they seek to partner them.

However, the most detailed guidance came in the 'six parts character and attitude' which I referred to earlier. The Chinese considered trustworthy those Western companies that demonstrated a willingness to share relevant information as a prelude to doing business or creating partnership. They specifically identified as inspiring trust those who were open and honest in exchanging knowledge and transparent and forthright in their business behaviour.

When asked how this attitude of transparency and cooperation could best be summed up as a characteristic, they replied 'a plain dealing person' or 'a straight shooter'. I have found this to be a widely-held aspiration for Chinese business people seeking to partner Western companies, and it is a highly logical one. If you are seeking to develop a business in which relationship will play a key role as motivator, facilitator and guarantor, then knowing that you are dealing with someone who is honest, plainspoken and plain dealing allows you to invest in the relationship in the teeth of cultural differences and contrasting business training. You know that with honesty, common objectives and a solid relationship where clarity will be to the fore, the business prognosis remains optimistic. This is the Chinese logic and it is ubiquitous, tried and tested, and perennial. It has worked for them domestically and internationally and has seen them through financial success and crisis with equal reliability and resilience.

Finally, the CEOs came back to the trust-building effect of Western businessmen showing appreciation for their culture and ways. A business interpreter in the group cited the example of an American investor seeking to do business in the province of Liaoning. When willingness to cooperate was agreed, and support for the overseas investment ratified by local government, the American general manager stood up and expressed his gratitude by drinking the entire glass of beer which had been placed in front of him. Since this is a traditional way of showing gratitude in China, his actions won applause immediately and created a warmer, more trusting and closer relationship with his Chinese counterparts.

In the spirit of building trust, respect for the high patriotism of the Chinese business community is also an important factor. As captains of industry, entrepreneurs and the lifeblood of commerce, Western businessmen freely offer opinions on governments, government policy and business legislation – and concur or defer robustly. In China, it is important to respect patriotic instincts towards a government which both historically and currently supports business intensely and 'up close'. Insensitivity to the patriotic appreciation this has created in the Chinese business community, or overt criticism of policies, is neither helpful nor welcome when building one's business profile with the Chinese. It marks us out as something of a loose cannon, insensitive to the opinions and reputation of Chinese counterparts and to their patriotic sensibilities. Moreover, at a time when many cultures are expressing admiration for the close cooperation of government and the private sector in China, it is not a particularly fertile ground for critical comment.

In summary, Chinese CEOs suggested that their ideal Western partner would be knowledgeable, plain dealing, sincere in intentions and cooperative. When asked what their final word on this topic was, they replied (affirmingly for the subject of this book) that they were looking for Western partners who were 'willing to achieve a win–win result through the business transaction'. This was their ideal partner – their partner of choice. I rest my case.

In concluding this response feedback, it is worth noting that the term 'mutual benefit' is more widely preferred in China than the term 'win–win', as the Chinese do not like the struggle/competitive edge inferred by the latter, even if the spoils are shared within such an approach. Their preference for 'mutual benefit' (I am indebted to Ming Jer Chen for this differentiation) suggests the kind of joint effort, harmony of objective and method, and shared happiness and profit derived from a business outcome which more accurately translates the preferred business trajectory of the Chinese towards success.

The Chinese respondents in this exercise are very representative of a tranche of current CEO-level business thinking. Moreover, they answered with candour and in detail. They are, without exception or doubt, extremely interested in closing the perceived cultural difference in business priorities, methods and approaches between China and the West.

Two things are noteworthy here. One is the sincerity with which these Chinese business people are seeking a comfortable business terrain of partnership and a common ground for cooperation. There is genuine enthusiasm and excitement about bridging the cultural contrasts that made a joint approach to business ventures problematical and uncomfortable in the past, for both Chinese and Western companies. Only a few years ago, this enthusiasm and excitement was more like bewilderment and apprehension or, at best, curiosity.

Today, the climate is different. China has many international partners and is creating new commercial partnerships in high volume, with diverse Western cultures every day. All aspects of the business dialogue between China and the West need to find a new comfort zone and spirit of cooperativeness.

And we, as a new generation of prospective business partners for China, are coming with a new and better intention, with goals such as mutual benefit rather than one-dimensional profit motives; we prepare well and this includes our best efforts at knowing and respecting Chinese culture and business culture; we know more of the Chinese business approach and the aspirations and preferences of our Chinese counterparts. We want to engage, we seek to partner, but above all we want to relate.

And this is the real opportunity at this time with China, from which all true or enduring business success will follow. It is our time to connect for the purpose of building meaningful business relationships, and by 'meaningful' we mean the kind of cooperation which builds mutual trust in both companies, and with reference to both cultural frameworks. In the West, this involves accommodating our concerns for accountability, professionalism and quality; in China, this involves a dedication to relationships, a commitment to people at the core of our business dealing, a desire to build and protect reputation and a person-centred, respectful approach to the carrying out of business marked by civility and a desire to create loyalty and longevity in and through our business partnerships.

These areas of concern and expression of preferences in business style may seem tantamount to different priorities; they are not. We talked earlier of the Chinese desire for knowledge and wanting to do things well and proficiently. What is this but professionalism and business development under a different guise? The Chinese desire to have high levels of business information and transparency from prospective partners prior to contracting with them is simply a good, diligent exercise in accountability under a different name.

Our goals are not dissimilar. Our methods have a common core. Often what differs are the degrees of emphasis. Even in the crucial, final area of 'relationship creation and management', we are not so different – though the Chinese may question our Western terminology for what they see as the state of being in multiple, highly-valued relationships, since for them this is the very 'stuff of life' and not something that is created or managed.

We in the West also value our professional, client and partner relationships, but typically in ways that are codified, limited and managed. Even the terminology we use reveals the more professionally structured handling of business relationships. And yet we have devoted much time and effort to understanding the dynamics of these relationships and how to improve them. There is much room for learning from each other in this critical area: the West with its extensive forensic learning about the dynamics of business and professional relationships, and China with its example of how committed relationships facilitate and power success.

Values like loyalty, business friendship, continuity and stability are gifts from China's business culture to ours. I would like to feel that we are reciprocating with more than due diligence, corporate governance or IPR protection models, immensely powerful and helpful as these are to our business cooperation with China.

I would like to think that each one of us in our own way might finally be ready to respond to the gift of relationships that China offers us, by simply saying 'yes' to the invitation concealed in the gifts, the invitation to relate. It is time. It is our moment to do so. And it is the right thing to do. Not least because of the mutual enhancement of relationship skills between our two cultures, because of the trust that will be built and because, in a world where now more than ever 'plans cannot chase change', relationships well made may yet prove to be not just our greatest business asset but our most trustworthy guide and ally in creating business success through mutual benefit and respect with China.

Chapter Eighteen

SUMMARY

This book has taken you far into the Chinese relationship model and its rationale. It has sought to guide you how to participate well in this model for effective commercial results and enduring business friendships. It has demonstrated how others have applied these core relationship skills, along the Chinese model, in their communication, behaviour and negotiations to the lasting credit of their businesses and reputations in China.

It may well appear to you that, in order to achieve this, we have asked much of you in terms of a quantum shift in your customary style of business relationships, and in expressing more of your identity and character than would be typical in your own or other markets. This is true. China demands effort and rewards it. But in the interests of balance, let me reassure you that this is a two-way process. China also wishes to make a proactive and dynamic contribution by adapting its business styles. I will use this final chapter to summarise areas of difficulty and mediated solutions involving a shift from both cultures for greater results and effectiveness.

Interestingly, as so often is the case in business and life, it is not the big things that cause anxiety and breaks in business relationships, but the little things. Let us examine some of the ways in which simple shifts in business styles and behaviour could help us to cement the relationship skills we are building.

One important area is accountability. Handled well, this supports solid relationships. Handled badly, it is a deal breaker and a terminator of relationships. However, it is not the more sophisticated overall parameters of accountability which are most problematical. We are increasingly getting these right with China, and China with us. Rather, it is the ongoing communication of progress and what this signifies that continues to be troublesome. China likes to be spoken to often to keep the relationship strong, and we in the West like to know what progress is being made in tasks allocated, frequently, and ideally in writing. This is because our business world is deadline-driven and job and project security are results-driven.

Often, in the mind of Chinese partners, when a task is allocated the crucial thing is to get on with it efficiently and until completion, whilst taking time to maintain one's business relationships and interactions wholeheartedly. This is excellent and something we hope to emulate to partner in China better. In return, we ask that in order to allay anxiety in our business model, we are told what progress is occurring and are told regularly until key common objectives are met. Often, the West does not need the full results of projects at these times, merely reassuring updates. A simple shift here from efficiency alone to efficiency with reporting would have enhanced almost every business partnership I have observed between China and the West, including some which failed because this was not present.

In some ways, the two approaches are simply culturally different versions of letting each other know that we matter. In China, this takes the form of focus on tasks once set as well as relationship maintenance, whilst in the West, it takes the form of sharing business progress before completion of the tasks to help with the ongoing accountability which is expected of us weekly and sometimes daily. One approach (China's) could be summed up as 'speak to me', the other (the West's) could be summed up as 'update me'; both are really a business version of signalling to each other that we matter.

A simple shift on both sides would prevent multiple business difficulties from arising or proliferating. Equally, the degree of detail and transparency in business information needs review. We have read how transparency in revealing business information was identified by the CEOs we consulted as a key property of potential partners for China. Equally, when the West requires business information from Chinese colleagues and partners, they are at times surprised by the brevity of the information they receive, wonderful as the quality inevitably is.

We understand the cultural reasons: the immense consideration China's business people give to the opinions and assessments and the reticence to tell others what to do in business. And we respect them for it. The West, however, is an information-driven culture where knowledge management defines results and protects jobs even at senior levels. Like reporting, we are assessed on the comprehensiveness of information and analysis we bring to our boards and stakeholders. So even the same information, more comprehensively analysed or explained in our culture, can make the difference in positive or negative perception from those on whom our business depends.

So greater transparency and knowledge share from us, and more comprehensive detail in business communications from our Chinese partners, including their valued and respected opinions and analyses, will advance the mutually beneficial climate of the business we are seeking to create as we go forward in partnership.

In essence, the key to a mediated path of success with mutual benefit for both cultures could be summed up in one word: reciprocity. In turn, the key to this is to understand that which causes business anxiety and strain in each other and to mitigate it.

For China, this has everything to do with reputation, and in the West, this has everything to do with performance. These are the areas where we are most 'on show' and 'exposed' in our respective business cultures.

Understanding what reputation means, with all its connotations, and being willing to create and support it for our Chinese partners, is perhaps the most valuable business investment we could possibly make. Understanding the high pressure levels that exist around performance in our results-driven Western culture and cooperating to create performance and its visible expression as reporting, is a huge investment for China in successfully partnering the West.

What is asked for, of both cultures, is a new definition of reciprocity – one that takes account of the business pressures and strains on each party as they are expressed in their specific business cultures.

Ask yourself how you felt the last time someone helped you to allay significant pressure in your business or professional life. Wonderful, I would suggest. Now imagine this experience multiplied within myriad business situations in China with both sides feeling supported, empowered and truly partnered.

Why should we settle for less at this magnificent, seminal moment in our business development and that of China? We have the tools. We have the will. And now, finally, we have the opportunity. If we use these tools, we will succeed, to the enduring benefit of all the businesses and people on our planet.

Chapter Nineteen

CHINA:
QUICK REFERENCE GUIDE

Because sometimes you need answers, not explanations

1 Think *relationships, relationships, relationships.*
2 Remember relationships drive business.
3 For China, think of your usual level of business preparation, then double it.
4 For China, do everything more thoroughly: prepare more thoroughly, research more thoroughly, enquire more thoroughly.
5 China requires a personal touch.
6 Who you are matters in China, just as much, if not more, than what you know.
7 The most important word in the Chinese lexicon is 'We', in the Western world it is 'I'. To be successful, make the shift.
8 From the beginning, handle as much as possible face-to-face.
9 Do your research in person, visit the sites, meet prospective partners.
10 Whenever possible phone, don't email.
11 Handle video conferencing with care as it puts the Chinese on the spot. If essential, table questions well in advance.
12 Remember the importance of face, of Chinese dignity and reputation.
13 Ask yourself constantly if what you are doing is building face or taking it away.
14 Set your intention for China; make it a 'we' based intention: mutual benefit.
15 Remember that respect and civility are your greatest business assets in China.
16 Understand the slower timelines in China, and make sure that your stakeholders do.
17 Learn to value patient progress and avoid ultimatums.

18 *Consult, consult, consult* with the Chinese.

19 Be open and transparent in your dealings. It wins great respect.

20 Remember that the protracted 'getting to know' phase in China is a critical part of the business process.

21 Value business banquets as a chance to show appreciation for Chinese hospitality, time and commitment to relationships.

22 Remember that the Chinese meet you outside the meeting room. Be ready for this important ceremony and greeting (no fumbling with business cards or coat buttons).

23 Remember that the Chinese will accompany you to your car, taxi, train, etc. Appreciate it!

24 Enthusiasm, knowledge and discipline are valuable assets in China.

25 Show that you are enjoying the business banquet Chinese hosts provide. This is their wish, and it helps them relax. The Chinese love shared meals.

26 Your good manners are your greatest assets in China. Show them to good advantage.

27 Present clearly, slowly and with conviction.

28 Get to know and brief your interpreters in advance of negotiations. Remember that they facilitate the transmission of your ideas as well as translating your words.

29 Be prepared to work long days and never refuse business hospitality for reasons of 'space' or tiredness.

30 Be crystal clear on your business objectives, especially in negotiating.

31 Remember business leaders set objectives and policy in Chinese negotiation; the detail is fleshed out by their team.

32 Observe the Chinese paradigm and match it with the requisite status and function within your negotiating team – it will help you reach your goals.

33 If you are a CEO or MD, act as one when in China, including and especially in terms of showing your status and having your team reflect it.

34 As a CEO or MD, avoid being seen to do any business task beneath your management level.

35 The Chinese value hierarchy and order and expect this in partners.

36 Remember what engenders trust in Chinese business partners: plain dealing, expertise, consultation, and willingness to share knowledge.

37 China thinks collectively and does business in teams. Modify any aggressively individualistic behaviour or language.

38 Show appreciation for your Chinese counterpart's efforts, long hours and dedication and be willing to 'go the extra mile' in your business efforts for China.

39 Build relationships, nurture relationships, preserve relationships as a priority, the priority every day of your business life with China.

40 Give gifts thoughtfully, carefully, sincerely and without ostentation.

41 Choose gifts which have meaning for your guests and for you: images of your city, a favourite Chinese landmark within your country, a practical object of use to your Chinese counterparts.

42 The Chinese find praise difficult. Couch it in terms of the team, the leader. If it is directed at an individual, express it in private.

43 Never lavish praise, the Chinese suspect excessive statements.

44 Respect silences in conversations; they are moments for mature business reflection.

45 Remember that the Chinese rarely say 'no' directly. Examine the 'yes' you have received.

46 Do not ask direct questions of individuals – this risks face.

47 Always give as much indication as possible of subject matter and questions to the Chinese.

48 Allow time for consultation and reflection. Never press for immediate answers or hurry dialogue.

49 Watch your relationship with timelines. Feeling harried often results in behaviour which the Chinese experience as pressurising or aggressive.

50 Demonstrate your company's solidity: emphasise the growth, its market impact, its sound financial basis and its benevolent people policy.

51 Show your trustworthiness. Visit often. Keep your word. Invest time, money and, most importantly, yourself in building relationships.

52 Keep your promises. Broken promises are total trust breakers in China.

53 Exhibit what you want to find in your Chinese partners.

54 Expect the best. We tend to find our expectations realised in China, so expect harmony, strong business friendships, positive dialogue and plain dealing. You are more likely to find it.

55 Allow the Chinese to achieve results their way. This often involves use of relationship networks and creative thinking 'outside the box'.

56 Reward in public, criticise gently and in private – it protects relationships.

57 Remember that your Chinese partner's face is your face; treat it with care.

58 Avoid knee-jerk reactions. They kill business opportunities in a world of 'face' and 'discipline' like China.

59 Leave your ego at home and replace it with a sense of collective benefit and harmony. You will soar in China if you do this.

60 Dare to show who you are and what you value, especially commitment to your business, employees and family.

61 Think of the kind of behaviour and care you would lavish on friends and family, then show it to the Chinese. You are building a family of 'business friends'.

62 Look for success after you have built the business relationship, not before.

63 Think before you prepare to speak, then think again.

64 Communicate gently.

65 Exercise restraint in all situations, in both your verbal and written communications.

66 Remember to put sincere connection, a desire to create mutual benefit and respect, at the core of your business approach.

67 When receiving Chinese business visitors, meet them outside your building and see them to their cars at the end of the meeting.

68 Extend hospitality to the highest standards when receiving Chinese guests. Remember how you were treated and reciprocate.

69 Plan meals carefully when receiving Chinese visitors and pay attention to quality, environment and matching status when receiving guests.

70 Failure to take care of and extend suitable hospitality to Chinese business visitors suggests disapproval.

71 Be willing to be the first to say sorry and mean it. It rebuilds trust.

72 It helps to like China. It helps even more to love it. This is not a hard task and the Chinese will know and respond!

73 Forget all the 'China Scare' you have heard, ditch the stereotypes and the judgements. China rewards courage and open-mindedness.

74 Remember that by applying relationship skills for your business success in China, you are making relationship history. View what you do in China as important. It is.

75 Keep your side of the street clean. If you behave well, China will always respond.

76 Embrace the differences in workstyle, culture and relationship approach – they will grow your skills and that of your business.

77 Release judgements on key values like trust, accountability, integrity, teamwork. Remember that these have different definitions in China but they are no less real and important. At the deepest level, we all want the same things in business and life. Dig deep for empathy.

FURTHER READING

Chen, Ming Jer (2001) *Inside Chinese Business*, Boston MA: Harvard Business School Press.

Clissold, Tim (2002) *Mr China*, London: Robinson.

De Mente, Boye Lafayette (2004) *Chinese Etiquette and Ethics in Business*, McGraw Hill.

Gascoigne, Bamber (1973) *The Dynasties of China*, London: Robinson.

Mia Kuang, Ching (2009) *CFO Guide*, Singapore: John Wiley & Sons (Asia).

Rudman, Stephen Todd (2006) *The Multinational Corporation in China*, Blackwell.

Sinha, Kunal (2008) *China's Creative Imperative*, Singapore: John Wiley & Sons (Asia).

Spence, Jonathan D. (1999) *The Search for Modern China*, New York: W. W. Norton & Company.

Stuttard, John B. (2000) *The New Silk Road*, John Wiley & Sons.

USEFUL WEBSITES

http://www.china.org.cn/
http://english.sina.com/news/china/index.html
http://www.cbbc.org/
http://www.ukinvest.gov.uk/en-CN-index.html
http://www.chinadaily.com.cn/
http://thechinabusinessnetwork.com/
http://www.chinabusinessreview.com/
http://www.chinaview.cn/
http://english.mofcom.gov.cn/
http://english.cctv.com/business/

INDEX

Index compiled by Annette Musker